A Hitler Youth

Growing up in Germany in the 1930s

Also by the same author and published by Spellmount Ltd

THROUGH HELL FOR HITLER

A HITLER YOUTH

GROWING UP IN GERMANY IN THE 1930s

by

Henry Metelmann

SPELLMOUNT
Staplehurst

British Library Cataloguing in Publication Data:
A catalogue record for this book is available
from the British Library

Copyright © Henry Metelmann 1997, 2004

ISBN 1-86227-252-2

First published in 1997 by Caliban Books

This edition first published in the UK in 2004 by
Spellmount Limited
The Village Centre
Staplehurst
Kent TN12 0BJ

Tel: 01580 893730
Fax: 01580 893731
E-mail: enquiries@spellmount.com
Website:www.spellmount.com

1 3 5 7 9 8 6 4 2

The right of Henry Metelmann to be identified
as the author of this work has been asserted by him
in accordance with the Copyright, Designs
and Patents Act 1988

Typeset in Palatino by MATS, Southend-on-Sea, Essex
Printed in Great Britain by
T.J. International Ltd
Padstow, Cornwall

Contents

Acknowledgements

As a two-finger typist, averse to anything as technological as a word processor, I could have hardly produced this book without the continous technical help of my friend Natacha Lane. Whenever my spirits sank low and I came close to giving up that most lonely of jobs of writing a book, it was my dear friend Ebby Napier who pushed me on, kept the noisy and grandad-demanding Dylan at bay, and finally encouraged me to produce what you now have in front of you. My thanks and love to both of them.

To my parents who ensured that I grew up with the potential to recognise life and the world for what they are, to my late wife Monika, my children Mark and Gisela, my grandson Dylan, and my loyal friends Joan and Evelyn, who believed in me.

Foreword

My father was an unskilled labourer, my mother came from the country and I was ten years old when I was told that we had a new Kanzler (Prime Minister) with the name of Adolf Hitler. Though I had heard his name and seen photos of him in the newspapers and cinemas, I had no real idea of who he was, nor what he stood for. It was only from my own observations and experiences that I knew of the turbulent times we were living in. But at the time it did not mean much to me, it all seemed a natural part of ordinary, everyday life.

Our flat was located in a tenement and was surrounded by smoking, loudly-hammering factories. Down by the river were the docks and when the wind was blowing our way, we clearly heard the sirens and the bells of the ships. Strikes, demonstrations and street fighting, which at times I had to run away from, were the order of the day.

Far too young at the time, not having had any opportunity to compare like with like, I was in no position to analyse the meaning and importance of what was going on around me. But I was wide awake and eager to learn and I watched all the happenings now described in this book with absorbing curiosity.

I had heard of and read the names of previous Kanzlers like Heinrich Brüning, Franz von Papen and General Kurt von Schleicher. They had all come and gone and meant little to me. And whenever they left, my parents exclaimed, they never took the mess they had created with them. That mess was for us to sort out and it grew steadily worse, pulling in wider and larger circles of the population, and hitting hardest those who could least defend themselves against it.

Even I, as young and inexperienced as I was, could see it. The evidence unrolled right in front of my eyes in the streets, at school and just everywhere. And when in bad winter weather, with snow lying on the ground, a number of my school friends did not turn up because they had no decent shoes to wear and no proper coat to protect them from the cold, I thought that this was just a natural and ordinary part of daily life. If one left sandwiches lying around in the class room, they quickly disappeared.

Such were the lives and conditions of the likes of us. But there were other lives as well. Not all that far from us in the green suburbs and along the wooded banks of the river Elbe, there were people who lived in large beautiful villas which mostly stood in well-tended gardens, and which were securely fenced off against intruders from the outside.

When I wondered why it was like that, why we too could not live in such good conditions but had to make do with the crammed and often unhygienic ones in our part of the town, my parents said that it was because those people in the suburbs were wealthy and we were poor. But when I asked why it was that some people were wealthy and we – so many of us – were poor, my father just laughed in a sarcastic way. He went on to say that if we could logically analyse that problem and find the solution to it, we would be on the way towards solving the dehumanising sting of poverty so common amongst us.

The word Nazi had already been a well-known one to me for a number of years before Hitler came into office. It was a short word for nationalist and was largely understood in connection with the brown stormtroopers who could be seen marching in military formations through the streets of our town. I could not understand why my father detested them so much and called them 'braune Pest' (brown plague). They were always friendly to me when, together with my friends, I ran alongside their column, dancing to their music and singing their songs with them. So what was so bad about them, I wondered?

And the months and years rolled by and then so much did happen. Even I could sense that in so many ways life had changed since the coming of Adolf Hitler. There was the Reichstagsbrand (burning of the Parliament Building), the Night of the Long Knives and the homecoming of the Saarland into the Reich. It was all very exciting and I was carried away by it all. It did not take long before I wore the striking uniform of the Hitler Youth. Never having been on a holiday before, for working people that kind of extravagance was as good as unthinkable, I loved going to the camps which were located in lovely parts of our country which opened my eyes to the beauty of Germany, my Germany. How proud all this made me and how sad at the same time that my father, whom I loved and admired, still called the Nazis 'die braune pest'.

Then came the time, no doubt being influenced by what I was learning at school and in the Hitler Youth, that I acquired my own individual opinions, which resulted in many bitter clashes with my father. The horror of mass unemployment which was so fearful in the German mind, had been as good as wiped out in Germany. Father pointed out that Hitler's armament programme had been responsible for that 'miracle'. However, there were no bounds any more to my excitement, my joy when I realised that my Germany, after the humiliation of Versailles, was becoming a strong power again, which the outside world, like it or not, had to respect.

I loved going to the big rallies especially when the Führer was present.

I saw him a number of times and remember well when he came to the shipworks at Hamburg to launch the battleship *Bismarck*. Then conscription was introduced. How happy that made me, now being able to look forward to becoming a soldier of the Führer. What greater pride could there be than wearing the field grey colours of the newly created Wehrmacht? But it was this that especially frightened my father. He had been a soldier in the 'Great' War, had fought at the Somme, at Verdun and in other bloody battles, and was now extremely bitter about it all. He called it the 'big betrayal' and again saw war and madness rising from the horizon.

He mainly blamed the churches, who though using hypocritical words about heavenly peace, by and large supported the warlike stance of the Nazis, instead of telling their followers that killing people was a sin against basic Christian principles. By that time many concentration camps had already been opened in all parts of our country. Everyone knew about them though few people mentioned that thorny subject. Though I never saw it with my own eyes, I knew that there was a concentration camp not all that far from us at Neuengamme. We were told in the Hitler Youth that anti-Reich elements, such as communists, gypsies, Jews, homosexuals, bible punchers, thieves and murderers, were collected in them and made to work for the good of Germany, which I thought was only right and proper.

Then King Edward VIII of England abdicated. Our newspapers were full of it. About ten months later he paid a private visit to our country with his new duchess, the former Mrs. Simpson. As a greatly honoured and welcomed guest he was received by our Führer, and when he made the statement that 'German youth was lucky to grow up in such a great society as ours', we were so proud and it strengthened our conviction that our cause, the one mapped by our Führer and Party, was the right one to follow.

Not long after that came the Kristall Nacht (Crystal Night) when Jewish shops were ransacked, synagogues set alight and many Jewish people beaten to death or drowned. My parents were aghast. And though I felt a pinch of dislike, I thought that it was perhaps all a part of the necessary ethnic cleansing of Germany. Next Austria came home into the Reich, and Chamberlain and Daladier abandoned Czechoslovakia to Hitler. We then sent the *Legion Condor* to Spain whose planes bombed Guernica and helped Franco to overthrow the elected government of that country, and we were so proud.

When war finally started with our attack on Poland, it seemed almost like a relief, like a clearing of the air after all the worrying uncertainties which the Göbbels propaganda machine had drummed into us. Father was devastated – but not surprised any more. As he said, his life's aim and work to guide his son on to a peaceful path lay in ruins. He became ill. But before he died, already much weakened, he made a last attempt to make me see reality, the truth, as he called it. But as much as I loved him, I could only promise him that I would think about what he had told me. But so young and with the Nazi drums drumming into my brain, I all too soon pushed that promise aside.

It was only several years later when I trudged through the snow during the Napoleonic retreat from Stalingrad, that I belatedly remembered my father's warnings, and that I began to understand what he had meant. Of course, it was too late then. I only wished that I could have said to my father: yes, you were right, a thousand times right in the way you saw things and events. It was I who was the fool.

CHAPTER I
Childhood at Home

My earliest memory is standing on the pavement of the Bahrenfelder Strasse. It was a very cold winter evening and we had just come out of a food shop and mother, carrying several bags in her hands, found it somewhat awkward to carry me as well. I remember yellow street cars with loud chiming bells going by. The drivers stood in the open behind their driving mechanism, with little protection against the weather. They were all muffled in thick overcoats, woollen scarves and fur hats, so that all one could see of their faces was the bit around their eyes. There were people with small wooden handcarts in the road, some of which were pulled by dogs. People rode bicycles, which had large oil or carbide lamps in front which fascinated me.

I must have been almost two years old then and when I recently went back to what was then the Prussian town of Altona and walked up that same stretch of the Bahrenfelder Strasse, I was surprised how easily this, in itself an unimportant event, clicked back like a flash into my memory. I was able to point to almost the exact spot where mother had picked me up on that grey wintry evening when dusk was giving way to early darkness.

Several of the grey five-storey tenements in that street are still standing, having survived the carpet bombings of 1943. Some of them still show the pockmarks from the bomb splinters on parts of the façade, but most of them have been replaced by modern red brick buildings. They now have open balconies which have altered the character of the street, if not the whole neighbourhood. It is still a poor part of the town, a typical run-down working class quarter. Many immigrants from Turkey and other mainly south and east European countries live there now, and have become the majority in some streets. The bumpy cobblestones have been covered with a smooth, dark-grey surface, and now carry heavy traffic so that one cannot cross the street so easily as mother did with me those seven decades ago. One now has to walk to the nearest corner where lights regulate all traffic movements.

The grimy, noisy factories we passed on our way home have long since gone, having largely given way to wasteland, where children have created all sorts of play paradises for themselves. Perhaps it is because cultures

1

from faraway lands have been implanted here, that I could detect an underlying atmosphere of uncertainty, if not mistrust and resentment which seems to permeate everything. Was perhaps a new kind of racism emerging in my town of birth? Or was I just imagining things?

My father's parents had both died before I was born, grandmother having missed my arrival on Christmas Day 1922 by only six days. They were said to have tried their hands at many an enterprise, had made money and lost it and had been forced to move home a number of times. Grandfather had been a miller by trade. At one time he had owned several windmills in the northern part of the country. One of the mills between Hamburg and Lübeck, I learned, had burnt down. He had tried for a period to run an undertaker's business, along with his milling activities. But luck had failed him and the whole lot had collapsed in shambles. Whispers had it, though I never heard father say so, that it had surprised no one because large amounts of money had been frittered away on race courses in the vain hope of getting something for nothing on the quick.

At one time the family had lived in Friedrichsruh, a sleepy town to the south east of Hamburg. In the middle of the 1890s Prince Otto von Bismarck, the 'Iron Chancellor', was sacked by the newly crowned and headstrong Kaiser Wilhelm II, and had retired to a villa in Friedrichsruh, not all that far from the Metelmann household. Throughout my childhood I understood, mainly from one of my uncles, that it was a matter of pride for our family that the Bismarcks and the Metelmanns had relations of sorts with each other. When I asked father what these relations were, he merely smirked and called it a useless indulgence in snobbery. He told me though, that as a small child he vaguely remembered an older brother of his father's had sometimes accompanied old Bismarck on his walks across the heath, and that the two had had animated conversations with each other.

I now sometimes wonder whether perhaps the family losses at the race courses, plus the fact that father came late in the lives of my grandparents, his oldest sister Alma being seventeen years older than he was, had something to do with father never 'having made it in life', as the saying goes. I am absolutely sure now that he had not only been an intelligent man but more so a wise one. He had never benefited from any education worth its name, had changed schools a number of times and had remained an unskilled railway worker from the end of the Great War to the early part of the next, when he suffered an untimely death.

He had been called up to 'the Preussen' (the Prussians), as army life was generally called in our northern part of the country and had served in a Pioneer Battalion (engineers). He had experienced the full horrors of war at the Somme, at Verdun and later for a short time, against the Russians in East Prussia and Poland. His bitterness about his experiences was constant. To him the war had been a senseless and criminal slaughter of

2

millions of young men, arbitarily put into different colours of uniforms, as well of totally innocent civilians. I noticed that to the very end of his life the mere mention of war evoked tears. He said that he considered it his most important duty to save his son from going through the same dehumanising experiences of war which had been his fate. He was in no doubt that the 'Great' War had from beginning to end been a terrible crime against humanity, on a scale hitherto unknown to human history. He went on and on about 'the ones on top', the real criminals who on both sides had driven their millions into the slaughterhouse of battle, and who had never been punished for what they had done. On the contrary, one could see them on newspaper photographs decorating each other with medals and titles, still strutting around in what they considered was their own important and rightful privilege.

Especially Verdun stuck in his guts. His brother, my uncle Wilhelm, who sported a twisted moustache like the ex-Kaiser and was full to the brim of proud patriotism, sometimes came to see us. I had the impression that he liked my mother more than he did my father, which at times caused angry words within the family. My uncle had served in the early part of the century in the Imperial Colonial Army in German South West Africa (now Namibia), which had suppressed with utmost recklessness and savagery the revolt of the Hereroes and Hottentot tribes against German colonial occupation. He had a very different opinion on the subjects of politics and war than my father. He was proud of what he had done for Kaiser and country. Sadly so often when he came to see us, tempers flared between the two with mother desperately trying to calm the heated argument, pointing towards me who was 'all ears' and pleading, 'please Fritz, please Wilhelm, how can I teach the boy about peace when he can watch you two going for each other like fighting cocks?'

Onkel Wilhelm – he had been decorated with the 'Iron Cross' while father had not – once tried to tell me in more detail about the great inborn heroism of the German soldier, fearlessly withstanding almost the whole world in the Great War, and always showing himself in heroic light. Father forbade him outright to poison 'the lad's mind' with his patriotic rubbish, under the threat of showing him the door.

Father took me aside afterwards and in his quiet manner told me about his own experiences at Verdun. He tried to ram into me that there was no glory or heroism in war and battle, only madness, desperation, fright and unbelievable brutality. I sometimes wondered why it was that father's and Onkel Wilhelm's reports about the same events, in this case Verdun, differed so much from each other. Which of the two was the correct account, which of them was the truth?

Father reminded me of people we both knew, ex- soldiers who had lost limbs, were blinded or had been maimed in other horrible ways and now lived out their miserable existences, waiting for death to relieve them from their sufferings. Some had been forced to beg in the streets, and when they explained that they had received their injuries as front line soldiers defending the Fatherland, no one wanted to be reminded of it any more. People wanted to turn their hearts and minds away from those gruesome happenings, as if by that they could make it appear that it had never happened. Father himself had been wounded in the hip and leg from which he still suffered, experiencing pain until the end of his life. Once every year around Christmas he visited his friend in Bremen with whom he had served in the same battalion at Verdun. Mother always packed him a food parcel, for Hans had lost both legs, lived alone on very little money, finding it hard to get around on crutches and in a ramshackle wheelchair. 'When you get older,' father said, 'I will take you with me so that you can listen to what Hans has to say. And then you can compare it with what Onkel Wilhelm comes trumpeting out with.'

Being still very young at that time, I naturally took in what father said. I believed in his assessments rather than in anyone else's, including Onkel Wilhelm's. But in later years when I approached my teens, no doubt due to what I was then being taught in the Hitler Youth and at school, I found Onkel Wilhelm's views much more exciting and began to soak up many of his meaningless assumptions like glory, greatness and heroism, from which I more and more developed arrogant Nazi attitudes. Though I did notice that this caused my father much distress, I suppose that I was simply not mature enough to be able to reach out to him on this. Mother told me several times how sad all this made him to realise that his son was slipping away from his guiding influence.

The older I grew, the more bitter became our arguments, so much that mother sometimes felt that she had to step in, almost crying and begging us to stop. However, our love for each other never broke, although it was only many years later that I began to look back with sadness to our confrontations and wished that he could hear me say: 'Papa, you were the one who was right all along, your assessments and predictions were correct, I sadly only woke up to the truth after my nose had been rubbed into the dirt and snow of the Russian battlefields. I am sorry. I hope that you can forgive me.'

But now, dear reader, having moved so far into the future, let me take you back to the very early part of my life. After my parents had married in 1921, they lived with my father's mother in a pleasant ground floor flat which had a nice large garden at the back. The Stresemann Strasse in Altona was named after a Foreign Secretary of the Weimar Republic. During the Kaiser's days it had been called Kleine Gärtner Strasse (Little Gardener's Street). When the Nazis came to power in 1933 they renamed it General Litzmann Strasse after a General who had beaten the Russians on the Eastern Front. Now it is called Stresemann Strasse again. What better indication than these name changes to describe the turbulent times of twentieth century German history.

I was born in that flat in Stresemann Strasse but cannot remember anything about the place. Due to the savage inflation raging in Germany in the first year of my life, resulting amongst other things in the far too high rent my parents could not afford to pay, they had to look for cheaper accommodation, which they found in a poorer part of the town before I reached my first birthday. I lived there throughout my childhood until I was called up in the army at the beginning of the war. To me, all things being relative especially when one is so young and has nothing to compare it with, I look back to the period of my childhood with much happiness and gratitude to my parents.

At the time my parents moved from Stresemann Strasse to the poorer part of Altona, the contents of the flat were divided up amongst my father's relatives. I could not help becoming aware throughout my later childhood that this was a sore subject which had brought about painful ructions in family relations. It was a direct result of this that some of my relatives, though they lived not far away from us, never really became known to me. Friends of my parents and later some of my own friends, expressed surprise about the unexpected quality of our furniture, so unusual they thought in an unskilled worker's family living in a poor part of town.

Mother, being a great homemaker, looked after it with loving care. Our home, always having an underlying smell of furniture polish and good home cooking, was not only spotless but very homely which, thinking now about it, was probably a reflection of my parents' loving attitude towards each other, as well as their great love for me. It was many years later when I had my own family and was building a life and setting up home in England, that I realised how important my upbringing was in developing the foundations of almost all my attitudes to life.

No one in our family was religious, except perhaps mother towards the end of her life. We seldom went to church, except for the usual ceremonies of christenings, confirmations, weddings and deaths. Although the general principles we adhered to in family life could loosely be described as Christian, they had arisen more out of natural human feeling than religious conviction, which never really penetrated our conscious understanding.

Though father was in every way a gentle and quiet person, I understood from family conversations, which I was not supposed to be listening to, that he had at times upset his parents and others in the family, especially after he had come back from the war. It was said that he had become very critical of existing society, calling it thoroughly hypocritical and dis-honest. He told me that his personal experiences at the Battle of Verdun had completely destroyed almost everything he had been taught as a child to believe in.

5

Mother's family background, firmly rooted in peasant stock, differed much from my father's. Her father had walked after the Franco-Prussian war of 1870/71 from Lippe Detmold in central Germany to the north in search of work. Nothing much more really was known about him. He had married a poor local girl with whom he had acquired a cottage at the edge of the Holstein village of Stapelfeld, to the north east of Hamburg, where he set himself up as the village butcher. He fathered six children of whom two were stillborn. He died before the 1914/18 war and left the family in very straitened circumstances. Mother's mother was the only one of my four grandparents who was alive when I was born.

Stapelfeld was a typical village of that area, nestling in the flat country-side. Its farmhouses and cottages were clustered around in loose fashion. Many of them were surrounded with high hedges behind which there were large vegetable gardens, and there were many fruit trees. English-type gardens with lawns were not yet common in those days, though some Stapelfeld gardens had colourful flower beds in front, which could be seen from the road over pretty wooden fences

The hub of village life was the pub in its centre, with a bakery and a food shop on either side of it. All this was owned by one family. The owner, Herr Ruge, and one or two of the larger farmers were the only villagers who had motor cars. He once gave mother and me a lift, which was an experience in itself. I sat on mother's lap and once on the move, the car rattled noisily over rough cobblestones, and it became impossible to hold a conversation without shouting. When looking through gaps in the floor, I was fascinated to watch the road streaking away underneath us.

Across from the pub, half hidden in summer behind huge chestnut trees in the large playground, stood a pleasant two-storey school house with a large red-tiled roof. In it one teacher, at that time a Herr Goldschmidt, taught all sixty or so village children at the same time. Mother as well as my aunts, uncles and later cousins went through that same teaching process. It is still a wonder to me that each of them had become very literate, good at basic mathematics, and had a fair general knowledge.

The nearest church serving the village population was in the small town of Rahlstedt, about five kilometres away, which had a railway station on the route from Hamburg to the Baltic town of Lübeck, of which the writer Thomas Mann was a famous son. A good bus service connected the station with most of the villages around, including Stapelfeld.

Grandmother's cottage stood at the very end of an unmade side road, running into a field track which was always very muddy after rainy weather. Right opposite the cottage was a shallow pond into which the cattle waded on their way between the meadows and milking stables in summer. We children loved to sit on the large boulders surrounding the pond with our feet dangling in the muddy water, making mud cakes.

The cottage's living quarters and the stables were all under one roof. At the far end one could get a horse and cart on to the threshing floor, above which was the hayloft where we children, though we were not really allowed to because of unsafe floor boards, loved to play. The lavatory was in a small shed standing away from the cottage. When sitting on the bucket one could peer through the gaps between the wall boards. Especially in winter darkness it was quite an undertaking to go to the toilet. Needless to say, at night we used chamber-pots. Water was supplied by a pump which stood about ten yards from the kitchen door. It was always a matter of honour for the one who emptied the kitchen supply bucket to go out and fill it up for the next person to use. I remember when electric light replaced the old oil lamps which hung from the ceilings in every room, grandmother proclaimed that it was the work of the devil. But once she got used to it, she became quite excited at using the switches with such instant success. Her attitude then became quite modern, reminding us children of the great wonders modern technology had brought into our humble lives. But she also loved to talk with nostalgia about the good old days when everything had been relatively backward and when she as a girl had to work so much harder than we ever would. Life had been so much sweeter in those days, she said.

A large iron hearth stood in the corner of the kitchen which had a cold stone floor. All through the year a fire was constantly kept going. While sawn logs and sometimes a shovel of coal were being used in winter, it was a summer job for us children to see to it that the wood box in the corner by the door was always full with dry wood, available in abundance in the hedgerows and lanes near by. All ceilings in the cottage were low, as were the door frames. A six-footer had to bow to enter. A white-tiled stove stood next to the wall in the main living room and reached almost to the ceiling, leaving a narrow recess in the corner, into which reclined the most comfortable chair in the entire cottage. A creaky staircase led upstairs where space under the sloping roof had been boarded up, creating two extra bedrooms for my cousins. But was it cold there in the winter!

Chicken, ducks and geese wandered all over the place and made quite a commotion when strangers arrived. I can still remember the sound, giving me a feeling of warm belonging. Sometimes when the door had been left open, they ventured into the kitchen and feathers flew, when with arm-waving and shouting they were driven out again. There was the usual house dog and several cats who diligently tried, not very successfully, to keep the mice and rat population down.

Max, the family horse, mostly roamed freely, grazing in the grassy lanes. When he was needed, someone had to go out and call him, and he loyally came trotting into the yard to be put into harness or whatever he was needed for. He and I became good friends. I went out of my way to look for him in the lanes and when I had found him, he always nudged me and wanted to be stroked. When one day, finding another horse in Max's stable and being told that Max had to be put down because of old age and sickness, I was extremely upset and found it hard to speak to my uncle Emil, who had slaughtered him. How could he have done it, I mused, to such a loyal servant and friend like Max?

When on a Sunday afternoon a visit was planned to family or friends in one of the neighbouring villages, a cart with soft springs was pulled out of the outhouse, given a wipe-over and was made ready with blankets and cushions for the trip. A step was let down at the back and everyone climbed through a small trap door on to the back with us children competing for a seat next to Uncle Emil to hold the reins. And by making all the correct tongue noises of an experienced horseman, we safely got Max into a steady gallop through the village and out on to the open Chaussée. On trips like that everyone was in a good humour, and there was much banter and laughter.

The only paid village official was the Bürgermeister who acted as elected chairman of a small council, with a new one coming in every three years or so. Most, if not all of the council meetings were held in the backroom of the pub, which was probably the reason why so many villagers were overcome by a kind of disbelieving wonderment, when decisions were announced on a notice board standing on two poles outside the pub. Some called them alcoholic orders.

Though everyone in the village spoke Plattdeutsch with each other, which is a curious mish-mash of German, Dutch, Danish and English, spoken in the region between the North and the Baltic Seas, as well as slightly further inland, High German was the official language and the only one allowed in school. As throughout my childhood years I spent most of my holidays with my cousins in Stapelfeld, and knowing most of the people there, I learned much about village life and loved it. Looking back now seven decades later, and with much turbulent life in between, I have no hesitation in calling it the happiest and most carefree time of my life.

Every autumn with all hands needed for Onkel Emil's potato harvest, mother considered it her duty to go and help. Needless to say, she took me with her and I loved trotting behind her over the rough fields, helping to fill her bucket and sack, which it was my job to hold open for her. Sometimes father also came to help. We then always slept in grandmother's room, and when one early Sunday morning I heard voices and looked out of the window, I saw many people, men, women and children walking in rows over a recently harvested potato field. They carried buckets and dragged sacks behind them while their cycles and small hand carts had been left by the side of the dirt track. Grandmother said that they were poor people from Hamburg who had come because Herr Westphal, the farmer, was a religious man and had allowed them to pick up what had been left over from the harvest.

She also told me that there had been thefts from as yet unharvested outlying fields. Apparently poor people from town had come in the night, had dug until the early hours and left with many sacks of potatoes before it was noticed and reported to the Bürgermeister who then rang the police at Rahlstedt. 'Surely,' I remarked, 'that was stealing and wrong.' Grandmother then became rather edgy, did not want to commit herself and said that there was 'stealing and stealing'. As much as I tried to press her, she could not bring herself to condemn poor people who took food from the earth to feed their families. She used to say that God made food grow for the use of all people and that there should be no need for poor people to steal it and, if caught, be punished or even go to prison.

This whole contradiction niggled me somehow, especially as grandmother was not at all forthcoming When I later asked father whether it was right to steal potatoes, he looked at me for some time and then told me that I was right to ask that question, but that I was too young to fully understand the implications of it. A question of that kind could not be answered with a straight yes or no. He asked me what I thought if both a rich and a hungry poor man walked into a baker's shop and both stole a loaf of bread while the baker was not looking, would I think that both had committed the same crime and should they both be punished in the same way for it? This was my father at his best, asking this sort of question, making me think for myself about the more intricate workings of society. And when I then wanted to know why there were rich and poor people in the first place, he just smiled and said that if I could find the answer to that question, I would be well on my way to understanding what society was all about.

Later in the morning, I went out to the field when some of the children came and talked to me. They had been sitting around a fire where their parents had made breakfast for them. They told me that they had left town in the very early hours when it still had been dark. I noticed that many of them looked thin and pale, that their clothes seemed to be shoddier than mine and I wondered whether that was the meaning of being poor. Though I was repeatedly reminded at home to be careful with everything, especially food, we never went hungry in our family. For that, I suppose, Stapelfeld with its ever-available food supply was partly responsible.

After my mother had left school, she had worked in service for a rich family on the outskirts of Hamburg. I loved to listen to her stories describing the poky and small cellar room she had to live in next to the kitchen, and about the bellboard with about a dozen bells on the wall below the ceiling, which she had to attend to twenty-four hours a day. There was no law in those days against a seven-day working week and no trade unions she could turn to for help. The pay, as her food was provided as part of her wages, was little more than pocket money and she felt at times an ill-treated slave, thinking of running away. When she once mentioned how a son of the family, a guard's officer, had tried to grab her in the corridor and elsewhere, I set off embarrassing giggles by innocently asking, 'but Mutti, why did he grab you, what did he want from you?' After that I was bundled off to bed.

But then the Great War had come which gave women a hitherto undreamt of chance to improve their lives. Mother grabbed the opportunity with both hands. Women were now needed to replace the young men who had been drafted into the forces and mother, with only her village school education, was courageous enough to go on a special course in Hamburg. Here she learned typing, shorthand, filing and other office skills which put her into line for a job much better paid than her service one, and she found work in the personnel department of a Hamburg business. I heard her sometimes say that this period, forgetting the horrors of war, was the most satisfactory and productive time of her life. She claimed that it had added enormously to her range of knowledge and the appreciation of her own abilities as a woman. She was happy, she said, that father not only understood but more so agreed with the need for women to struggle for better recognition in life.

She took a room in the poor working-class area of Hamburg-Rothenburgsort with a family who were wonderfully friendly and helpful to her. I vaguely remember when I was still very young that she went back to visit the family, taking me along with her. No doubt, she wanted to present me, her child. We sat in the kitchen with the mother when one after the other of the family came home from work. Each time there was a joyous surprise of welcome. The docks were near by; from the kitchen window I could see the cranes and the masts of the ships in port. Most of the family worked in the docks. Over coffee and cakes came the spell of reminiscences: 'do you remember this? – do you remember that? – do you recall that funny man?' – and so much more. Much fuss of course was made of me, with one of the girls running down to get me a bag of sweets. All the time there was loud talking and hearty laughter. When we came away on the tram, and also later in life, mother instilled in me that on the whole, the poorer, working people were much more genuine and helpful than their counterparts, those further up the social ladder, who regarded making money as their main objective in life. She claimed that the latter in general, though much more articulate and polished in their behaviour and manners, do not speak from their hearts but from their calculating brains, which in most cases makes them cold and hard human beings.

However when in 1918 the war came to an end and the 'undefeated' German armies, as the leaders called them, arrived back home, the opportunities for women abruptly ended. Mother expressed much bitterness about this. 'When our masters needed us, we were good enough,' she said, 'and when it was all over, they gave us the boot.' She was eager that I should understand all that and when I became a little older, she talked to me about the deeply ingrained injustices against women in our society. She was so angry that most people accepted these injustices as if they were natural, handed down by God. She felt very strongly that women's potential to add to the development and well-being of society were squandered because of those deep-seated prejudices. She fiercely condemned the docile Kinder-Küche-Kirche (Children-Kitchen-Church) attitude, and wanted to see women organise themselves to change society. But when father asked her 'How?', I felt that she was unsure about where to begin.

When my uncle Otto once suggested that it was only right and proper that women should not work in peacetime as there was not enough work for men anyway, a bitter argument resulted with mother questioning at root the very concept of unemployment, economic crisis, recession, war and poverty, arguing that all were connected with each other. She accused him of blindly accepting all these manmade phenomena as if they had come from God, handed down from on high. 'Try to think, Otto,' she said, 'think for yourself with your own brain and don't throw stupid slogans about which others have formulated for you.'

One of her most valuable possessions, it seemed to me, was a small collection of Käthe Kollwitz prints of superb drawings, depicting the suffering in poverty of ordinary working people, caught in the nets of an economic/social system which, according to her, should have been discarded a century earlier. She was firmly convinced, and of course father supported her on this, that poverty was unnecessary given the existing state of advanced technology, and that it only existed because of an economic system based on private profiteering.

My parents brought me up to always be truthful, never mind what the circumstances. To lie, they taught me, would be a terrible thing as it would destroy all trust, especially within the family. If ever I did something wrong, I was not to be afraid of owning up. Even if as a consequence I should be punished in a small way, that would soon be forgotten. But the trust, the love and my own clean conscience would still be intact and very much alive.

One day, I must have been about four years old, mother had to go somewhere for a few hours and left me with a kind old lady, Tante Lubitz I called her, who lived a flight of stairs below us. In a way I looked forward to it as until then I had never been away from mother. Tante Lubitz went out of her way to produce all kinds of amusements for me. That was fun, but when she made me sit down to have cakes and cocoa and I found that the cakes were hard and the cocoa tasted like water, I didn't really want any of it. I swallowed it down nevertheless. Mother had told me beforehand to be a good boy, and after I had finished and Tante Lubitz asked me whether I had liked it, I said: 'Yes, Tante Lubitz, thank you, it was very nice.'

11

After mother had fetched me back I told her truthfully that I had not liked it at Tante Lubitz because her cakes and cocoa had tasted awful. She said very little then, but when father came home from work, she told him in a joking manner that I had liked her cakes better than the ones Tante Lubitz had given me. And when they both laughed, I could not hold back any more and burst into tears. Both looked puzzled at first, unable to understand why I should burst out crying and asked me what was wrong. I told them that I had lied to Tante Lubitz and would they please not send me back to her and make me say sorry. But they hugged me instead, told me that would be the last thing they would do, that I should not worry, that everything would be all right. But then, I suspect, they both realised that they were in a bit of a quandary, that it was they who had some explaining to do as to the subtle difference between telling a fib and an outright lie.

Father took me on his knees and said something like, 'Oh dear, oh dear, you are learning rather early what a confusing place this world of ours is where it not always pays, and indeed sometimes is better, not to tell the truth.' We were very close at that moment, which gave me a feeling of protection and safety. The explaining was probably not easy for my parents as they had hitherto taught me that white was white and black, black, and to tell a lie was bad and wrong under all circumstances. And they had to explain now in a manner which would not make me lose trust in them. Mother fidgeted a bit and then told me that I had acted correctly when I wrongly told Tante Lubitz that I had liked her cakes and cocoa as otherwise I would have made her very sad, the last thing I surely would have wanted to do.

I think that I did understand and probably matured a little, advancing a small conscious step forward in understanding how complex life could be. What I did not quite grasp – and of course I had to absorb many more such lessons from that day onwards – was why it should be so, why so much of the art of living smoothly together should depend on not telling the truth. What sort of humans were we? And I imagined that animals were much more honest and straightforward in showing their real, true feelings, their instincts, than we were.

Mother had a friend, a Polish woman with a long and almost un-pronounceable name who had been transported to Germany during the war to do what mother called slave labour. Afterwards, having decided to stay in Germany because of a man friend who later let her down, she had fallen on hard times. Mother had found her one late evening freezing in a waiting room at Hamburg Main Railway Station. She took her home to her room, helped her to find work in the kitchen of a restaurant and the two became and stayed friends until Olga died when I was about five years old. Mother kept a framed photo of her on the sideboard in our flat which stayed there until it was burnt with the rest of our belongings during the great firestorm which destroyed Hamburg in the high summer of 1943, at the time I was doing my stint for the Fatherland, retreating from the Russian Front.

When at the time of the beginning of the war against Poland in 1939 I once made one of my typical racist Hitler Youth remarks about the so-and-so Poles, mother was shocked and severely took me to task, forbidding me to ever speak in such terms again in her presence. She said that she had met a number of Polish people who had come to Germany as forced labour or because of poverty back home. She had found most of them nice people and thought that it was a crime and a tragedy that Germans and Poles should fight and kill each other now again in a war, which was not of the making of the ordinary people on either side.

Another friend of mother's had been a tram conductress whom she had met on tram journeys to and from work during the war. This friend had married a docker, had a baby who had died, and lived in one of the poorest parts of Hamburg near the docks. We visited Frau Schlater several times. To get to the place we had to walk along the dockside of the busy port, which to me was very interesting, but I did not like the tenement where Frau Schlater lived. It gave me the creeps because it was a very small place which could only be reached by walking through an archway and then along a back alley. Everything about it smelled of poverty and neglect. The small courtyard which we had to cross, and which the sun never reached, was filthy and when we climbed up the dark stairs, we found the damp smell overpowering.

After some knocking, Frau Schlater opened the door about a couple of inches before she took the chain off to let us in. My young instinct told me that she was bothered by our unexpected arrival because she kept apologising for the dreadful state of her flat and the unbecoming circumstances she was living in. I was told to behave and be very quiet, although I did not understand why. The two friends whispered to each other about something which was not intended for my ears. But then, all of a sudden, the cause for it became all too clear, when with a loud bang the door to the bedroom opened and Herr Schlater, half-dressed and obviously the worse for drink, came tumbling out. He shouted at his wife, threatened to hit her and when mother tried to intervene, threatened her too. There was screaming and shouting all round. I was terribly frightened and all that mother could do was to grab me and run down the dark staircase, leaving Frau Schlater on her own with that brute of her husband. We both felt depressed when we walked away from the place and when I asked mother what all this had been about, she did not want to tell me, but kept saying something about poverty often bringing out the worst in its victims.

Once a month the rent collector, a Herr Appell, a dapper little man of about sixty who was always immaculately dressed and never without his black Homburg hat (we children called these hats 'Eierkocher', egg boilers), visited each flat in our tenement to collect the rent. All we knew about the owner of the tenement was that she was a rich lady who lived in the Bavarian Mountains near the Austrian border and never bothered to even have a look at the flats.

Mother often asked Herr Appell in for a cup of coffee and a piece of home-made cake. On me he made a sad impression. Never once, and I did know him for a number of years, can I remember having seen him smile. His main conversation was the weather, the hard times we were living in and the steep stairs he had to climb. There were other tenements in the neighbourhood from where too he had to collect the rents. He complained that many tenants looked at him as an enemy as if it was his fault that they had to pay rent. He told mother that he had to make his rounds at irregular times, not only because he was afraid of being robbed but because a number of tenants simply would not open the door if they suspected it was him. Then one day we heard that Herr Appell had been taken to hospital by ambulance and that all the money he had collected had been stolen. Father said that with so many poor people around it was not really surprising. After that a much younger, stronger, tall man came to collect our rent. Mother never asked him in. But she visited poor Herr Appell in hospital and we were all sad that he had lost his job on account of his age and frailty

Our flat together with two others was on the fourth floor, the highest in the tenement. The view from our front windows facing west was rather pleasant. We looked down on to the busy life in the street. We could see the green of the trees further on and behind them the brick-built church, the Kreuz Kirche (Church of the Cross) which had a high, slim spire. From our kitchen window at the back we looked into a busy coal yard. Mother often moaned about the dust rising up from the shovelling of coal, that it dirtied her washing which she hung on to a wooden frame sticking out from the window.

While quite often beggars climbed up the stairs and knocked at every door, others did it the easier way. They walked into the coal yard, either alone or in small groups and sang a song or two. Especially when they had instruments with them, their performances seemed to me very good. Mother as well as the other housewives then wrapped coppers into bits of newspaper and threw them down to them. I loved to do it, but when mother discovered that I tried to hit the singers, she told me off.

When these people came to the door, mother never gave them money but always asked them whether they wanted a sandwich, a bowl of soup or fruit. Sometimes mothers came with small children and told heart-breaking stories. Mother always listened and gave advice, but she never let them into the flat. With poverty all around us, terrible crimes occurred daily and I had strict instructions never to take the chain off the door unless I knew the caller.

We children called the coal yard owner 'Onkel Bernhard' because he was a kind and friendly man and let us play in the yard. We called his nice wife 'Tante'. At least once a week Onkel Bernhard asked us to help him put ten briquettes each into a brown paper bag to be neatly stacked at the side against the wall. They were then taken away for general delivery or sold singly. Many people living in the neighbourhood bought coal by the bucket-full. Some had so little money that they could only buy half a bucket and Onkel Bernhard never liked it when customers tried the never-never approach with him. He explained that he would like to help but that he too had to pay for his coal. Those of us kids who had mastered the art of counterweighing the bucket on the scale, were allowed to serve the customers, which was not only great fun but also made us feel very important. When a customer arrived with a bucket, we asked: 'what is it to be, Ruhr or Yorkshire and how much?' and then filled the bucket accordingly, reporting the weight to Onkel Bernhard or jotting it down on a bit of paper to hand to Tante Lenchen. When we knew the friendly face of the buyer and about her or his difficult circumstances, we put an extra lump in after the weighing and I think Onkel Bernhard knew about this little cheating trick of ours but never said anything because he had a good heart.

His customers who lived in the outer districts had more money, as he told us, and had their coal delivered by the hundredweight in sacks which Onkel Bernhard loaded on to the cart pulled by two horses. It was great fun when we were allowed to go with him, to sit on the sacks to make sure that they did not fall off on uneven roads. We loved to lead the horses out and back into their stables or walk them backwards into their harnesses, which demanded some skill. We loved to sit in winter in the pleasantly warm stables on the straw or even better to climb up the rickety ladder to the loft from where we threw down the hay for feeding.

We ourselves, father being a railway worker and therefore entitled to buy cheap coal from his employer, never bought coal from Onkel Bernhard. Father every autumn hired a handcart, allowed some of my friends to climb on to it with me and pushed us to the railyard near the station, where we held the bags open for him to shovel them full of coal, cokes or briquettes. It was always a joyous and loud trek through the streets where everyone shouted so that their friends could see them sitting proudly on the cart. Father then had to climb five flights of stairs with a sack on his back while mother helped him by carrying some coal in buckets. After he had unloaded them in our lock-up storage room under the roof, he felt exhausted and needed a good rest after a wash.

It was always quite an upheaval when father needed his wash, which he did every time he came home from work. We had only one tap in our flat which was in the kitchen above the Handstein, a low sink. But as the kitchen was also our living room during the week, the table had to be

15

pushed back, a couple of chairs removed and mother and I had to get out of reach when father started splashing water all over his upper body. It was a great relief when mother afterwards had wiped the wet floor, when everything had been put back into position and ordinary life could be resumed once again. When I sometimes made a sour face because of all that upheaval, my parents reminded me that we were lucky to have our own private tap in our flat and not to have to share one with other families, which was the case in quite a few other tenements in our town.

Most flats had electric light though some of the older ones still had gas lamps. I well remember several cases of whole families dying in their rooms from escaped gas. A number of tenements had common lavatories on the ground floor with three or four cubicles to be shared by about a dozen families.

From an early age I intensely disliked washing day which mother undertook every second week or so. There were no other facilities available in our tenement, and so it had to be done in the kitchen. As we always kept a continuous fire going in the iron kitchen hearth throughout the winter, the heating of the water created no great problem. But it did in summer when mother had to heat large saucepans of water on two small gas rings which took a long time. The tin bath was then placed on to two chairs by the open window, with mother standing behind it for hours with a bent back, rubbing and rubbing on the metal rubbing board until her fingers became sore and painful. The drying presented no difficulty in summer when the wet clothes were hung out of the window on to the frame which father had made himself. But in winter or on rainy days, the entire performance became a great nuisance. Washing lines were then strung in the kitchen from wall to wall under the ceiling and we had to dive under the hanging pieces to move anywhere. However cold it was outside, the top window had then to be open to prevent the condensation from dripping down the walls and the smell of strong soap from creeping into our nostrils. What a welcome relief it always was towards evening when mother started to take down the dried washing and the more cosy atmosphere of ironing-time took over, and sitting around the table became a pleasure again. Especially during the long winter evenings when I had become a bit older, we put a soft blanket on to the table, pulled the kitchen lamp which was hooked on a pulley right down so that our eyes were shaded from the light and my parents taught me card games, always great fun to play.

For a whole month every year before Christmas the Hamburger Dom, one of Germany's largest fun fairs, took place on the Heiligengeistfeld (Holy Ghost Field) which was a large open area near the centre of Hamburg. It was a matter of tradition and also of honour to take me to the Dom. Needless to say, we walked there and back in order to save tram fares. About half-way we crossed the Prussia/Hamburg border at the

16

Nobis Tor (gate). Father was well informed about local history and had many interesting tales to tell. He was eager to impart them to me as I was eager to listen and learn. Many concerned the Nobis Tor, some were crude and brutal but others were pleasant. We had a large book at home with drawings of the Nobis Tor. Some of the houses, being several hundred years old, still stood and I stared with fascination at their ancient gables.

When I expressed my thought that it must have been great to have lived in those olden days, father discouraged that line of thinking and urged me never to fool myself with such illusions. He explained that life must have been very horrible in those days, especially for the poor people who then as now were always handed the bucket to empty in the end. Not many children survived to the age of five due to malnutrition, hygiene-related diseases and the very poor living conditions their own parents had been born into. Almost all the poorer sections of society were illiterate. Schools, if there were any, were run by the churches who liked to claim that they did so from the goodness of their hearts and their concern for the well-being of the people. But the truth, father stressed, was of course otherwise. Churches then as now were very much part of the establishment which was based on owning property and were therefore immensely interested in filling ignorant minds with nebulous hocus pocus to keep them from thinking about the real causes of their poverty-stricken existence.

On the Hamburg side of the Nobis Tor was St. Pauli with its main very wide thoroughfare, the Reeperbahn, about which many songs have been written. Father said that the word Reeper relates to rope making and it was here where tradesmen with their workers made ropes for the ships of the port of Hamburg which was only a few hundred yards away.

All buildings on both sides were well illuminated and at night the whole street was an ocean of coloured lights. Inside them were amusement places of all sorts, pubs, shops, wine bars and even a couple or so theatres, as well as many cinemas and night clubs. There were always many people on the Reeperbahn twenty-four hours a day, and all year round. The entire area attracted many foreign sailors and with them criminal gangs who made it their business to rob them of their belongings. There were drunks lying about on the pavements from whom my parents tried to screen me. To me, life there was extremely fascinating, it seemed so full, so varied and consisted of so many colours. A street or so away were the Chinese Quarters. I begged father to take me and show me one day. But he told me that even the police were scared to go in there and never patrolled with less than four constables.

I was too young of course to understand the life of vice which was and still is probably the entire underlying pillar of the Reeperbahn entrepreneurs. I had no idea what brothels were, in two of which – the Lohe and the Herbert Strasse – hundreds of girls traded their business. But I did notice many pretty teenage girls walking apparently aimlessly around and talking to men. When my parents said that it was mainly poverty which made them do that and I then asked what they meant by 'do that', they simply did not respond to my question.

Most of the boys in my area were keen footballers. Needless to say, none of us belonged to a club nor possessed any kit and sometimes we found it even difficult to produce a decent ball to play with. At times we played with a tennis ball which might have been a blessing in disguise as it made good footballers of some of us. Then there was the problem of where to play. Usually we did it on pavements and when the game spilled over on to the road, it mattered little as most of the traffic was horse-drawn and horses, if we got into their way, stopped of their own accord. Seldom did we manage to get two full teams together, but as long we were at least six, three on each side, the game was on. We used our jackets as goal posts and we sometimes drew the outline of a goal with chalk against a wall.

There were a couple of parks with green spaces where we were allowed to play, but as few of us had bicycles, it was too much of a long walk just for playing a game of football. However whenever we arranged to play against another street, we did walk there. Never having a referee for these matches, and some of us were real hackers, quarrels often broke out which easily developed into fights. In that case the game came to a sad end and we trudged home, all twenty-two of us, but well distanced from each other. Even when we had lost the game, we were in high spirits, more so if we had managed to give the victors a good hiding afterwards. Walking home like that, we usually sang the currently popular songs, many of which we had learnt in the cinema. On Sunday afternoons there were special performances for children. One of the films was Tarantella with Nelson Eddy and Jeanette McDonald. Of course all talking and singing had been translated into German and we noticed by the lip movements of the actors that they were really speaking and singing in a different language. We thought that it was very funny. For weeks afterwards everyone doodled the Donkey Serenade which we called Esel Serenade until everyone got fed-up with it. One song we all knew was the International. It was a kind of signature tune with us. Why that should have been so, I don't know and I cannot remember the circumstances under which we picked it up nor who put us up to it. I am sure that it was not my father, though he liked me singing or whistling it.

It was at the time when I entered school that I became aware for the first time that there was something called politics. Naturally, hardly having an idea where the country of Austria was, I nevertheless gathered that something unusual and important was developing there which very much distressed my parents and at the same time made them very angry. I also realised that in matters of politics, which father called the organisation of life, my parents treated me differently from how most of my friends were being brought up by their parents. In most households as far as I could make out from visits to my friends, politics and religion were taboo, never spoken about, at least not when the children were present. I remember one of my aunts, and that was in relation to the Austrian issue, looking towards her children, and saying that talking about these subjects would deform their characters. My parents told me on our way home that they totally disagreed with this sentiment and strongly impressed on my young mind that such an attitude was not only nonsense but also unfair to the young ones who one day would have to face the real world, and then would discover that they were ignorant of it. Everything in their view, just about everything, given the right time and circumstance of course, should be openly talked about. In connection with this they strongly impressed on me that I should never be afraid of asking questions about anything and everything.

When I then wanted to know about Austria, they told me that serious unrest had broken out in Vienna because poor people at the very end of their tether and unable to see any other way out of their poverty had taken to the streets in open revolt against the harsh policies implemented by their government. Street fighting had been going on in Vienna for days and was now spreading to other cities. And when the police had failed to stem the revolt, the army had been brought in, and at first had machine-gunned the crowd consisting of men, women and children, old and young, mostly unemployed and often hungry demonstrators. Of course the government, press and church were saying that it all was due to nasty agitators who were bent on causing trouble. Many had been killed by the gunning. But the masses of the poor were desperate. Food shops had been plundered and law and order – father called it the laws and orders of the rich – was breaking down. It was then that the army pounded the living quarters of the poor with artillery. The carnage from that was horrible. Father said that the Catholic Church was playing a cunning game in it all. The Vatican came out with all sorts of sweetly sounding words, urging the poor to stop their protesting. Please, be sensible and let us have peace. There was no appeal to the well-offs however. After all, they were not rioting, on the contrary they were well behaved. 'No wonder,' said father, 'they have no need to ransack food shops, they are not suffering from hunger and deprivation. Whenever there is any move towards democracy, real democracy which expresses the economic and social needs of the majority of the people, you can be sure that the Vatican will step in to stop such nonsense.' I was aware that my parents were making the rounds of their friends and workmates to collect money for the Austrian workers and their families.

Sometimes in summer when father had his day off or his annual week's holiday, he took mother and me on a long walk to the village of Othmarschen. It was a pleasant stroll mostly along country lanes and pleasant paths which had high hedges on both sides and could be very muddy after the rains. I loved these walks because, out of their daily unchanging routines, my parents were then in an easy loving mood, often holding hands, observing everything around with great interest and making me aware of it. Taking our time leisurely, this walk could last for up to two hours.

Othmarschen was a quaint old place, almost as if time had stood still. Naturally it was very different from the industrial town of Altona where we lived. But it also differed a lot from the village of Stapelfeld which had a much more rural character, with the farmsteads in the village still very much in operation with herds of cows tramping along its lanes and even the cobbled main village street, leaving their mess everywhere.

As father explained, Othmarschen had been like Stapelfeld up to the beginning of our century. It was at that time that the industries of Altona had grown and spread and with them the tenements of the workers. Altona crept closer and closer towards Othmarschen. That's what people called progress. When we walked there in the early thirties, there was still a wide, green belt between the two. But my parents could foresee that one day Altona and Othmarschen would grow into each other with the latter totally losing its character.

The real change arrived at Othmarschen when the railway line had been built from the town into Schleswig Holstein proper which gave Othmarschen a pleasant small station. The economy being at the best of times unpredictable, the farmers grabbed the easy opportunities and sold their fields to clamouring developers who anticipated huge profits from building on it. With the railway there, Othmarschen was now only half an hour's train ride from Hamburg and fifteen minutes from Altona. Those industrialists and others who had done well for themselves in town were now only too eager to buy property in the country and live there.

Though the village council could not stop that development, probably they did not want to as in monetary terms it was profitable, they nevertheless restricted the building of new houses in the village centre which had a pleasant pond with masses of ducks on it and kept its character pleasantly rural. The great change, of course, was that now so many of the people living there did not work in the village any more. Feudalism had gone forever from Othmarschen and capitalism with all that it meant, good and bad, had fully arrived.

Next to the pond was a Gastwirtschaft (pub) which had a large garden with a children's playground with swings, roundabouts and climbing ropes where I enjoyed myself. My parents sat in the garden at a small table, father with a large glass of beer and mother with a lemonade while I had a glass of something or other. I remember those kinds of outings with my parents with great pleasure and gratitude.

With the years flying past and getting older, I did not fancy walking with my parents any more but wanted to make discoveries under my own steam and go roaming with my friends to Othmarschen and other places. The village cottages, of which many were still thatched, had large gardens surrounding them. A number of families already owned cars and most of the properties were well hedged-in to keep peeping eyes like ours at bay. In autumn we took our rucksacks, knocked at the doors and asked whether we could pick the fallen apples from the lawn under the trees. Most owners gave us permission, they were probably only too glad to get rid of the fallers. And when no one answered the door and the tree was on a convenient escape route, we picked the apples nevertheless and when the fruits were hanging reachable in the trees, they too found their way into our rucksacks. We realised that according to the law such acts were really stealing, but our instincts also told us that as God had made the trees and the apples grow on them, there was something wrong with the law which gave so many trees and apples to the wealthy and none at all to poor people like ourselves.

Sometimes we met some of the Othmarschen village children. We sensed that they were very different from us in almost every sense and thought that they were really not like traditional village children at all, at least not in our accepted sense. None of them went to our schools, some said that they were being privately educated, whatever that meant; and our instincts somehow told us that there was something wrong here. We felt that all children, never mind from which background they came, should have the same kind of education and thereby the same opportunities in later life. Unlike ourselves, they only spoke High German and when we spoke in Plattdeutsch to them, they simply did not react, thinking perhaps that we were common. They were able to express themselves far better than we could which made us think that they were stuck-up. Both sides must have felt that there was a barrier between them. They seemed to have nothing to say to us while we felt the same towards them. The few exchanges we had with each other were artificial with even a sprinkling of contempt. It happened once or twice that when their mothers saw them talking to us, they called them in. Once we heard one saying to her son not to get involved with us town children which made us feel as if we were dirt. As a response we all went close to the fence, poked our tongues out and shouted that next time we would give them a good bashing.

It must have been around that time that my parents allowed me to go to Sunday School at the nearby Kreuz Kirche. I was well aware that they were not exactly in favour of it, but I think that they finally caved in to my pestering them because I made the point that as so many of my friends went, I wanted to be with them. However, before I went for the first time, they told me to keep my eyes and ears open, to be attentive to what was being done and said and above all to ask questions if there was something which I did not understand.

I attended several Sunday morning sessions and in a way I quite liked it because everyone there was very friendly. Each time it started off with a short service whose meaning mystified me, but I let it go. Then an old lady and sometimes the pastor himself took a group of us into a quiet corner and told us stories from the Bible. There was so much which simply made no sense to me and at first I assumed that it was I who was at fault, that I simply was not clever enough and that I was probably the only one who had really no idea of what was going on. The more I concentrated and tried to understand, the more confused I became. And then I went home and announced to my parents that I had had enough and was not going to Sunday School any more.

'Why not?' mother wanted to know, 'surely, you must have a reason.'

'I don't like it because neither the pastor nor the old lady will answer my questions.'

'But what did you ask?' mother wanted to know, and I told her that I had asked where heaven was, what kind of bench Jesus sat on to the right of God and what God looked like, was he bald with a few hairs above his ears and did he wear a blue coat?

When I had asked that, the old lady just looked at me and then went over to tell the pastor who came and chided me, saying that I must never look at these holy events with ordinary eyes and ask questions in that way, but that I must believe that God and Jesus are all around and in us. And when I asked why I must believe what I did not understand, the pastor told me that I must not upset the others with such stupid questions and that one day in the future when I was a few years older, the all-pervading truth would dawn on me. To top it all, on our way home some of my friends had teased me, saying that I was stupid because the pastor had said that I was.

Mother took me into her arms, told me that she loved me, that I must not let these people upset me and that she was not really surprised that things had turned out in this fashion. Then father came in on it and told me that I was not at fault, quite the contrary, that indeed I had been more than right to ask such questions and that he was proud of me for doing so. The pastor had probably become angry because I had shown him up in front of the others, he was afraid that they perhaps too would realise that he did not know what he was talking about and that for that reason he simply had not known the answer to my question. He mentioned the word brainwashing and when I asked what that meant, he related what had happened to him when he was a little boy, only a year or so older than I was now.

'It was during the Kaiser's days and every morning before school started, all of us boys and girls had to assemble in the large school hall for prayers. The school rector (headmaster) started it off by saying "God bless our Kaiser and the Royal Family", which we all had to repeat. Then came general announcements and it all ended with a prayer. That is what I now realise was brainwashing. We were made to say words which none of us had the faintest idea what they meant. What no one was allowed to mention was that the Kaiser's family as well as the church were amongst the richest institutions in the land. And we, the ones who owned next to nothing, were ordered to pray for them, to support them in their endeavour to keep us down so that they could hold on to what they already possessed and add more to it.

'And then the Great War had come in 1914 and almost all of us boys were put into uniforms and sent to the battlefront where we had to fight and kill and possibly be killed and lose our limbs for Kaiser and Church. Those very few who refused to do it, who had the courage to stand up for their fundamental Christian conviction that to kill other humans was to deny God's command, were put in front of the firing squad so that others should not get the same idea.'

Father had been present when two of his comrades had been shot in that way, one of them had reminded the officer commanding the squad that Jesus had taught to love one's enemy. But it had not helped him, he was killed just the same, Christian principles or no Christian principles.

And when the war was all over in 1918, with millions of innocent people killed and vast tracts of land with thousands of villages and towns, mainly in France, devastated, the Kaiser and his lot simply crossed the border into Holland to settle in a castle in a large estate near the town of Doorn not far from the German border. He had wisely bought it beforehand 'just in case'. 'That was all His Christian Majesty cared for, his own safety and wealth, for he had not forgotten to take his gold and diamonds with him.'

Mother, of course, always supported father. She complemented what he had told me and added that it had been exactly the same in her school, as it had probably been in others all over the country. She gave the example of how the whole brainwashing machine had worked there. The children had to learn by heart the names and birthdays of the royal princes and princesses. If I remember correctly, there were seven boys and one girl in the Kaiser's family. And when their birthdays came along, the school day started with a special prayer for the birthday child, followed by an hour or so of mechanistic and grovelling discussion about his or her achievements, how hard-working they were and what superior qualities they had. Mother told me all this when she was in her early forties and she was still able to rattle off the names of the royal family with their birthdays. Looking back at it then, she was fully aware that this had been done to discourage the young from thinking about poverty and other problems in their own lives.

CHAPTER II
The Last Days of Weimar

I started school at the age of six. Everything around that important event excited me. Aunts and uncles as well as friendly neighbours reminded me that this was a totally new step in my young life which then finally arrived after Easter in 1929. Older children had somehow managed to put fear into me by saying that teachers were nasty grown-up creatures whose aim was to dish out punishments to those who did badly in class. And I wondered on the quiet how I could possibly cope with all that.

Of course mother came with me on that first all-important day. I carried my large Schultüte, a cardboard cone of about eighteen inches long filled with all sorts of goodies like sweets, fruits and pralines. This custom, I think, is still observed in Germany and other Central European countries today.

The school itself, a large Wilhelmenian building, probably built in the early part of the last century, was about ten minutes' walk from home next to a busy suburban railway line. It had two entrances, one for boys and the other for girls.

Mother had tried to cheer me up on the way, had kept telling me that I must not believe what others had tried to frighten me with and that teachers were really nice and friendly people who would teach me so many new and exciting things, which father and she could do no more. But she was unable to wipe away my overall uneasiness which my imaginative mind had created. Everything seemed so strange and so threatening. What was my fate to be? Life suddenly seemed so full of problems, with the building itself looking more like a prison than a school. But then I noticed a boy with his mother whom I knew who also looked miserable and carried his Schultüte, and when we then finally sat next to each other on the double seat with the desk in front, I felt already a little bit easier.

Then however came the crunch when all the mothers had suddenly disappeared. Up to that day I had never really been without mine. One minute they were all standing by the door – and in the next they were gone. Some of us started to howl and I was not quite sure any more whether to join them until Fräulein Wulf, our teacher, quickly managed to pacify us all. She was a nice young lady, probably in her late twenties, rather buxom with a bunch of blond hair, neatly tied together at the top of her head. Foreigners probably would have called her Gretchen. She had friendly eyes which one could trust and an easy way which I liked and which gave me much-needed self-confidence. She told us nice stories and played games with us and there was much laughter. I got so absorbed in it, that I was almost disappointed when it was suddenly all over after the school bell rang and the mothers had come back to fetch us home.

On the whole I had liked my first school day, at least I told father that. There was one bother, though, an unaccountable fear about which I told no one. It took a year or longer before I was finally able to overcome it. It was about the Rector, a Herr Clausen who, no doubt, was a kind and considerate man who always gave us a friendly smile when he came into our class room. But when he then went to Fräulein Wulf and quietly spoke to her at her desk, I imagined that it was about me and that he had especially come for that reason. There was nothing I was aware of that I had done wrong, but I had fixed it into my mind that one day he would come to take me away and punish me for something I had not done.

The school playground at the back had a rough cover of black cinders which produced many nasty cuts on knees, hands and elsewhere. Fights broke out quite often between a couple of aggressive boys around which a crowd quickly collected, egging the fighters on, who then had to be quickly separated by the teacher who was in charge of the playground. In the absence of a fence, a demarcation line had been drawn on the cinder surface which separated the boys from the girls. Anyone who overstepped it had to report to their teacher and received a telling-off and a warning. We played many games during the breaks, most of them innocent ones. But there was one which we called 'Kriegserklärung' (Declaration of War). It was a very popular game and always watched by many. A square of about eight metres was scratched into the cinders which again was equally divided up into four smaller ones of about four by four metres. Each of those squares then took the name of a country such as Germany, England, France, Russia or others. The four players then stood closely together in the centre, each in his own square when one of them announced I declare war on so and so. At this the other three had to make one jump away from the caller and stop. If the latter who had declared war was able to touch one of the others, it was his right to take a piece of land from that one's square. The one who at the end occupied the largest bit of land was the winner.

I am aware that this was only a children's game. But by playing it with enthusiasm, we grew up thinking that declaring war and taking land from one's enemy was the most natural thing to do. Needless to say, each of the four players wanted to be Germany.

It was about that time that I joined the Christian Jungschar, a boy scout movement with rather strong patriotic, nationalistic undercurrents. Much of the set-up was based on the English Baden-Powell movement which was quite often mentioned at our meetings. There were scandals, I remember, with some leaders having interfered with boys about which my parents warned me. Our uniform shirts were of a dirty-green colour, the trousers beige and the blue necktie was held together by a metal ring under the chin. We wore a wide-brimmed South Westerner on our heads which had been worn by our soldiers in the Imperial Colonial Army during the suppression of the natives' uprising in South-West Africa and which, we thought, looked smashing.

The weekly meetings took place in a large upstairs room in the Gemeindehaus (Parish Hall). On some Sundays we went on outings by either bus, train or river boat or we marched. The parish verger, a kind, elderly and completely bald-headed man, always opened the meeting with a prayer followed by a Bible quotation which he then related to happenings in everyday life. No one took much notice of what he was saying and when it lasted too long, a telling restlessness developed amongst us. All we wanted was to move on to the more interesting parts of the evening, like games, telling stories, and so on. Then the real leaders of the Jungschar, the older boys of about sixteen to eighteen, took over and religion was not further mentioned. They organised all kinds of competitions and we learned many songs. I liked best the ones which reached back to Germany's past, which were melancholic and had a patriotic flavour. The expression 'Fatherland', we were taught, had a holy meaning and was often on our lips. When a more cheeky one amongst us once asked, and we all burst out in loud laughter, why we did not call it 'Motherland', the verger became very angry and warned him not to make a silly joke about something for which countless heroes had died in bloody battles.

In summer when it was warm and the evenings were dry, we were allowed to go out into the large garden which had smooth lawns with tall trees standing on their edges. I loved it out there as most of us, coming from working class families and living in town flats, were not used to such luxuries and judged them as something only the wealthy had a right to enjoy.

As seen through my eyes at the time, and completely unable to compare like with like, it seemed to me that life was rolling along nicely and totally securely. I heard, mostly from remarks by my parents, that there were upheavals and unrest in the outside world which posed a threat to us all. But being totally unable to understand why that should be so, I pushed these worrying thoughts aside. I heard about politics but did not really know what it meant. The name of a Herr Brüning, the Reichskanzler (Prime Minister) and leader of the small Catholic Centre Party, was often mentioned at home and I noticed it on the front page of the newspaper. He apparently had issued emergency decrees and when I asked father what that meant, he said that they had something to do with our big-mouthed and small-brained leaders having again got us all into a holy mess, not knowing how to get out of it and trying the usual remedy of shifting the burden on to the backs of poor working people, of whom more and more had become unemployed as a result.

When I was about seven or eight years old, father arranged for me to go on a holiday in a railway children's home on the North Sea island of Föhr which was not far from the Danish border. I was rather homesick at first but quickly got used to the new surroundings and made many new friends. The Home was in a lovely old villa in large grounds from whose upper windows one could see the sea, which at times was wild and grey. I discovered there that such a wild sea fascinated me and I could have stood there by myself for hours, just watching.

On fine days we walked down to the almost white sands and un-dressed. There were dunes all around us with bits of dune grass growing out of them. We liked to lie in their hollows, watch the sky and the screeching seagulls above us and let the always present breeze blow over the tops, only touching the tips of the dunes. At the early age of about four, mother had taught me to swim in our local Bismarck Baths. This now came in very handy as I was allowed, under strict supervision of course, to swim in the shallow sea. It was my first holiday and when I arrived back home after four weeks, happy, healthy and browned with bleached blond hair, I noticed how pleased and grateful my parents were with the way I was growing up. I knew that they loved me and of course I loved them dearly.

Naturally not realising it then, the Weimar Republic went deeper and deeper into crisis and closer and closer towards collapse. Had someone asked me what the Weimar Republic was, I would not have known. All that I was sure of was that I was a German boy and that my country, my Fatherland, was Deutschland, Germany.

Father at least on one evening in a week went to a meeting. When I asked him where and of what kind the meeting was, he patted my head which he did whenever he was thoughtful and responded with: 'One day when you are a little older and therefore have a better understanding of the ways of the world, I will tell you.' I knew that he was proud to be an active member of his trade union of which, I am sure, he was one of the local leaders. But the trade union meetings were usually straight after work and I now have little doubt that the evening meetings were of a more political nature. He often spoke in terms of needing a close and continuing contact with like-minded people who saw the world through the same eyes as he did. He had a dream, he told me once, the deep yearning of his generation of breaking free of the humanly degrading and smothering clamp which the power of money had over people. He was sure that if not

28

his generation or not even mine, one generation one day would succeed in that necessary task, to set people free to develop their limitless potential.

During the Weimar days our town was in many ways a political beehive. There were so many political parties sticking their posters against walls, hoardings or windows of empty shops and so many demonstrations, marche, and protests with meetings on squares, in parks as well as in open streets. Ordinary people seemed to be at the end of their tether. When one came by chance upon such an event, one at first could not be sure of what party or political grouping it was. There were so many leaflets driven by gusts of wind into doorways and other sheltered nooks, which we children picked up at random to redistribute to the first puzzled and then perhaps understanding passers-by.

The largest groupings of course were those organised by the working people, for they, as compared with the others, were by far the largest in numbers. Father called the working class the as-yet sleeping giant. The middle class, the bourgeoisie as they were called, who lived in more healthy surroundings away from the smoking factories and the city centre, did not see the necessity or the point of coming together in such ways. They did not feel the need to march and sing and shout political slogans.

The communists seemed to be the most active, at least in our poor part of the town. They, at least the activists amongst them, wore a very simple sort of uniform, consisting of a seemingly too large greyish cotton shirt which hung over the top of their trousers and had large pockets. Most of them had not even that and dressed themselves in ordinary poor-quality workers' clothing. They showed the hammer and sickle on their lapels and gave their greetings by raising the clenched fist to a height of their ear. They greeted each other with 'Rot Front' and we called them generally 'Die Rote Front'.

Then there were the Sozis, the social democrats, grouped together in an organisation called 'Der Reichsbanner'. They had three silver arrows as their emblem on their lapels, raised their clenched fists high above their outstretched arms and used as a greeting the word 'Freiheit' (Freedom). Though they had no real uniform, they seemed on the whole much tidier than the communists. Perhaps, father suggested, they had slightly more money than the latter. These two parties, though they did not show much liking for each other and went their own often divided ways, never clashed with each other in the streets, at least as far as I know.

The third main groupings were relative newcomers, the National Socialists or Nazis as everyone called them for short. They differed much from the others in so many ways. In the early days they were simply called 'die Hakenkreuzler', the ones of the swastika, because the Hakenkreuz, the crooked cross in a white circle on red cloth was their emblem, which was mostly carried by the Fahnenträger (flag carrier) in front of their column when they marched in town. Their marches were never ones of protest but simply of showing their colour and strength. Their movement had originated in the south of Germany in the Bavarian capital Munich and probably for that reason found it difficult in the early years to make meaningful political inroads in the northern and western industrial cities like those in the Ruhr, Berlin, Hamburg, Dresden or Cologne.

The Nazis were well organised and outwardly so much more disciplined and stricter than any of their opponents. Their main political arm was the SS, short for Schutzstaffel (Protector Team), and though many of its members were said to have come from the huge army of unemployed, every member wore a uniform consisting of a brown shirt, necktie, breeches and a funny looking round cap with a flat top. They also wore nailed jackboots and often had music with them, mainly drums and pipes. Their songs were loud, almost of the shouting type and when they were marching in the streets, going round and round in our town, almost entirely in the working class quarters, we children liked to run next to them on the pavements, waving our arms and trying to sing their songs with them. They always behaved in a friendly fashion towards us, often patted our heads and sometimes even allowed us to make up the rear of their column. They always marched firmly in step, there was no slackness about them, and I could not understand why father did not like them and called them 'Die Braune Pest'.

Whenever the Nazi Party organised a political meeting, their brown stormtroopers were always present in large numbers. And when other parties organised theirs, they were also there. When they did not like the speeches, and they of course never did, they started shouting mainly from the back of the hall. When the stewards then moved in and attempted to call them to order, the trouble started and fights broke out which in many cases brought the meeting to a close. Father was sure that had been their objective anyway.

It was obvious and there was evidence that the Nazis as an organisation had much more money than their main political opponents, though they loved to accuse the communists of receiving 'Moscow Gold'. The most obvious evidence was that they all wore expensive uniforms including jackboots. They sometimes wore these, which they were not supposed to, for private use which were then partly hidden from view by their trouser legs pulled over the upper parts. There were many jokes about their hidden jackboots making the rounds. As to the number and sizes of flags and banners, their supply was prolific compared to those of other political parties, especially the communists who, it was too self-evident, had made their red flags and banners themselves.

The same went for musical instruments, trumpets, drums and flutes, which played an important part in their propaganda activities. The instruments of the Nazis were often brand new and were safely stored and locked away in their own depots, while one could see the members of the other parties carrying their own instruments from home to the meeting place and back.

It often happened, especially during the long winter evenings, that friends of my father's dropped in, each with a bottle of beer for which mother provided the glasses. They then sat around our kitchen table and discussed various political and historical topics. One evening they talked about the sources they thought the Nazis were getting their money from, and on the whole they agreed that much came from the industrial barons in the Ruhr.

I liked my father's friends. They were always friendly to me, sometimes brought me sweets and mother a bunch of flowers. As long as I kept quiet and it was not too late, father seemed to like my presence. I then sat in the corner by the warm stove and was all ears. Naturally, much of what was being said went well over my head but some of it, and I only realised it much later, submerged into my memory to help me later to better understand and be able to analyse the happenings and events around me.

Though the meetings were always male, there was a time when a middle-aged woman came to join. She was well-spoken, considerably better than the others present and I gathered, though I cannot be sure any more, that she was lecturing at Hamburg University and did not want it to be known that she came to this kind of meeting. Whenever she spoke, the others listened with concentrated attention. She always came later than the others and left earlier which, I think, was all part of her concern not to draw outside attention.

All this must have happened around 1931/32 before the Nazis were appointed to government because I heard the woman say that Hitler was the only party leader during the election campaign who could afford to travel by plane from election meeting to election meeting, thereby easily covering every big city in the Reich, sometimes giving as many as three main speeches in one day. There was general agreement around the table about the source of Hitler's money. The woman mentioned Fritz Thiessen, a leading industrialist, who was one of the richest men in the world. Thiessen had a vital interest in pushing Hitler for the Chancellorship, as the latter had promised to bring in an armament programme which would help the ailing industries in the Ruhr, reverse the bitter recession and ease the massive unemployment problem which at that time, with the Russian Revolution still very much a memory, was developing a threatening revolutionary outlook amongst many working people. Apart from that, it was beginning to bite into the middle classes as well and there was evidence that they were shifting their support towards Hitler. She reminded those present that not all that many years ago the red flag had been flying above the town hall of every major German city and, given the right circumstances and conditions, that situation could arise again.

Capitalism, she said, was in dire trouble and its beneficiaries were afraid that workers would organise themselves against that system.

One at the table pointed out that Nazi recruitment was being helped by the provision of free and reduced-priced beer at the SA meetings. Father explained how sad and disappointed he had been when he learned that two of his old mates, drinkers both, had turned their coats, as the saying goes and like Judas, not for a coin this time but for a glass of beer, had given up all they had so fervently believed in.

I witnessed many clashes in the streets during those years. The Nazis were always prominently involved in all of them. They were not always very serious, sometimes not much more than a fracas which had a funny side to it, when we shouted and laughed from the sidelines, cheering the fighters on. Abuse of course was always plentiful, blows were struck, the shouting was loud and human rings were quickly formed around the fighting men who got entangled with each other and rolled around on the pavement or cobblestones. Sometimes there was blood gushing from a broken nose and screams of pain from perhaps too much twisting of an arm or neck. Often there was also a quick all-round disappearing act when someone shouted 'police!'. Those who were too slow were taken in a police van which we called 'Maria' to the station.

I think it was in the summer of 1932 when a terrible clash occurred in our town which is still remembered in the annals of inter-war years as the infamous 'Altonaer Blut Sonntag' (Altone's Bloody Sunday). That catastrophe took place not far from where we lived in a rundown area which had many narrow streets and alleyways between crumbling tenements. I cannot remember how many people died, but the numbers were considerable. The ensuing fighting had spilled over into several other parts of the town afterwards. As I understood it then, there had been a mass demonstration against poverty, unemployment, rising rents and prices which had been called and partly organised by the communists. Thousands had been on the march which was to lead to the town hall when troops of the SA had moved in from several side streets, which seemed to be in a concerted manner.

Many men, women and children were in the demonstration and when the SA intervened, so many tried to escape, that others, not being able to get away, were trampled on. Police had been present in the side streets as the event, so I understood from father, had been cleared beforehand with the authorities. But as so often in those days, a heavy smothering cloud hung over their role and actions and nothing seemed to be clear-cut afterwards. Those on the right of the political spectrum preferred to see in the police the upholders of law and order, while those on the left, probably also understandably, saw in them nothing but the upholders of a repressive status quo. No doubt, my father, like all others, must have held a prejudiced view of some sort in a situation like that. It must have been almost impossible to hold a totally objective one. Nevertheless it was my own observation at the time, and I had many opportunities to see what was going on, that there was a covert co-operation between police and Nazi stormtroopers. Many members of the police in our part of the town had come from the ranks of the military and were generally suspected to be of a politically right-wing persuasion.

Suddenly from amidst all the chaos and confusion a machine gun had opened up from a commanding rooftop of a tenement at a corner. Later, we thought that we too had heard the clatter of it, had looked out of the window and had seen agitated people running in the street below. Mother went down to find out what had happened and then abandoned the idea of taking me to where she had originally planned.

When father came home from work – he often had to work on Sundays and then had the Monday off in lieu – he was very agitated and distressed. He did not know much more than what we had already gathered and there were so many wild rumours making the rounds. But he was positive that the SA had actively helped the police to arrest many demonstrators while they themselves had been allowed to get away scot-free.

Since the collapse of the Kaiser's Reich at the end of the First World War in November 1918, the German people had achieved some social advances after much struggle. As father told me, by having thrown out the Kaiser and abolished the monarchy, an important step towards democracy had been made. But he stressed that it had only been one step on a long stony road which still had to be trodden. The Kaiser as a person, he impressed on me, was not necessarily important, but the whole economic/social system was based on private land ownership, then still in the hands of about two hundred rich families, and this was something the November Revolution had been unable to dislodge.

As I had been born only four years after Kaiser Wilhelm II had been forced to abdicate and as he was still alive during my childhood years, it is perhaps understandable that the mere mention of his name evoked in me a sense of fascination and mysticism. What did this aura around the Kaiser mean, why was his name so much connected with glory, what sort of a person was he and why did some of the older people when they talked about him lower their voices and still called him 'His Majesty'?

At school he was no longer on the curriculum, certainly not after Hitler had become the Führer of the Reich. When during history teaching his name simply could not be avoided, I had the impression that our teacher always tried to speedily skid over it. He was hardly ever mentioned in the Hitler Youth, but at home and in the streets the expression 'in the Kaiser's time' was most commonly used to compare something in order to score points of one sort or another. There were songs about him, street songs, funny ones in connection with him having been found out and chased across the border, which we children sang with much delight.

I must have pestered my parents to tell me about the Kaiser, what he was like, had they ever seen him, why did he have that funny upward twisting moustache, so for once they told me what they thought about him. They said he was a millionaire many times over and always wanted more for himself and his large family. 'And the Reichstag, our feeble Parliament, votes for it,' my father said. It was said that the Kaiser had fathered many children out of wedlock with chambermaids and others who were probably proud to have been the Kaiser's children, and that there had been more unsavoury things about him which only became known to the general public after he had been dethroned.

Father had actually seen him once in Hamburg. I think it happened after the launching of one of his warships. It was known that he was very keen on building a powerful navy to challenge the British. The up and coming Japanese were somewhat of an obsession of his and the coining of 'the Yellow Peril' was said to have originated with him. But father had only seen him from afar when he had stepped into his horse-drawn coach. Accompanied by Uhlans on fine horses he had waved from the coach window in a theatrical manner.

I tackled father about what he had meant by saying that the Kaiser as a person was not really important, that he was crippled, had a short right arm and was not very clever but that the system he symbolised was. 'For a start,' he said, 'the very existence of monarchy flies in the face of any pretension of being a democracy. On the contrary, these two institutions are total opposites. The Kaiser was surrounded by a chosen group of advisors who knew exactly what they were up to. All of them were very rich, most belonged to the aristocracy and were therefore powerful in their own right. Working people were usually told that these people had a private income the meaning of which was never explained nor discussed. And all of them were hell-bent on continuing a system in which ordinary people, in spite of the smoke screen of the Reichstag, had no input whatsoever. The royal families, and there were a number of them in Germany, only sat on their thrones by accident of birth, intrigue, corruption and probably worse. What is important to remember is that the unelected ones around the Kaiser in effect decided all important policies. In his name, they could make war, sign treaties and make important key appointments, without any meaningful interference by the rubber stamp Reichstag.'

No doubt thinking that it was important for me to understand the historical background of later developments, he explained how the modern German Reich had come into being only as late as 1871. The first Reich had collapsed in 1806 after the Prussian Army had been beaten by Napoleon at Jena in Thüringia. Sixty-five years later however, the time for German revenge had arrived when the Prussian armies beat Napoleon III at Sedan, where the French Emperor had to hand over his sword to the arrogant victors to concede defeat. While artillery duels could still be heard from near-by Paris, victory celebrations were being prepared in the large historic mirror hall of Versailles, where the Prussian Chancellor Otto von Bismarck had summoned the kings, grand dukes, dukes and other reigning princelings of the German states, except the Kaiser of Austria. At that time the area of Germany consisted of several hundred small states which all had their own capitals, some their own currencies, hindering the free flow of goods and capital desired by the increasingly influential class of capitalist entrepreneurs. A journey from say Cologne to Berlin included something like thirty border crossings with customs and other hold-ups.

Von Bismarck, the Iron Chancellor, so father explained, was a most reactionary Prussian Junker but clever enough to foresee that modern capitalism could not be stopped from replacing outdated feudalism, which in so many ways was still under outright aristocratic dominance. Such was the logical flow of history. The establishment of Bismarck's Second Reich, based on an alliance between the dominant classes of land, high finance and industry resulted in the bringing-together of the German Länder under one crown.

Thus on the 18th January 1871 King Wilhelm I of Prussia was pro-claimed Kaiser of the Second Reich at Versailles which was the birthdate and place of modern Germany. Father showed me a famous painting depicting the proclamation ceremony. Each one of the several hundred present was male and wore military uniform. To father that was an ill omen not only for the fate of the ordinary people of Germany but for the direction of that so potentially powerful state right in the heart of Europe. Working people, having had no say in the Reich's creation, should therefore have no duty nor sense of loyalty towards it either. 'Our future,' he repeatedly stressed it to me, 'can only be with the working people of all other countries and not with our rulers.'

Following the Versailles set-up, the Reich's rulers put much importance on 'educating' the masses of whom a considerable percentage was still illiterate. These rulers were no fools and clearly realised that a thorough basic training of working class children was of absolute necessity for challenging Europe – and later perhaps the world – militarily and economically. Their plans for education of course did not include the encouragement of independent thinking, which they were fully aware would lead to a challenge to the established order, the last thing they had in mind. The ancient devout religious beliefs of the peasantry were replaced to a large extent, at least in the Protestant parts of the Reich, by an almost equally religious belief in the state and its leaders, in Deutsch-land.

After Wilhelm I's death, Friedrich III came to the German throne. But already suffering from cancer, he died a hundred days later which made

Wilhelm II German Kaiser. After Wilhelm's inglorious flight on November 9th 1918, Germany was declared a Republic and President Friedrich Ebert was elected as its head.

Ebert, the leader of the Social Democratic Party, had been a saddle maker by trade and was thought by many to be a man of the people. But father said that from the word 'go' many thoughtful people were very doubtful about the real powers of his office. Ownership of land and capital still dominated all life in Germany and Ebert was not strong enough to lead the nation towards necessary fundamental change.

However, he did acknowledge that in spite of all the doubts, many worthy social and other advances were implemented. For the first time children, mainly working class boys, had a chance of meaningful education and training. There was a flowering of newly set-up workers' education groups all over the country which in turn helped to open up hitherto unheard of opportunities for the rest of the population. But the great danger, as father put it, of sliding back to the rule of the old rulers was always lurking in the background.

As to workers' education groups, now looking back on my life, I consider myself lucky to have benefited from one of them. My parents had heard of a holiday play school which had been set up by a progressive group which had rented a sandy stretch of beach on an arm of the River Elbe right opposite the port of Hamburg. I was then seven or eight years old. Being a bit fearful at first of adventure away from home, I was not very keen to go. But I was talked into it and afterwards was very glad that I went.

The organisers of the camp, having got hold of some building materials, had somehow erected a long shed which was open towards the river side and had a make-do warm-up kitchen. There were enough tables and benches under cover to keep and entertain about one hundred children in the rain. The overseers were young men and women, some of them unemployed teachers, victims of the economic recession which was gripping Germany in the late twenties/early thirties.

Mother took me to the collection point at the landing stage early every morning, from where she picked me up again about eight hours later. We crossed the river by ferry and landed at Köhlbrand close to our assigned beach. Though strict discipline was the order of the day, we were allowed maximum freedom to roam the sands of our well-marked beach. Buoys clearly showed the limits which we were not allowed to cross in the water and a boatman kept a watchful eye on us at all times.

There was sand, sun and water, all the things to make young hearts happy. But as I only realised in later life, there was also much more. We built countless sandcastles, had balls to play with or rubber rings or just lay on the sand, softly stroked by the pleasant summer breeze from the river. Well organised games and competitions of all sorts took place all the time. It was there at Köhlbrand where I picked up the basic rules of chess which father then helped me to develop to such an extent that about a couple of years later, he had to lovingly admit that I had become the better player.

We had to bring our own food and took warm tea from an urn. There was community singing every day which I loved. To this day I still know the words and songs which I learned at Köhlbrand. Most of the songs had something to do with walking in nature and being kind to people and animals as well as about simple love. They were totally devoid of the subjects of war, patriotism and 'great' leaders, which were the themes of those I learned years later when I became a member of the Hitler Youth.

Because I loved it all so much, a girl neighbour Ilse came with me and though I had made a number of friends already, Ilse became my closest playmate and we stayed good friends until many years after the war, when life sent us in different directions and we sadly lost touch with each other. Whenever we met, we talked and laughed over the lovely time we had together at Köhlbrand.

Hamburg itself was clearly visible to the east, rising gracefully from the river's edge towards the commanding ledge on which stood the huge Bismarck monument. Hewn into a huge block of granite, the Iron Chancellor was slightly leaning on his sword in front of him, reminding all incoming visitors of our country's might. Within the panorama at the back of it rose the many beautiful church spires of which Hamburg can be so deservedly proud. Amongst them were the famous St. Michaelis Church which every true Hamburger knows as the 'Michel'.

Amidst all the fun and laughter we had an hour of story telling every day and, looking back on it, I am pretty sure that this was perhaps one of the main reasons why my parents had arranged for me to go to the Köhlbrand Camp. The story telling was called 'Geschichte' which in German means story as well as history. Amongst our overseers was a husband and wife team who did most of the lecturing. They were both well into their thirties and we were allowed to call them by their first names, Hans and Ida, which in those days was a clear departure from well-established convention but which, we thought, did much to establish a more trusting relationship than a more formal one would have allowed.

Hans and Ida, who had made it their job to know almost everyone by name, then sat on a kind of sand throne with us children, all of school age up to about twelve, sitting around them in a wide circle. After Hans one day mentioned in front of us that he knew and respected my father, I felt very proud and liked him the more for it. We listened to many stories about the Bauern Krieg (German peasant revolts against their feudal masters) in the fifteenth century, about its leaders like Goetz von Berlichingen who rallied and led the starving peasants against the ruthless landowners, the squires, who bled them white and lived in fortified castles

37

and Herrenhäuser (manor houses), guarded by their own troops of mer-
cenary soldiers. The people's poet Friedrich Schiller had written a play
about that episode out of which Hans and Ida read sections to us,
introducing us at the same time to the largely unknown wealth of German
anti-establishment literature.

They read to us the stories about Rübezahl, the German Robin Hood
who, as the story goes, had operated in the Riesengebirge (Mountains of
the Giants) which separated the flat lands of Silesia from Czech Bohemia,
right in the heart of Europe. Rübezahl relieved the rich of their ill-gotten
loot and gave it back to the poor from whom, so we were told, they had
stolen the land in the first place, the foundation and basis of their wealth.

We loved to listen to it all. Of course, our hearts warmed towards the
poor people with whom we could so easily identify. For the rich and
ruthlessly powerful we only felt contempt. Ida reminded us that, though
much had changed since the days of Rübezahl, the fundamental causes
why some people were so very rich and the many were so very poor had
not really changed to the present. When someone suggested that perhaps
it would be a good idea to have another, a modern, updated Rübezahl, Ida
just smiled and said, 'well, perhaps that might be a good idea.' From then
on Rübezahl became our hero. Kaisers, kings, generals and popes were
not fit to lick his boots. And when I came home and told my parents what
I had learned about that hero of the people Rübezahl, they smiled, and
understood. And when father came home next day from work, he brought
me the book Rübezahl, so that I should go on learning about the real
problems of life.

After the Nazis came to power in 1933, camps like Köhlbrand and other
workers' educational groups were either shut down or taken over by the
Nazi movement. When several years later, I had soaked up much of what
I was told in the Hitler Youth, one of our leaders mentioned Köhlbrand
and claimed that it had been a breeding ground for Reds. I did not have
the courage to protest and admit that I had been there and even more, that
I had liked it and thought that his claim was untrue. On my way home I
thought about what the Hitler Youth leader had said and I remembered
how at Köhlbrand we had been encouraged to strive for friendship
amongst ordinary people and peace between nations and countries, and
wondered what had been so wrong with that. And I also found myself
wondering about what we were now being taught in the Hitler Youth,
which stressed conquest, fighting and war. Deep down it bothered me a
bit, logic suddenly did not make sense any more, but by that time I
hesitated to ask my father questions of this kind, because I knew very well
what his answer would be. And I did not want to hear it. As I see it now,
the Nazi teaching had significantly changed my attitudes and thinking.
Also, I wanted to be like all the others – if they didn't ask questions, why
should I?

All around where we lived were many factories, quite large ones, employing thousands of workers as well as smaller ones and workshops in backyards where two or three people tried to make a meagre living. The banging and grinding and blowing filled our atmosphere throughout the working day. We did not really mind, on the contrary we had got so used to it that in a sense it was music to our ears, the music of work, of life itself. Thinking about it now, I am sure that there could not have been much social planning in the Wilhelmenian age when most of the factories around had been built. The living quarters of the working population were so unhealthily intermingled with the industrial sites that it was no surprise that many of us living there were afflicted by asthma and other respiratory diseases.

Right next to our tenement was a gas cooker factory, the Haller Werke, which at the Nuremberg Tribunal a dozen or so years later in 1945/46 was found responsible for having designed and produced gas oven equipment which had been used at Auschwitz. The building stood wall-to-wall with ours and when the factory conveyor belts were switched on, the continuous rumbling could be heard in every flat. On Sundays when it was switched off we thought that there was something missing.

Being so young with no experience whatsoever, I was obviously unable to assess and analyse working conditions. By turning my thoughts back now, I realise that they must have been terrible in the machine rooms. We children climbed up to the ground floor windows which in warm summer weather were often open and looked into that strange beehive of enforced human activity. Even then we realised that it was regulated by the speed of the conveyor belt which put all the workers in the hall under time pressure. Amidst the loud clanking noise and that strong and yet somewhat attractive smell of metal and oil, there were rows of machines, lathes, presses and cutters lined up almost like soldiers on parade. The floors were uneven, filthy and dangerous. Standing in front of the machines were their operators, doing their same repetitive tasks throughout the whole working day. Even to watch them at their work became boring to us after a while. Most of the workers were friendly towards us, gave us a nod while a few ignored us, perhaps being too engrossed in what they were doing. They all looked grimy, some of them pale and hardly anyone smiled or talked and if they did, they had to shout to overcome the noise. Feeble electric lamps were hanging from the ceiling over the machines which had to stay switched on although the sun was shining outside. Between the rows were passages through which youngsters, just out of school, pushed heavy trolleys on swivel wheels, collected the finished products and took them to another large hall at the back for assembly or temporary storage. When they came back, they brought fresh materials for the machines to consume. Everything was well organised to the last detail so that no working time was wasted.

In the far corner with a few steps leading up to it was a glassed-in cubicle which was occupied by the Meister (overseer) and his clerk who were busily working their way through heaps of paper and coming out from time to time to check on something. They had a clear view of every machine through their large windows and we noticed by the bothered glances some of the workers threw at the cubicle, that they hated and feared that watch tower. When I discussed with father what I had seen in the machine rooms at Haller's, he said that only the devil could have invented and planned such an effective torture chamber. 'Human beings,' he used to say, 'never matter when the making of profit is at stake.'

Perhaps it should have surprised no one that under such conditions strikes broke out at almost regular intervals, and when it happened, there was always much excitement, at least for us youngsters. As father so often growlingly said, there were so many sparks in the industrial atmosphere only waiting to be ignited. Suddenly the large iron gates and some of the smaller side doors were pushed open and masses of workers came streaming out. Most of them looked hurt and angry, there was loud talk everywhere and shouting, and when there were laughs, they were of the hoarse, the sarcastic kind. They then stood around on pavements and sometimes also filled the street, blocking the traffic and not caring that they did. All of them were still in their working clothes, they had no time to wash and one could also sense the general uncertainty in their minds. They had decided to come out all right, but what were they going to do now? There was obvious boiling anger, frustration and a foreboding gloom in the air which one could almost cut with a knife. Heated arguments and quarrels quickly developed and we kids had moved right into the middle of it all. Though we did not really understand what it was all about, we felt with and for the strikers and when they shouted at the windows where an overseer or other appartaschnik looked out, we shouted with them and raised our threatening fists into the air just as they were doing.

Usually police arrived quickly on the scene. They came in their buses, blue Minnas we called them, parking them in the side streets. Like the strikers they too, at least in the beginning, looked lost, did not quite know what to do or how to behave, while some walked over to the strikers to make enquiries. But they still looked baffled. Of course I don't know what the strikers had told them but I do know that they did not trust them. Strikers had long memories and were aware that police possessed hard rubber truncheons which they had sometimes used on workers and, needless to say, never on the bosses. Even I could see it, there were now two groups of people, both German, both speaking the same language and living in the same neighbourhood. They looked at each other with suspicion which sometimes looked to me close to enmity. I once heard one of the strikers say, 'as civilisation means the art of living together peacefully, what kind of civilisation is this?'

I seldom witnessed any fighting at this stage. There was much loud disorganised talking though, and after the first emotional reaction the situation tended to calm down. Afterwards, the strikers sorted themselves out a little and agreed on one or two spokesmen who then went back into the factory to do some talking. But as soon as management appeared on the scene, either from inside or outside, tempers began to flare again and the police then proceeded to ferret out the unfortunate spokesmen, accompanied by loud verbal abuse from the crowd. Shoving and pushing then started up and I remember how one of the strikers turned livid when roughly handled by a policeman, and shouted that he had been good enough to have fought for his country at Duaumont in the war, had been wounded for his troubles and had an Iron Cross to show for it, and would never have believed that a young lick-spittle of a policeman would have dared to threaten and order him about like this in his own country.

On that first day the bulk of the strikers went home in the late afternoon with only a few of them staying on at the main gate. They had placards saying that the workers of this factory were on strike because of hardship and made it their job to stop transport into or out of the factory and talked to anyone who claimed to have business there. Several policemen also stayed on and I think they, like the strikers, were relieved every few hours throughout the night.

Almost all the strikers came back next morning. It all seemed a bit calmer, as everyone knew what to expect. The noise and loud excitement of the day before had given way to determined sullenness which did not bode well. Some had come with their womenfolk and children. But then the strike dragged on and when management tried to bring in strike-breakers, mostly unemployed workers from near-by towns, more serious troubles broke out again. It seemed as if the strikers had set up a successful network of communications because they always knew well beforehand about the time the scabs were likely to arrive so as to be ready for them. They then marshalled themselves into close lines across the main gates which the police then tried to open up, dashing and hitting in between them, using their truncheons and trying to push them to the sides. But mostly they were unsuccessful, for whenever they managed to break the human cordon, the gaps were quickly shut again by the powerful pushing and shoving from all sides. 'We are many, they are few' was one of the shouting slogans I often heard, and father told me that it had been coined by the English revolutionary poet Shelley.

Suddenly the convoy of lorries, covered with tarpaulins, came into sight, rumbling up the narrow street. There were about ten of them. That was the moment when the simmering bubbling noise changed into sharp fury, when the turmoil at the gates started to boil over and the human waves of desperate people, pushing into and crashing against each other, became dangerous to everyone. There were shouts of pain and the faces on either side looked very agitated if not wild, at which point we children tried to get out of the way.

With helmets flying, the police sometimes managed to get a lorry or two through one of the wide gates. But they mostly failed, the lorries then had to drive on and trundle down the street out of sight. Even we children saw a victory in that and shouted 'Hurrah!' in unison with the strikers. It was an obvious tactic of the police, whatever happened, to keep the lorries on the move. For them to come to a standstill was dangerous and I once witnessed how one of them was turned on to its side by the strikers, shedding its pitiful human load from underneath the tarpaulin on to the hard cobblestones. Fists then flew and truncheons rained down on those who could not get out of the way quickly enough. And the noise all round rose into a crescendo. Sometimes ambulances arrived for which the strikers always opened a passage. Though the crowd worked in an organised way against it, the police sometimes managed to arrest one or two whom they then bundled rather unceremoniously into their blue Minnas.

All the time the strike lasted, speakers of all descriptions arrived from all kinds of organisations and political parties. Some brought their own wooden boxes on which they then stood, mostly on the pavement opposite the main gate to address the strikers. Some talked in a loud, rousing way, others cool-headed and advisory. There were shouts of general agreement but also boos. The main speakers, as far as I could make out, came from the trade unions, the communists and the social democrats. I remember one clergyman coming along one day who behaved and spoke quite differently from most priests, with their whining voices. He was young, down-to-earth and tackled the problem head on. He said that if Jesus had been present, he would have been on the side of the strikers and certainly not on the one of their masters. His speech received very warm applause as most strikers probably recognised that he was risking his professional reputation, to say the least.

One day there was a change to the general pattern. A car arrived in which sat a number of Nazis in their brown SA uniforms. From the word go they were regarded with suspicion. But after they had talked to one of the stewards who wore a red armband, one of the brownshirts was permitted to mount the wooden box and make an address. Unlike all the other previous speakers who were jostled in a friendly comradely manner, this one was treated with cold disdain. The crowd stood away from his box and was unusually quiet. He did not get off to a very good start because he addressed them as comrades, to which several shouted their objection. His technique of speaking was not bad which suggested that he had probably been trained to address crowds. Also his educational level seemed to be higher than that of his listeners. I stood very close to the box and understood his every word. When he mentioned the hard times most people had to go through in this recession and that it was a great shame that Germans argued and sometimes struggled and fought against each other as was happening now at this factory gate, there was muted nodded agreement by some.

He went on to say that the convulsions of social/industrial unrest now gripping Germany, were largely due to the vile machinations of international financial intrigues mainly instigated by Jews and other German haters. He then stressed that all the directors at Haller's were aryans, pure Germans with not one Jew amongst them and continued that they, the strikers, should recognise this when they considered further action. He went on that there was a severe economic recession in Germany which was threatening to move into a slump and could possibly, if they were not careful, wipe away all their jobs. At this a restlessness was developing amongst the crowd and someone called from the back, 'who made this recession which always seems to be an excuse to push our wages down? Has it been handed down from God, or is it all a logical part of this idiotic economic system which is having us all by our throats?' But the speaker ignored that interception completely and went on to what was probably the main part of his speech. He came back to what he had said in the beginning, that he was saddened to see that German work-givers and German work-takers confronting each other in this outdated way, and that the strikers should realise that the directors, the same as the workers – at this stage someone shouted, 'and what about the profiteering shareholders?' – had to do their job, that it was a fact that money was scarce and that wage demands for the sake of the country should be measured and reasonable.

With this there was no doubt left that he had shot his bolt. Pandemonium broke out all around. It was not only verbal insults which were hurled at him but solid objects like tomatoes and eggs from which he had to get off his box and duck. We kids thought that it was all very funny until one of us had his laughing abruptly stopped when a soft pear hit him on the head, after which we scrambled to the edge of the crowd from where we continued to observe what was going on. The brown-shirted speaker had hurriedly left his box and was escorted by his bodyguards to the safety of their car. 'Who has sent you, who has paid you to speak to us?' were the main insults directed after him. After the police had cleared a passage for their car, someone produced a brown Nazi cap, held high on a stick which looked like a sort of trophy. He then donned the cap on his head, back to front, put his finger under his nose to imitate Hitler's moustache, rolled his eyes, raised his arm in the Nazi salute and hoarsely shouted 'Heil, heil.' As far as I know, no uniformed Nazi ever dared to come and address the strikers again.

Whenever there was a strike near-by, father made it his job to go and express his solidarity with the strikers. Once, when there had been no sign of trouble, he took me with him. I loved to listen to what he said to them, words of encouragement and also caution, that he was a worker himself and that he knew exactly what had driven them to their action and that he was sorry that he could not give them much support. I found it remarkable that at occasions like this his eyes sometimes misted over and his voice choked. When I asked him about it afterwards, he explained that he was very moved by it all.

Mother too when going to the shops made a point of walking past the main gate, talking to the strikers and wishing them well. Both my parents arranged to collect money for the strikers from amongst friends, work mates and sympathetic neighbours. And when the strike was over, there was no victory nor defeat, only sadness, frustration and a sense of utter helplessness. I stood at Haller's main gate when the strikers went back to work one lunch time and saw grown men weep. It gave me a lump in my throat as I sensed somehow that their struggle was also our struggle, that it was for our future, for me. I too felt like crying. But I was too young and totally unable to give that feeling any shape or form. For weeks afterwards there was sadness in our streets and though life went on as it had to and with the strike not having settled anything, it all seemed an anti-climax.

The early thirties with its ever deepening economic recession was an extraordinary period in our country. Under several of its governments, all right wing ones, the country was sliding from one crisis into another to which there seemed to be no end in sight. Father remarked sarcastically that throughout his entire life he could not remember one period when there was no crisis of some sort. Mass unrest in cities and towns was the order of the day, and it was spreading and becoming increasingly severe. There were large demonstrations, marches and protest meetings at town halls. But by that time the Nazis had become a dominant street force in the cities. They, the Nazi stormtroopers were the only ones of the political groupings who wore full uniforms. They were also well organised under one command and disciplined if not actually trained in street fighting. And whenever and wherever demonstrations against the established laws were called, the Nazis were there to be counted upon to disturb if not break up the plans of the organisers.

Of Chancellors of the Reich at that time, I can remember the names of Heinrich Brüning, the leader of the small Catholic Centre Party, Franz von Papen whom they called 'the fox' and who was known to have close connections not only with the Vatican but also with big business, and General Kurt von Schleicher who, it was being said, had his fingers in many pies, political and otherwise.

So many rumours of attempted coups and counter-coups were making the rounds. Everyone was worried about the extreme uncertainty of the situation and had different ideas and proposals for what had to be done to prevent a total collapse. Though many mostly self-acclaimed intellectuals spouted their contradicting ideas, no one, it became clear, had any real solution. All that was clear, was that the general situation was steadily and surely sliding into deep chaos.

The burdens most feared by the working people were those of unemployment, inflation and rising rents. Father's job – he was working as an unskilled fitter at the railways – was not under immediate threat, but many of my friends' fathers' jobs were. I used to visit their homes as they visited mine and I knew of the cloud of fear they were living under. When the long expected sack from work suddenly materialised, there was hanging of heads and tears and a feeling of helplessness, not knowing how to pay the rent and feed the children. I sometimes felt almost embarrassed to admit that my father was still at work, at least for the moment. What was worst of all was that there was no hope, no sign of any recovery, no discernible light at the end of that long tunnel of abject misery. Talk was about seven million out of work in the Reich with the industrial cities like ours hardest hit. Real poverty was stalking the streets every living day.

One knew and heard of large and small business closures, many shops were forced to put up their shutters and even some of the banks were said to be in serious trouble. Thousands lost their homes as they simply did not have enough money to pay their rents. The number of homeless people was rising all the time. One could observe whole families living in make-do sheds and even tents on waste ground from where police tried to evict them, resulting sometimes in ugly and humanly degrading scenes and fights. Many families, including some of my school friends, were living in garden and tool sheds on their allotments. According to the law, that was forbidden, but the laws had been made by rich people who had no need to live in sheds. At school we were asked to bring extra sandwiches for those who had none to bring. Even I with my very limited understanding of what all this really meant, did notice the hungry eyes with which some of my pale friends watched the teacher distributing the gift packets during break time. When snow was lying on the ground a number of my class mates did not come to school because they simply possessed no shoes good enough to keep the snow and slush out.

Though we ourselves were poor in monetary terms, our home was well-furnished, always superbly clean, a good fire was always on the go in the kitchen stove in winter and we always had enough to eat. When I once called at the downtown flat of my friend Johnny, I was shocked by what I was confronted with there. The door from the public landing led straight into their kitchen/living room. At home we had at least a corridor. There were no curtains in front of the window, only bits of paper, and mainly to keep the draught out. The floorboards were rough and uncovered and everything seemed cold and bleak. A bare table with a couple or so chairs stood forlornly in the middle of the room under a supposed-to-be lamp which had no shade. On the chair by the stove sat my friend Johnny on his mother's lap. She held her protective arms around him and both looked at me, the unexpected intruder, with large eyes.

I had come to collect money for hungry children in Africa, organised by the local Sunday School, and after I had said my piece, standing just inside the still open door, quietly rattling my collection tin with the inviting slip on top, Johnny's mother forced out a painful laugh and told me to look around the room and to make my own assessment. She said that though she was sorry for the African children, her Johnny was a German child and she did not know how to find the money to feed him properly and that indeed he was hungry right now.

In a rather muddled and embarrassed manner I apologised and left in a hurry. I did not knock at any other door but went straight home to tell mother. Without much ado she sent me back to the Pastor and told me to hand that collecting tin back to him with her compliments and to ask him to please go himself and see Johnny in his flat. After he had opened the door for me he asked me to come in and tell him. But I did not want to and almost fled from his doorstep, sensing that his friendliness was not clean, not genuine. I do not know whether he ever picked up the courage to see Johnny – and I never asked the latter whether he had done so. Perhaps we were both far too embarrassed.

And into all this fertile seeding ground for trouble strode that man Adolf Hitler. It was as if the political stage of fertility had been set up especially for him. He was said to have the gift of the gab – but not much more – that he was a mere tool of others and in himself totally unimportant. Father said that he also had the talent to make black look white and he promised anything to anyone who cared to listen to him. Though his face appeared on photos in newspapers and on advertising boards all over the town, I had never seen him in the flesh. However in those days early in the thirties hardly a day went by within our home without his name being mentioned either by my parents or my father's friends who regularly came to see us. I think that I somewhere had heard his gruff voice either on the radio in friends' homes or the newsreels in the cinemas. It was difficult for me to understand what he was saying because of his unfamiliar Austrian accent.

In his many speeches up and down the country he pointed out the economic and social horrors the German people had to endure at the hands of the corrupt Weimar traitors. If the German people would give him their votes, he promised, he would not only get rid of their shameless oppressors but bring them to task for the crimes they had committed. His first and overriding aim would be to erase unemployment which in turn would stimulate the economy and make the necessary inroads into the ever deepening spiral of mass poverty. He emphasised that speculative activities of parasitic Jews and other anti-German elements in financial and economic life would be thoroughly investigated and by doing all that he would lay the basis for making Germany great again. He would give us back our former glory so that foreigners, instead of using us as their door mat, would again look up to us and our achievements with admiration and due respect.

Who of the poverty-stricken people could shut their ears to these promises, who could afford to, as it became clearer with every new day that all else had failed? And those who believed his words, how could they not vote for him? After all, almost all people agreed that something very drastic would have to happen and that mere attempts to patch things up would only worsen conditions.

And suddenly it did! At first it had only been a rumour – most people in those days had no access to radio – which quickly transformed itself into a bombshell, which had almost noiselessly fallen from the sky. There were still some who thought that it was not true, surely, it could not be? This all important issue of a new Prime Minister had not even been discussed in the Reichstag and there had been no elections. Many working people were aware, and I heard it often enough in our home, that our rulers, should their position of wealth and privilege ever become seriously threatened, would be ruthless enough to set up a military-backed dictatorship to restore order. But few were prepared for them to go as far as placing the reins of government into the criminal hands of a brown-shirted bunch of gangsters.

CHAPTER III
After Hitler's Rise to Power

There can be little doubt that the 30th of January 1933 was one of the most, if not the most, important dates in German history. It was the day when Adolf Hitler was appointed German Kanzler (Prime Minister) by Reichs President von Hindenburg. It happened at a time when public support for the Nazi Party, largely because of the brutal behaviour of its brown storm-troopers, was actually on the wane. A special ceremony for this important occasion had been arranged in Potsdam's Garrison Church where all Prussian Kings had been crowned. It was known that not all that long ago von Hindenburg had called Hitler dismissively 'that stupid Bohemian Corporal'. My parents were devastated. Mother almost cried and kept repeating, 'how can they do that to us, how can they do that to us? Surely they must know that the Nazis are nothing but gangsters?'

I think it was on the same evening or the one after that some of father's friends came round to our flat. None seemed in the mood to give vent to the usual jokes and laughs. They just sat there silently around the table and obviously waited for father to say the first words. Some held their chins in their hands and even I, just over ten years old, could sense their feeling of sadness and frustration, if not of downright hopelessness, which seemed to have engulfed them.

Father rose to what was expected of him and pointed out that probably to keep a balance and certainly a watchful eye on the expected antics of the 'bohemian corporal' or 'housepainter', by which he also was known by working people, Herr Franz von Papen, 'the Fox' of German politics and ex-Kanzler himself had been appointed as Hitler's number two by Hindenburg. The only other Nazi besides Hitler in that first Cabinet was Dr. Wilhelm Frick as Home Secretary, while Hermann Göring was made Minister without Portfolio. All other ministries controlling the main levers of power in Germany like finance, defence, industry, energy, and foreign affairs were given to right-wing conservatives. By all counts it would have been an overstatement to call it a Nazi Cabinet. There must have been many reasons behind this establishment choice, one of which was that the Nazis had absolutely no experience in government and another that from amongst them, it was extremely difficult to find anyone fit for high office.

Father used to say at that time and also later that to join the Nazis voluntarily was in itself an indisputable proof of either downright viciousness or extreme naivety.

It was on one of the following evenings that father and his friend Otti took me to the Kaiserplatz (square) behind Altona's main railway station where the Machtübernahme (taking of power) was to be celebrated. Mother was not only against him going, as the last thing he wanted was to celebrate, but certainly against taking me who, she thought, was much too young for such a thing and because she feared that there could be trouble. But father's view was that it was important for me to watch history in the making, never mind whether good or bad prevailed. And to this day I am glad that he took me.

It was already dark when we arrived and the streets were wet from earlier rain. Many people were standing around in groups and hundreds more were arriving all the time. The wide façade of the new town hall was lit up from behind us and stood out starkly against the dark sky and the trees at the sides. A long balcony ran along much of the front of the building and two long swastika flags hung from top windows on both sides almost down to the ground. The symbol of the Nazis – the black hooked cross (Hakenkreuz) in a large white circle against the backdrop of the red flag – was very imposing. It hit right between the eyes and generated a mixture of power and fear. As to the Nazis themselves, there was no gentleness whatsoever about their symbol – and that was probably as intended.

After the brown stormtroopers, the SA, and the black-clad SS had taken up positions on both sides of the square and a line of honour in front of the building, the long torches were lit throwing a dancing flicker of light over us. Then the musical troops, mainly consisting of drums and pipes, started playing. And when two beautifully tuned fanfares blared their 'silvery call to arms' into the night from an open upper window, everyone was aware that the Nazis had arrived, that times were going to change from now on and the official part of the evening's ceremony was to begin.

The large doors behind the balcony opened and one by one the main actors strode out towards the stone balustrade and greeted the crowd with the Nazi salute. Some of them wore brown or black uniforms, others wore civilian clothes and there were several ladies amongst them. At that phase father nudged me and said in a quiet voice, so that no one could hear, that he had seen it all before in the Kaiser's days, that I should not forget that this was all part of the game of impressing and fooling the masses. The only difference being, that in those days they wore ermine, had crowns and brilliant studded tiaras, while now they had donned simple brown shirts, making themselves perhaps more acceptable to ordinary people.

It also happened that on that day Altona had got a new mayor. Herr Brix who wore a brown uniform was introduced to the crowd and it was announced over the loudspeakers that the Kaiserplatz was forthwith called Adolf Hitler Platz. The official speeches were difficult to understand because of an underlying scratching sound from the loudspeakers. There was plenty of 'heil' shouting, while swastika flags were being waved everywhere, but there were also some boos coming from the rear. The main theme was that the Almighty had given Adolf Hitler to the German nation so that he could tear the shackles of Versailles asunder and set us free. Once he had done the necessary tidying-up, the Germans would be no more the play-things of others but a powerful nation and one Reich brilliantly led by a strong Führer.

But then trouble broke out at the back with stormtroopers and police rushing about and father thought that it would be better to take me home. He and Otti were very depressed and when they agreed that this was a sad day for Germany and probably for the world, I did not understand why that should be so and when I asked the question, father merely shook his head and said that he would try to explain to me later. When they kept talking about how vicious the new government doubtlessly would become, I wondered on the quiet what kind of viciousness they were talking about. Why should the brown SA be so dangerous to us? After all, I knew Nazis personally, several young men from down the road who were members of the SA. Only the other day my kite had been caught up in the branches of a tree and one of them had climbed up and had fetched it down for me. They had both been very friendly, had called me 'little Henry' and had given me a sweet. So why should I be afraid of them?

I mentioned this incident, and Otti put his hand on my head and said, 'look here, little Henry, it has nothing to do with the friendly man in brown fetching your kite out of a tree and giving you a sweet. All that you have seen here tonight on the Kaiserplatz does go very much deeper than that. You know that we have had so many governments in the recent past. You yourself know the names of Cuno, Brüning, Papen and Schleicher. They have all made such a mess of governing us, that the working people as a whole have become poorer and poorer out of which a reaction has occurred which could so easily have developed into open revolt against the government and established law and order. The thing is that a revolt of the lower orders is something the rich fear like brimstone and fire. So what they have done to stop the rot is to bring in a new government under Hitler, who will act in a brutal and reckless way against any opposition to the way the country is run.' When he asked me whether I had understood what he meant, I said 'Yes, Herr Prautsch, I think so' – but I really hadn't.

There was an interesting sideline to the happening of the evening. The Bürgermeister (mayor) of a German town in his capacity as fully-paid administrative head, appointed by the ruling political party, holds down an important post as he has a dominant influence on all spheres of policy making. Our mayor was Max Brauer who held the post for a number of years before the Nazis came to power. Though he was bound to have many enemies, my parents had faith in him and were fully convinced that he tried to do his best for our town Altona and its people against a background of difficult circumstances. As father kept stressing, it was capitalism which was in deep crisis and how could a socialist like Brauer react to it.

I already knew his face from the newspapers, when one Sunday morning my parents took me to a tree planting ceremony in the Friedens Allee (Avenue of Peace) where he planted a sapling which he called Friedens Eiche (Oak of Peace). Quite a number of people were present and stood round in loose informality. In his speech Brauer expressed his hope for peace for the people of Altona, for the whole of Germany and the entire world and that the tree should grow strong without hearing one shot from a gun or witnessing people fighting. Afterwards he came over and, amongst other people, he talked to my father whom he knew. He asked my name, patted my head and said something about when I grow older, to always stand up for peaceful solutions to problems however difficult they might appear to be.

Not many weeks after this, father came home from work very sad, telling us that the peace oak had been pulled out by vandals. He had talked to shopkeepers across the road who had told him that they had no idea as to who had done it. But then an old lady informed him that she had seen a troop of drunken SA who had trampled all over the flower bed, had stood around the tree in a circle, raised their arms in the Hitler salute, had urinated on the tree and then had pulled it out by its roots. When passers by had called them to order, they shouted that peace was a stupid sentiment, and war was better as it was glorious, and that if the protesters did not shut their stupid traps, they would bash their faces in. They then painted black swastikas on the seat on the tree triangle and also on house fronts across the road.

Max Brauer made a statement, condemning the act as political vandalism, after which troops of SA marched up and down in front of the town hall and shouted 'Brauer out!', 'revenge!' As I mentioned earlier, the very night that Hitler was appointed Kanzler, Brauer lost his job. As it was, the Nazis were making life difficult for him and he had to leave the country for his family's and his own safety.

His chauffeur, a Herr Droschinski, who changed his name to the more German sounding Geestmann, and joined the black SS, lived in our tenement. It did not take long before he became chauffeur to the new Nazi mayor Herr Brix. He had a telephone installed in his flat, the only private one, I think, in our whole neighbourhood and the black mayoral Mercedes was often standing outside our tenement front door. Whenever we children came too close to it, making faces against the mirror-like exterior, Herr Geestmann opened the window of his flat and shouted to us to go away. He told people that Max Brauer had been a corrupt mayor and had now turned up in China, where he worked as an advisor to the city council of Shanghai.

Father on hearing this was not keen to have anything to do with Geestmann but neither was he surprised that the Nazis were trying systematically to smear Max Brauer's character by every possible means. After the end of the war Brauer came back from China and became Oberbürgermeister (Lord Mayor) of Hamburg which, in a way, was a double promotion. He was to Hamburg what Willy Brandt became to Berlin. At that time I was still a PoW in England, when I received a letter from a friend of my then late father, telling me that he had been to a meeting in Hamburg's Rathaus (Guildhall) where he had met Brauer. They had been talking about common friends and my father's name came up. In his letter he included a piece of paper on which a few lines were scribbled in strong handwriting, saying something like: – met you as a little boy when you came to a tree planting ceremony in Altona with your parents. I am sorry that they have died, they were fine people and that you are still a prisoner. I know that your home has been bombed. When you come back to the Heimat please come and see me.

signed Max Brauer

The note made me very happy as well as proud because of what was said about my parents. When I came home to Hamburg after having been released from PoW camp in 1948, Max Brauer was not in town for a reason I cannot remember. But then I left again after only a month's stay and did not bother to send a note to him. I went straight back to England and worked as a farmhand for Colonel Courage, the brewer in Hampshire, before I became a cleaner/porter on the railways. I sometimes wonder what would have become of me, what different direction my life would have taken, had I gone to see the then Lord Mayor of Hamburg and had told him that I was looking for a job.

With the Nazis' arrival in government, the entire teaching process in schools was subjected to many changes, the curriculum of history received very special attention and was altered drastically. I think it took less than a year before we were issued with much revised history books which showed a very strong underlying emphasis of the need for German Lebensraum (space to live). Those kaisers, kings and military leaders who since the early Middle Ages had battled to find it in the east, were described as wise and forward-looking and given historic prominence, while those who had foolishly sought glory in the west and south of Europe were presented as selfish adventurers, who had not understood the essential flow of history. We were taught that former Germanic lands, having reached as far as the Black Sea and into what was now the heart of Russia, had through neglect been settled over many centuries by lower-raced Slavic people who had come from behind the Urals, from Asia.

Much history was explained in terms of battles, wars, kings and great leaders, as if it was a process almost ordained by God. No real effort was ever made to make us think about the deeper underlying causes of war and how kings had become such in the first place. If someone ever dared to ask a question of that sort, he was usually given short shrift and was told to never ask such silly questions again.

Lost battles were usually put down to German disunity while we were reminded that the main content of our anthem 'Deutschland über Alles' (Germany above everything) was that of brotherly holding-together, come what may. Lost wars were always connected with another dawn, another opportunity for collecting our might once again and trying anew. The teaching of history was presented almost entirely from a strong nationalistic point of view and it was instilled into us, that our cause had not only been righteous but that we Germans, especially in a military context, were racially superior, that we as soldiers were by far the best in the world.

A powerful historic symbol, which we were never allowed to forget, was the Treaty of Versailles. Though of course already strong on the curriculum during the Weimar days, Nazi teaching used it to explain almost everything that had gone wrong in Germany. Hitler in his many speeches simple called it 'der Schandvertrag' (treaty of shame) or 'das Diktat'. It set the tone of so much in our young psyches to be directed towards revenge.

In the first place I had never really understood why something as holy as our modern German state, Bismarck's Second Reich, should have been created just outside the gates of Paris and not in Germany itself. Was it implying that our country lacked splendour? For it was there at Versailles that on the 28th of January 1871, Reichsgründungstag (Reichs Foundation Day) we called it, the King of Prussia had been proclaimed German Kaiser by all the other numerous kings and dukes and princelings of the German Länder (states and statelets), who had all come in their coaches. Only the Kaiser of Austria had not been present, probably seeing more potential wealth and glory in lording it over his Hungarians and Slavic-speaking people in Central Europe and the ever troubled countries of the Balkans. Our teacher suggested that had Austria, the largest of all German Länder, joined the newly created Reich, the German capital might well have become Vienna instead of Berlin, with the Habsburgs sitting on the German throne instead of the Hohenzollern. German history in that case, he thought, would have been much more eastern-oriented with the map of Europe looking very different from what it was now.

The second major event stressed by our history teacher was the Treaty of Versailles at the end of the first world war. The line given to us at school was that Germany had been forced to sign under duress with a threat of Allied occupation. Hardly ever before in history, we were told, had

Germany been so humiliated as at Versailles in 1919. Not only had we been forced to accept that our country alone bore total responsibility for the war, but we were presented with a reparation bill which would take at least three generations to pay off. A fifty kilometre wide stretch to the east bank of the Rhine from Holland to Switzerland was demilitarised and the remaining German Army, the Reichswehr, allowed to consist only of 100,000 soldiers.

When our teacher explained all this to us, as well as the colossal loss of territory to Poland and other surrounding countries, he worked himself into such a rage that he dragged us all behind him into a similar state of depression and fury. As good Germans, he urged us, we must never forget and never rest until the shackles of Versailles had been removed from our ankles and wrists. Still so young and impressionable, the very name of Versailles produced in me, and I am sure in most of us youngsters, a feeling of supreme helplessness and degradation. I hated the French for what they had done to us and kept my mind busy with thinking about how one day I could help to turn the tables on them with bitter revenge.

Father too was no friend of the Treaty of Versailles, but that was for a very different reason. Having battled in the Kaiser's Army in France, he could understand the French trying to keep the German military in a weak state. He described the devastated areas of France over which the war had raged with hundreds of cities, towns and villages totally destroyed. 'A monument to the activities of the modern Christian nations' he called it and told me about the horrible, almost unbelievable suffering, which had been inflicted on the millions who happened to live there. After what had happened he in no way disputed German guilt, but he also felt that the Treaty's driving force should have been inspired by human wisdom in a sincere search for lasting peace on the basis of reality, and not on blind hatred which in turn would only plant the seed of revenge. He feared that the payments to France of massive German reparations, largely in the form of finished products like steam engines, telegraph poles, machines etc., would not only lead to turbulent economic situations in both countries, but also provide an effective propaganda weapon for demagogues like Hitler. It was his view that the victorious Allies, especially the French with their nationalistic blinkers, were making a fundamental mistake in assuming that chaining Germany into the Treaty of Versailles would protect them from their aggressive neighbour. He was convinced of the opposite, namely that the power of Germany could only be contained by roping it into an equal Federation of European states and in the longer run only by the institution of socialism itself. Until then, he claimed that there would not and could not be a lasting peace in Europe.

In the years to come throughout my youth until I became a soldier, I listened to many of Hitler's speeches. I cannot recall one in which he did not get mad over the 'Schandvertrag von Versailles'. He always appealed skilfully and indeed successfully to the shallow prejudices of millions of us Germans. He probably made Versailles one of the most effective propaganda weapons in his very aggressive armoury.

Talking about history, my great-uncle Fritz in Stapelfeld was a very old man aged over ninety when he died, when I was probably around twelve years old. As a young man he had served as a Hussar in Moltke's Prussian Army and had fought in the battle of Sedan which decided the outcome of the Franco/Prussian war in 1871 in the latter's favour. He loved to talk about it to anyone who was – or was not – prepared to listen. The older he became, some irreverent tongues claimed, the longer and more involved his story became. I had the impression that he bored the adults to tears who, whenever he went on one of his story-telling trips, made a face as if to say, 'here he goes again!' But what he was telling greatly fascinated me and my cousins.

With our youthful inability to measure time, the 1870 War was almost biblical. But there was Onkel Fritz in flesh and blood, right in front of us, one could touch him and he was still alive and kicking, well, just about, and telling his version of how he had almost single-handedly beaten the Frenchies at Sedan. 'Those were the days,' he said with a vibrating voice, 'when men were men, when we relied and charged on our horses and had none of those devilish driving machines which do not more than make the air stink.' How he made it out, I do not know and he never explained, but according to him one either fought like a hero or died like a coward. He called the French 'die Rothosen' (red trousers) because their soldiers at that time wore red trousers and he made no secret of having gruesomely struck through many of them.

As history now informs us, Emperor Napoleon III was captured in his coach on a muddy field path not far from Sedan. A painting exists somewhere depicting that occasion. But listening to Onkel Fritz, history teaching had been a bit wrong on that because the truth was that he had been captured in a village thanks to Onkel Fritz and a handful of his buddies, who had broken through the French lines unscathed and undiscovered, and had found the Emperor shivering in fear in his coach, with most of his guards having run away, at the sight of Onkel Fritz coming over the brow of a hill!

'Silly old buffoon', father used to call him, though not to his face. But all that did not matter to me. And though we kids had enough sense to realise that he was probably putting it on a bit, he was nevertheless our hero. And when he patted my head I felt I was being touched by history itself. But when in a history lesson at school one day I could not restrain myself and tried to pass on Onkel Fritzen's heroism and foolishly announced that I had an uncle still living who had captured Kaiser Napoleon, our teacher coughed rather uncomfortably, and there was a giggling in our class which made me feel a real fool. However, teacher quickly picked up the theme, calling it the unbreakable chain of history, saying that when we looked at a picture of our President von Hindenburg, we saw someone who as a small boy had sat at the feet of an old man, who had been a drummer boy in King Frederick the Great's Prussian Army during the Seven Years War against Austria.

That gave us a tangible perspective of the dimension of time in history and a feeling that somehow we were all part of it, because Friedrich der Grosse, one of the undisputed 'Greats' in German history, was to us someone right out of the dark Middle Ages. The Führer too admired him so much that when he moved into the new Reichs Chancellory in Berlin, he had a painting of Frederick hanging against the wall in his study behind him which prominently drew the eye of every visitor he received.

When I got home and told father the gem about Hindenburg and Frederick the Great, he, as he so often did, dampened my enthusiasm by saying that I had learnt another load of useless rubbish. He was sure that the world would be a better place to live in without these 'Great' warlords. He questioned why we were encouraged at school to admire these militarists and other corrupt parasites, and taught almost nothing about really valuable people, who had made positive contributions to humanity's well-being in so many fields and whose names were not even known to us.

The early weeks of 1933 went by and with Adolf Hitler just having been put into the saddle of government, there seemed to be a political lull which left some people wondering what all the fuss had been about. Life, at least from my low vantage point, went on as usual and nothing much out of the ordinary happened. The usual friends came to see father on the long winter evenings to sit around the kitchen table and talk. Father then always pulled the shaded lamp down from the ceiling so that the light did not fall into their eyes. They all agreed that this made it easier for them to think more undisturbedly, allowing them to express their thoughts more freely. I loved to listen to what they had to say even though most of its meaning was well beyond my grasp. They talked quietly, and as long as I kept myself to myself and out of the way, sitting on the floor in the corner by the warm stove, no one minded my presence. Even I could sense that their very approach to tackling the topics of the time had changed. Where as before they had shown a positive attitude to do this or that, they now seemed to be far more hesitant and above all much more subdued than before. This Nazi advent surely had done something to them and they were not sure at all how to tackle it.

One of them kept saying that the Nazis simply could not last long in government, that none of them had any experience in that craft what-soever, that they would soon make an unholy mess of it all which would leave the establishment around Hindenburg no choice but to get rid of them in the same quick manner as they had been installed in the first place. But most of the others seemed to be doubtful about this and leant more toward old Otti's theory, namely that the real rulers of Germany had no illusions about what kind of ruthless fools the Nazis were. It had been exactly for that reason that they had brought them in from the cold as the only political party which had enough popular support to stem the growing restlessness in the streets of the cities, and to channel the inwardly directed revolutionary tendencies into nationalistic ones. They would keep the Nazis holding the reins of formal state office until that job was completed, and only then would get rid of them.

But the all-pervading political lull was an uneasy one. Everyone sensed that there was tension in the air as if people were waiting for something to happen. And suddenly it did! It came like a storm breaking out of the sky. One night a neighbour knocked at our door after I had already gone to bed. Had my parents heard what had happened? No, how could they, after all we had no radio. 'Well,' he said, 'the Reichstag (parliament building) is on fire and Berlin is in turmoil, with people being rounded up and put away into what seem to be specially prepared camps.'

When mother woke me next morning, I recalled what I had heard before I had gone to sleep and I could see that she was excited but also disturbed. She explained to me that the Reichstag, the place where the peoples' deputies met to discuss and argue over policies, had been gutted in the night. When I arrived at school, the teacher confirmed it and added something about Deutschland being in danger and that the one who had done the burning, a Dutch communist with the name of Marinus van der Lubbe had been caught red-handed and arrested. He said that a communist plot had been averted just in time which could so easily have led to a bloody revolution. I did not know what to make of all that, it was all mere words to me, nothing more.

On one of the next evenings father's friends gathered again. But the meeting was a short one this time. There was fear in the air as one of them said that many of the arrests had been made in workers' flats. I heard father say that van der Lubbe was mentally handicapped, that at the best of times with police all over the centre of Berlin it would have required much planning and luck to break into a solid building like the Reichstag without being seen and challenged. He questioned the possibility that one man, not quite right in the head, could have smuggled a can of petrol into the building and start so many fires necessary to set it alight. Otti thought that there must have been much more to it: that it could well have been planned as a pretext for doing something sinister and that we would just have to wait and see what would develop out of it.

And develop it did. It was on one of the following days that Hitler asked for Hindenburg's permission to issue an emergency decree which gave the government special powers to declare the Communist Party illegal, to control the media and search suspected flats and houses without warrants.

From then on we had no more meetings in our home. Mother was frightened that neighbours might inform on us and she begged father to stop the meetings. The following evenings were awful at home. We three sat alone in our kitchen and I could see that my parents were afraid. Whenever we heard steps coming up the communal staircase, mother looked worried and asked father to go to the door when there was a knock. Watching my parents in that state, I too became frightened. I wanted so much to know what was going on, what had happened. Surely, we had done nothing wrong, had we? But they told me that we had a very vicious government, that times had become very uncertain and that from now on just about anything could happen. My father stressed that he thought that I had now become old enough, even though it might still be all too much for me to understand, to show an inner strength which was needed for the turbulent times ahead.

From then on hammer blow fell after hammer blow. Having lived through them all, I realise now that they all did nothing but confuse me, as I simply did not have the capacity to understand what was going on around me. However, these events screwed themselves firmly into my memory as they had become the main conversation subjects in our home, to which I had no choice but to listen. Sitting around the kitchen table, having our meal, walking or having a lie-in on a Sunday morning – having no bedroom of my own, I slept in my parents' – the hammer blows were all that was talked about. The real digestion of what happened came only many years later when it was all over, when the horrendous crimes had been committed and my parents were not alive any more. It was with this advantage of hindsight that I then tried to assess and also judge what my father had attempted to make me understand. And again that process took many years to germinate and though the awakening was painful and made me sad, it pulled me out of my erstwhile smothering confusion.

At first there were only rumours about concentration camps, KZs we called them, being set up all over the country. We had one at Neuengamme up the River Elbe on the other side of Hamburg. But that was a year or so later. I had never seen it and neither, I think, had my parents. I realise now that issue alone must have presented them with a very difficult dilemma. On the one hand they wanted me to be fully aware of everything going on around me, while on the other they must have realised that too much knowledge of what was really happening would possibly bring real difficulties into my life. After all, they had brought me up to be always truthful and to speak out without fear what was on my mind.

There was an instance when I noticed that my parents were in possession of a letter whose contents had obviously upset them deeply and which they kept discussing. Whenever I came on to the scene, they abruptly stopped talking. I suspected that the letter was a kind of round robin which they had received and were going to pass to their 'safe' friends. A few slipped comments, though, made me gather that it contained information about concentration camps, about who had been taken there and what was going on inside them. When I asked my parents about that, they told me that I was too young to understand and in any case it would be better for me under the prevailing circumstances not to know anything about it. It hurt and bothered me a great deal and I challenged them about the obvious contradiction between what they had always taught me and what they were actually now doing to me, keeping me in the dark and feeding me perhaps with untruths.

It must have been around that time that Hitler made an important speech to the remaining deputies of the Reichstag in the Kroll Opera House in Berlin which was now serving as the Reichstag and was in viewing distance of its burnt-out predecessor. The main theme was the Ermächtigungs Gesetz (enabling law). I cannot be quite sure any more but I think that it was formally put to the vote. Counting the hands, of course, was no longer necessary. Those deputies who would have voted against it, the communists, were by now all safely locked up in concentration camps and the result of the vote was therefore a foregone conclusion.

Having agreed to that, Parliament had effectively dissolved itself, had voted itself out of existence and had given the Hitler Government a free hand to run the country for four years without any cumbersome interference from Parliament.

Father was in no formal way religious. But when he heard about that, he said 'only God can forgive them (the deputies), for they don't know what they have done.' The main and overriding sentence of Hitler's speech was: 'Gebt mir 4 Jahre Zeit und Ihr werdet Deutschland nicht wieder erkennen' (Give me four years and you will not recognise Germany any more.)

Well, as it so happened, he was not quite right, four years did not make all that much difference to Germany. But when about fifteen years later I had been released from PoW captivity, returned to Germany and tried to find my way through the ruins of my home town and heard about all those many people I had known who had died in the bombings, I thought back to Hitler's bombastic statement in the Kroll Opera: 'you will not recognise Germany any more.'

The next blow was when news came through about the symbolic book burning session in a square outside the University Library in Berlin, where books were thrown out of windows on to a huge pyre. The same was then repeated at other places of learning on a smaller scale. There was no doubt that Josef Göbbels the then Nazi Propaganda Minister had organised it all. Cinema newsreels showed how brownshirts and Nazi students threw stacks of books out of open windows on to a huge bonfire. All books on all subjects by authors, thinkers and scientists whose names sounded remotely Jewish were fed to the flames, as well as those of 'pure' German writers, musicians etc. some of world renown, who were either known to be against or did not fit into Nazi ideology, the Weltanschauung (way to look at the world), as it was called. Perhaps as an indication of what was to come, all anti-war books like *Im Westen Nichts Neues* (*All Quiet on the Western Front*) were fed to the pyre. Little time was lost afterwards before Göbbels' sheets, as librarians named them, were issued to all public libraries listing the authors and titles of all books which were banned, so as to prevent German readers from being poisoned by the devilish works of anti-German elements.

My parents, though they were no great readers themselves, were severely shocked by what they called this sinking into cultureless barbarism. Mother stressed the point that any society which forbids its people to read books its leaders disapproved of, was showing its inner weakness by hiding something. In this she compared the Nazis with the Catholic Church who by way of the Vatican Index forbade their believers to read books which were critical of the Church. It was around this time that Hermann Göring made a speech in which he said 'Wenn immer ich das Wort Kultur höre, möchte ich nach meiner Pistole greifen.' (Whenever I hear the word culture, I feel like reaching for my pistol.)

One direct result of this was probably that a number of well-known people began to leave Germany. My parents, probably heard through the grapevine, of which there appeared many, about our nation's blood-letting. But nothing was reported in our media. Father had always tried to tell me that the basis of all dictatorships rests on the control of the information services.

Marlene Dietrich was said to have refused support for the Nazi regime and had gone to America. So did Albert Einstein, Thomas and Heinrich Mann, Kurt Weill, Fritz Lang, Richard Tauber and Bertold Brecht, who were only a few on a long list who had left. At school we were told that a cleansing process of German culture and science was being carried through. Father laughed sarcastically when I told him about it and he remarked that though he could understand that famous people did not like to live under the oppressive regime of the swastika, most of them were rich, had made their packet when times had been good for them and had no real difficulties to pitch their tents abroad. But we should not forget that there were hundreds of thousands who would equally have liked to go but could not because they were poor and for that reason other foreign and so-called Christian countries did not want them.

Of course everyone in Germany knew the names of Richard Tauber and Marlene Dietrich. Even to us children they were big household names. When we played the game 'Theatre', the girls wanted to play Marlene while the boys wanted to be Richard. Some said that Tauber was an even greater tenor than the Italian Caruso, but father thought that this was because of deep-seated nationalistic jealousy. We were aware that Dietrich had a beautiful deep voice and had come to prominence and fame in the film *Der Blaue Engel* (*The Blue Angel*) which was shown all over the world.

Tauber's was the voice every male wanted to copy. All this was of course before Hitler was made Kanzler. After that event the attitudes changed fundamentally and Tauber, then known to be half-Jewish, was simply not mentioned any more. We had an old gramophone at home and father loved to listen to his wonderful voice, he even tried to accompany Tauber when he thought that mother or I would not hear him. I remember how very angry and sad he was when Tauber had to flee his native country because of the Nazis.

Rumours were that Marlene Dietrich, though not Jewish, had very un-German if not anti-German attitudes. Father said that there was nothing un-German about her, that in any case this Nazi-invented expression was in any intelligent sense meaningless. Dietrich simply hated Nazism for what it stood for and everything connected with it, that's why she went to America.

During the first years of the Hitler Government the names of these two especially were still very strong and fresh in all our minds. So when one of us once mentioned their names at a Hitler Youth meeting, he was told never to do so again, as one was a dirty Jew and the other a common traitor. I heard many years later that Richard Tauber had died in England. As he had been rather careless with money throughout his life, he was penniless when he was close to death and unable to pay for his medical treatment. It was known that Marlene, who had been a friend of his for many years, paid for everything which Tauber needed.

From birth onwards whenever I had something wrong with me, mother took me to a child specialist, a Dr. Spielberg. My parents had not cared about him being a Jew and I, not even knowing what it meant, did not know. For them it was important to be sure that he was a good and reliable doctor who came when he was needed. Mother came home one day and told us that she had met Dr. Spielberg in the street and that he had stopped to talk to her. He had asked after me and when mother told him that nothing was wrong with me, he retorted that was good, but should I one day need him, he hoped that we would remember him. Mother said that he had looked ill and, after having made sure that no one could overhear her, she told him that especially at times like this, she felt ashamed to be a German and hoped that the Nazis would soon run out of their time. He had not responded to that in words, had just looked sad and had slowly walked away. Father reminded mother to be careful in future and not to make statements like that in the street. He added that as far as Dr. Spielberg was concerned, it would have been too dangerous to have responded to that. It was years later after the end of the war that someone told me that he and his whole family had not returned from the concentration camp.

It was not long after mother's meeting with him that I came home from school and told her that though Dr. Spielberg had always treated me well and had been kind to me, I did not think that it was really right that a Jewish doctor should be allowed to touch a German child. Mother was aghast at this and asked me what had come over me, making a stupid and wicked statement like that. I told her that we had a special meeting in the school's Aula which the entire school had to attend. A doctor in a brown uniform had come and given us a lecture on 'keeping the German race clean'. I had liked his talk as it had been an interesting one. The doctor had been young and good-looking, had spoken in a friendly manner and afterwards encouraged us to ask questions. He took the trouble to answer every single one and when one of us boys had made rather a fool of himself and everyone had laughed, the doctor had stayed serious but had kindly explained to the boy where he had gone wrong. That attitude had put him up a rung on the ladder of our estimation.

I too had asked a question, had put my hand up, then had not been quite sure any more and took it down, hoping that no one had seen it. But the doctor had, probably also realised that I was a bit shy and had come in the gangway in the middle towards me and encouraged me freely to ask my question. 'After all,' he had said, 'we are living in a free country.' Afterwards he said that my question had been a good and thoughtful one and that I must never be afraid to ask questions. By now everyone was looking at me and I felt very proud.

'But what was your question?' mother wanted to know.

'I had asked that if the Jews despised the Germans so much, as he had told us they did, and were so nasty to us, why had they come to our Germany in the first place, where had they come from and would it not be a good idea now that we had a strong Führer, to throw them all out again?' He then told me and the whole school, all the teachers and Herr Duggen, the Rector, had listened, that the Jews had come from the Near East in the Middle Ages when the German nation had been inattentive, probably did not realise how bad they were, wanted to be kind really and help them. And when they woke up to what a ghastly mistake they had made, it was all too late. Later, at the turn of the last century, they had come in droves from other Eastern European countries; from Russia, Poland, Hungary and Rumania etc. That shows that none of those countries had wanted them – and probably for good reason, having found out that they were greedy, ruthless and shifty. They were clever all right, far too clever for their own good and very cunning. They had wormed their way into the professions of teaching, banking, medicine and all those other branches from where they could spread their poison amongst the good and unsuspecting people of Germany. But now their time had come and he himself as a doctor had written a letter to a Frankfurt newspaper, as well as to the Ministry in Berlin, demanding that Jewish doctors should no longer be allowed to touch German children, and better still, should be struck off the Medical Register. He agreed with my suggestion that the best solution would be to throw them all out of Germany.

Mother looked angry and shocked all the time she was listening and did not interrupt me once except by saying a couple of times 'go on'. Then she asked me whether I had mentioned Dr. Spielberg. 'You didn't, did you?' she said. 'Yes, I did because he asked me whether I had ever come close to a Jewish doctor or whether I knew of one. But I did say that I did not think that Dr. Spielberg was a bad man.' 'Oh my God,' was all mother responded with. And when I got worried and wanted to know what I had done wrong, she retorted that we were going to leave the matter for the time being and wait until father came home from work.

As usual we had our Abendbrot (tea) together after which we stayed sitting round the table. I knew that mother had told father and there was tension in the air. Then father said that he wanted to tell me something: 'Look here, Junge, mother has told me what you have been taught in school today and what you yourself said to the visiting doctor. No doubt you now know that it has upset us very much. Now listen very carefully. When you were born you had not asked to come into this world, you just arrived and no one asked you whether you wanted to be German, French, Jewish or anything else. It was only we who told you, when you were a little bit older, that you were a German.' What he had said made sense to me and I nodded in agreement. But then he went on: 'And the same happened to all other children in the world as it also happened to mother and myself. No one of us can help what they were born as, can they?'

'No.'

'So can you think of any reason why anyone should be so stupid to think that as she or he has been born German, they are better people than those who have been born English or Jewish or what?'

I could not do other but agree with his logic. But he then went on to enlarge on the subject, or perhaps his ideal, his dream, that if someone like me or another of my generation went into other countries with an open heart, met people there, learnt their language or they ours, we would find that there was more binding us together than dividing us. Both sides would then learn that so many of our national assumptions, prejudices and superstitions would have no real bearing any more and that we could so easily live together as friends to our mutual benefit. He reminded me that I did not like the boy Helmut from around the corner, that we were always fighting each other whenever we met and that I might find that some boy on the other side of the French border might be much more to my liking and with whom I would get on much better than with that German Helmut.

He rammed it into me: being good or bad has nothing to do with being born German, French or Jewish. What it has to do with is the background of one's upbringing, with what one has been taught by one's parents or at school. 'People who tell you otherwise, however nice they might appear to you and however smoothly they can talk like that brown-shirted doctor, are the ones who are either bad or downright stupid.'

'But shall I not believe then what I am being taught at school?'

'Oh, Junge, you pose a good question there. What your teachers teach you about figures, laws of physics and languages you must of course accept as correct and try to learn and remember. Your sense must tell you, that is only good and right. But you are old enough now to sort out your own observations in your own mind. You must always be thoughtful if not sceptical if someone wants to pass something on to you which cannot be more than an opinion. An opinion can be right or wrong, good or bad and more often than not depends on circumstances or the way one looks at it. It might sometimes be a good idea when you are not quite sure about something you have learnt at school to talk it over with mother or me. We do not claim that we are necessarily right and you wrong, but talking it over might help to clear possible cobwebs from your mind.'

'Shall I tell the teacher then tomorrow that what the doctor had told us in the Aula was not only not right but bad?'

With this he again looked perplexed and I realised that he was thinking deeply about it. 'No, Henry, you must not do that and neither must you tell anyone at school about what we three have been talking about in our kitchen. It might seem dishonest to you, but with you growing older you will soon learn that our world is not the most honest of places to live in, that indeed some of its people can be very dishonest, purposeful liars, and that it is not always easy to handle things correctly. Look at it this way: you carry your pocket money in one of your trouser pockets and that bully Helmut grabs you and asks you where you have hidden it. Would you then say: ah, Helmut, it's in my left trouser pocket or would you tell him that you haven't got any on you and had left it at home?'

'Yeah, I would tell him a lie of course.'

'You see, that's exactly what I mean, in that case you would be quite right to lie. And if politicians and salesmen try to convince you that their ware is good, better than that of their competitors, would you trust them? For if you do, you would soon find yourself cheated and in queer street.'

After they had kissed me good night and mother had helped me into bed, I lay awake for quite some time and thought about all the contradictory things I had heard that day. I thought about what mother and father had told me and the doctor and my teachers and then also thought about Dr. Spielberg, how kindly he had always treated me and I regretted having mentioned his name to the doctor in school. And I felt so confused and did not really know any more what to think, where I could find the truth – and what was the truth.

As to the truth and being honest, another in itself rather unimportant but for me disturbing event took place at about that time. During much of the summer holidays I stayed with my grandmother, uncle, aunt and cousins in Stapelfeld. My uncle Emil, mother's brother, took me one sunny afternoon to the neighbouring village of Papendorf to collect a pig for slaughter. The road was little more than a field track and as there was as good as no traffic, Onkel Emil allowed me to hold the reins to lead the horse for a steady trot. Sitting on the coachman's seat, I felt proud and important. If only my school mates and friends at home could see me now. I also wanted to prove to Onkel Emil that I was able to do the job without fault.

However, we then had to go into a sharp bend at a crossroads, at the side of which stood a warning sign nailed to a tall post. Acting no doubt too eagerly, with the horse having enough road sense to take the bend correctly without my interference, I pulled the reins too early and knocked the post down with the back wheel of our cart. Well, of course, I was sorry and expected some telling off from Onkel Emil. But all he did was to look around to make sure that no one had seen me do it, and then told me to go on, not to look back and behave as if nothing had happened. He then laughed and said that I should not worry and that it did not matter in the least. The main thing was that no one had seen me do it and that anyway the post must have been rotten, as otherwise it would not have been so easily knocked over.

When I suggested that we'd better report the accident, he guffawed loudly and told me not to be such a silly fusspot. When I said that father had taught me to always be honest, especially if I had done something wrong, he retorted with something like, 'well, your father has woolly ideas. He believes in the ultimate goodness of humans. I on the contrary have learnt that most of them are lying bastards and if I now go to that supreme village idiot, our Bürgermeister, and tell him that we have knocked the post down, he will only think that either someone has watched us doing it or that I have gone barmy for telling him.'

Well, I did not pass this on to father, but it did upset me. Of late many of my idealised visions of the world and its people had taken serious knocks. More and more doubts were somersaulting into my mind which I found it hard to deal with. And with it all I felt that somehow I was arriving at an important crossroads which I would find difficult to analyse and digest but from which I could not run away.

With the Enabling Act now passed, the Nazis lost little time in making use of it. One of their first major actions was the bringing in of trade union legislation. The assumption that trade unionists could not be trusted in important state institutions was artificially spread in the media. That was the mental preparation for legislation and the latter itself was disarmingly simple: all individual trade unions were forthwith abolished and then re-instituted into a government-regulated organisation called 'die Deutsche Arbeitsfront' (German Workers' Front). Father claimed that this was a pure masterstoke on their part, perhaps the main reason why the Ruhr and other major industrialists had given so much money to help Hitler and his henchmen into government. He predicted that from now on the employers could do with their employees what they liked and could shape and dictate working conditions without bothering to even consult their workers.

With one stroke this legislation alone had swept away all meaningful opposition to the profit-making plans of the big employers of labour. They were now called 'work-givers' and the workers 'work-takers' as if that was something natural, that those who had the money were providing the work and those who had none were doing it. The press presented it as a creation of harmony in industrial relations where only chaos and con-fusion had reigned before. Strikes, though not really forbidden by law, had no place any more in modern Nazi Germany, and the world looked at us with utter wonderment and envy, or so we were told. Inner German conflict had been abolished with one mighty swoop by the genius of our Führer Adolf Hitler. There was now only one great happy German family, no matter whether they were the General Director of Krupp's and his family members or his lowest-paid sweeper in one of his many factories.

When in the evening father read that juicy bit to mother, he remarked 'what, no matter? The owner of Krupp's income is at the very least 100 times that of his low-paid workers. If the workers really fall for that tripe, then they deserve what they get.'

The head of the Arbeitsfront was of course appointed by the govern-ment, not elected by the workers any more, and was a trusted party friend of Hitler's with the name of Dr. Robert Ley. Jokes about his appointment quickly made the rounds, as it was said that with a name like that, Ley, he surely must have at least one Jewish pint of blood in him. But in our new times, now with the reception rooms of the concentration camps so invitingly open, no one outside their own four walls said so openly.

After the collapse in 1945, Robert Ley when waiting to be called to give evidence at the Nuremberg Tribunal, hanged himself with his braces from the cistern of the prison lavatory. From then on the accused top Nazis were not allowed to wear braces in their prison cells and the lavatory doors were taken off their hinges.

Father then made a move which I found difficult to understand. Having been an active organiser in the Railwaymen's Union for many years, he now threw himself into trade union work in the new Arbeitsfront Rail Section. Of course I was well aware that he detested the whole set-up, he was saying it often enough at home. And while every year during Weimar it had always been a matter of honour to him to march with his workmates in the May Day demonstration, I knew how he now detested to march on that day behind the Arbeitsfront banner which contained the swastika. It was after he had died and before I went to Russia as a soldier, that I asked mother about this. She told me that he had done this for two well-considered reasons which he had previously talked over with his mates and to which they had agreed. One was that within the Arbeitsfront he thought that he could still do something for his workmates as well as being able to stay in touch with important industrial developments; the second was that by actively getting involved in that way, he hoped to disappear from the open political scene, go a bit underground, so to say, in the middle of the enemy camp. Mother thought that it had worked exceptionally and unexpectedly well. Though his political reputation had initially brought some suspicion with it, it was probably assumed that he had seen the light as he was never seriously questioned.

Father in so many ways was a curious man, so very different from most of the other fathers I knew. In no way could he have been described as an educated man, at least not formally so, as he had left school at age fourteen. It was really only many years after his death that I reached the full comprehension of how extremely intelligent and wise he was. He had developed an understanding of life as lived by ordinary people, what lay behind it, what the reasons were for it and what it all meant, as few others whom I have met in my lifespan of seven decades have reached. At times he dabbled in the spheres of philosophy, not in a nebulous way, so difficult to understand by ordinary people, but on simple lines which could easily be grasped by most. Whenever he ran into difficulties on that, he made use of the principle of going back to basics. Amongst others he showed much interest in the theories of the French philosopher Jacques Rousseau whom he considered as one of the intellectual fathers of the French Revolution. He quoted Rousseau more than once to me saying that 'the fruit of the earth must belong to all its people but that the earth itself, the land with its minerals, the water etc. must never belong to anyone privately and certainly not be traded for monetary profit on the market.'

While the disarmament negotiations at Geneva were at least showing some pale light of hope, Hitler dropped another bombshell by announcing in a speech that Germany was having no more part in it. He made much of the humiliation Germany had suffered at the hands of the victor nations and said that he was sick and tired of the French and British who were busily building up their own arsenals under all sorts of hypocritical pretexts, were selling arms around the world wherever they could and at the same time making statement after statement that rearming was bad and threatening the peace of the world.

That speech was a clear signal for taking the cover off a German armament programme which, according to father, had been secretly going on already during the time of the Weimar Republic. Across the road from us stood the Ottensener Eisenwerke (Iron Works), a large factory complex employing hundreds of workers in which, the rumours had it, military hardware was being produced. It was unusual in those days, but guards were stationed at the factory main gates who did not let anyone in without a thorough check of their papers. Suddenly after Hitler's speech the truth came out into the open, for on every working day at a certain hour in the early afternoon we children waited at the gate to watch one cannon, hooked on to the back of a military lorry, come rolling out.

Being reminded all the time by my parents' conversations, I accepted somehow that the time we were living in was not only difficult but dangerously explosive. When mother exclaimed that life was a struggle, I merely heard the words but could not fathom their meaning. After all, I lived in a loving home, had always enough to eat, mother sewed all the clothes I needed and I had many good friends to play with in the street. Was it then so surprising that I simply could not see these hidden dangers?

This was the time in my young life when I was beginning to make my own observations and spinning my own thoughts. As my parents had always encouraged me to, I began to try to assess what was happening around me, not only in my own country but everywhere. That this was only possible on the basis of receiving information from at least two opposing points of view, I could not yet see. I watched the Nazis almost daily in their striking brown uniforms marching in the streets. I ran along with them, danced to their music and sometimes even filed in at the tail end of their column, trying to march with them in proper military step. They were friendly to us kids, we loved their music and tried to sing their songs with them. So why did my parents not like them, saying that they were an evil lot? I began to feel that confusion was tearing me in two different directions. Whom should I believe, the Nazis or my parents?

One winter's evening when father was sitting with some friends around our kitchen table, the doorbell rang and my cousin Alfred, who was in his late twenties, arrived. He had been in America for a number of years and had just come back. I had heard of him, had seen him in photos but never in the flesh. To us children America was something very special, something that had the aura of adventure. Woven around its mere name was the veil of gold, millionaires, skyscrapers and paradise. Every American, we assumed, must be rich and have at least one car, and with this in mind when I first set eyes on my cousin Alfred, I was more than disappointed. I rather naively asked whether he had his car downstairs. He merely shook his head and said: 'What makes you think that I have a car?' And when I answered, 'because you are an American', everyone around the table laughed, Alfred looked perplexed and I felt like a fool.

Working people in Germany at that time were anything but well-dressed but cousin Alfred, at least to me, looked very much down at heel. He wore a tattered overcoat, had shoes of which one was split at the side and looked thin and pale as if he had not had enough to eat. He was introduced to everybody and was asked to sit down in the table's circle and tell us all about his American experiences. As we had already eaten, mother offered to make him sandwiches which he eagerly, all too eagerly, accepted.

'Well,' he said, 'America is a very large and rich country.' He had left Germany several years before, I think he said during the recession in 1930 because he had been out of work and could find no other. Shortly after his arrival on the new continent he had been lucky and had found work in Bethlehem Steelworks. When I asked him why the name Bethlehem, had it anything to do with Jesus, father told me to stay quiet and to just listen as otherwise I would have to go to bed. Alfred went on, saying that the wages had not been all that good and the work had been hard and dusty. He then left the steelworks and had gone west as far as the mighty Mississippi River where he had worked in several jobs, one of them as a farm worker, but then recession had gripped America and the entire economy was threatened with collapse. The situation had become as desperate as it had been in Germany. Everywhere one looked, one stared into the eyes of poverty and hopelessness but also noticed the enormous riches of some. I think he said that twenty million people in the States were unemployed and for the many there was no dole money nor healthcare. In one of the larger cities he had seen dead bodies lying in the streets with everyone just walking past them as if it were something commonplace. Many people in that supposedly very rich country were homeless because they had no money to pay their rent, for most there was no social assistance whatsoever and one could actually see entire families making their homes in some sheltered corners on the pavements, just as he had seen on photos from India.

Now he had come back in the hold of a freighter after only about six years in the promised land. He had spent his last dime on the homeward journey. He reckoned that he would now find work in his native Germany after the great Adolf Hitler had taken the reins of the state into his safe, strong hands.

Up to then it had been quiet around the table. Everyone had been listening with close attention, but after his last statement, a suppressed snigger went round the table and I could hear the words 'the great Adolf Hitler' repeated several times. Straight away father's good friend Otti went into action and said that though the unemployment catastrophe had somewhat eased, it was only by reason of Germany's rearmament programme. Hitler's sorcerism had nothing to do with it and when Alfred remarked that he did not care what the reasons were as long he could find a job and earn money, one of the friends chided him for that, telling him

that he did not know what he was saying and that indeed he was expressing a very selfish and callous view. The friend made the point that an
economy in which unemployment was an almost natural part of a recur-
ring cycle, was or should be totally unacceptable to working people. For
that reason alone, he thought, working people should organise and get rid
of that system, for their children's sake if not for their own. What Alfred
also should realise, was that mass rearmament like this would almost
inevitably lead to war, but that this was probably what Hitler and his rich
backers were planning anyway.

But Alfred did not care to listen to that, he told the friend that he was
talking nonsense and in any case that if war was good for the economy of
the country, gave people work and money, so be it. I could see cold anger
rising in the faces of some around the table when mother again managed
to diffuse the threatening explosion and offered Alfred another sandwich
which he wolfed down, apparently forgetting what he was going to say. I
noticed father quietly nodding to his friends after which he asked Alfred
to tell us more about America. Again he told us what a great and free
country it was. He reckoned that it was a proper democracy as the people
had the chance to vote for the President they wanted every four years and
that it was up to everyone to become a millionaire or not.

Otti quietly chuckled at this, threw his head back and looked towards
the ceiling. 'I am glad that you were saying "or not" because obviously
like more than another hundred million people, you did not become one.
Instead you left America, spending your last dime on the homeward trip
so that you can find work in Hitler's armament factories. Do you know
that in the Opel Works in the west they are already producing tanks and
that Opel belongs to a large extent to General Motors in America?' As to
democracy he asked him whether anyone without millions of dollars had
the slightest chance of becoming American President. And when Alfred
just shrugged his shoulders, he asked what kind of millionaires' democracy he thought that was. While another quarrel now seemed close to
exploding, I found it all very exciting and I listened to every word. But
then father cut it short and asked Alfred about President Roosevelt who
had come to office about the same time as Hitler and how his 'New Deal'
was working and what the American people thought of it.

'Well,' Alfred went on his warpath again, 'it's just great. Everybody
loves it, the trouble is that it takes such a long time to filter through and I
could not afford to wait.' He told us about the Tennessee project which
now employed large numbers of formerly unemployed for admittedly
low wages and which in fact had taken about a million off the unemployment register. Father pointed out to Alfred that he thought that the
root problem lay with the working of capitalism itself, that it was the
entire system which was in trouble the world over and not only with the
German economy, the American, the British and the French. They might

not see it that way but they are all in the same boat, threatened with the same disaster and all struggling against each other to get the best seat. And in the end it will drag them all into a war. 'And who do you think will suffer and will have to pay the price?'

Alfred just shook his head, saying that wars had nothing to do with capitalism but with human brutality. And when everyone around the table laughed, father screwed up his face and mumbled something, more to himself than to others, that those who do not want to see, will not see. He suggested to Alfred to carefully watch further developments, to also look behind the meanings of the nicely sounding words spouted by the politicians and perhaps to learn that Hitler's steady move towards a war would be appeased by western rulers because they too were at their wits' end about how to find a solution to their mounting troubles. He feared that no one in western countries really had any idea how to solve the threatening social/economic problems without a war.

I felt a bit sorry for cousin Alfred as I could see that he was like a fish out of water, how he wriggled and twisted on his chair, not really knowing any more what to say. While he had felt free enough to contradict all the others around the table, he felt too respectful towards father to argue against him and said: '– ah well, Onkel Fritz, if you say so – but now I must be going because I want to look up a friend.' With that he shook hands all round. Everyone wished him well and mother took him into the corridor to see him off. I heard them talking quietly after which mother came back into the kitchen, shut the door behind her and told father that Alfred had asked her for money. One of the others, realising the embarrassing situation, cut the Gordion knot and proposed that each of them should put a few coins on the table so that the failed American millionaire could pay for his tram fare back to his room in Hamburg. After that the table was rather subdued. They all expressed a degree of pity for Alfred. Then Otti said 'Well, we have all heard his sad story. He left Germany for the paradise in the New World but he found it wanting and came back with his tail between his legs and now wants to find his luck in helping Hitler to build his mighty war machine.'

CHAPTER IV
And into the Hitler Youth

Strange things began to happen in the Christian Jungschar weekly meetings in the Gemeindehaus (parish hall) that I regularly went to. One of our leaders, Herbert Stiebert, who was about seventeen, turned up in a different uniform. He wore a brown shirt instead of our usual dirty green one. I noticed that the old verger, who usually opened the meeting with a prayer and a short talk, was visibly upset. But he went on behaving with his normal friendliness, greeted Herbert and made no comment about his uniform. Of course none of us asked any questions, we just sat around the table and stared, though we all wondered what it was all about.

The meeting, the games we played or whatever it was we did that evening, went on as usual. But the general atmosphere was lost, decidedly disturbed, the usual tranquillity of our being together had been destroyed. What was more, all of us sensed that something had to happen, had to give way, to clear the air. I saw that Herbert was speaking quietly to the verger who towards the end of the meeting announced that Herbert had requested to say a few words to us. It was obvious that he felt very uncomfortable to say the very least. The colour of his face went dark red as he clumsily rose to his feet. Not being the best of speakers, he had to clear his throat several times, before he came out with what was nothing more than a terse factual statement that he had joined the Hitler Youth and was not going to come to our meetings any more. He then clicked his heels in a military salute, raised his right arm into the air, shouted 'Heil Hitler', to which no one knew whether to respond or not, and strode out of the room. We all sat there quietly for a long while, not really knowing what to say until the verger came out with a few general words, but without any explanation about what had happened, and we all went home.

A week or so later all of our parents were asked to come to a coffee meeting in the Gemeindehaus. Mother went on her own. I was already in bed when she came back and I heard her quietly talking to father about what she had learnt at the meeting. I tried to listen but could not understand though I could make out by the tones of their voices that they were upset. Dropping off to sleep I wondered why of late so much in our lives had gone topsy-turvy.

The next Jungschar meeting was on a Sunday morning. We were about a hundred strong in our group and lined up in the street outside the Gemeindehaus, which in itself was unusual. Our leaders stood about on the pavement, talking to each other in a somewhat nervous manner while the verger stayed inside the house, watching the goings on outside through a large window. Next we heard the sounds of a marching column, someone shouting 'left-right-left-right', we also heard the sounds of a large drum and several flutes. Then we saw them, it was a troop of Hitler Youth, nosing round the corner and coming towards us. They carried a swastika flag in front, followed by the lone drummer with the flutes behind him. They marched into the gap between us and the pavement, when a sharp command brought them to a halt right in front of us. Everything seemed to have been pre-arranged. We just stood there and wondered and stared at this very unexpected spectacle. The leaders of both groups came together, shook hands, not exactly friendly but in a militarily correct fashion, exchanged a few words and raised their arms to each other in the Hitler salute.

It did not take very long before the Hitler Youth leader again bellowed a command and his troop marched off. Before we knew what it was about, our senior leader stepped off the pavement and called us to attention. His command sounded much gentler than that of the Hitler Youth leader: 'follow the column in front of you, march! left-right-left-right. ' At that moment we had not fully realised that we had just joined the Hitler Youth. We quickly caught up until the two columns were almost one, with only a bare gap between us. We too now marched to the same drum beat through the streets of our Sunday morning sleepy town, in front the brownshirts, and us, the dirty-green ones, in the rear. The passers-by looked on in surprise at this strange spectacle. No one had any idea about the destination of our march. We hardly talked to each other, it was all so strange and unexpected, we just marched on until we arrived at the headquarters building of the Hitler Youth. Before we were dismissed, the venue of the next meeting was announced and nothing much more was said.

When I came home, I told my parents that it looked like I was now a member of the Hitler Youth, and not the Christian Jungschar movement. I also told them that when we had left the Gemeindehaus to follow the Hitler Youth troop, I had seen the old verger standing bareheaded on the top of the steps, watching us marching away from him. He had looked so miserable, almost with tears in his eyes. 'Yes,' said mother, 'it really was he who built up the Jungschar movement in our town, he had been so proud of his work. And to see you all just marching away from him behind the swastika must have been a bitter, bitter pill for him to swallow.'

Father just sat there, looking glum and fed-up, for he had never made it a secret that he hated everything connected with the Nazis, and he had never been over-enthusiastic about the Christian Youth Organisation. As he had so often stated he wanted me to grow up freely without the danger of being brainwashed from any side. I only realised much later how much it must have hurt him, a down-to-earth working man, to watch his only son being sucked into the Nazi movement.

We then sat together at the kitchen table to talk the matter over. Father asked me whether I really wanted to belong to the Hitler Youth. Well, I wasn't quite sure, in a way I did not mind, but the last thing I wanted was to appear enthusiastic about it in front of him. I said that I wanted to be with my friends and all the other boys of the neighbourhood and, anyway, as I understood it, the Jungschar was no more. Even though my 'enrolment' had not been exactly voluntary, was I now to go and tell the Hitler Youth leader that I did not want to be one of them? And what then? What sort of reason was I going to give him as he surely would ask me for one? Father, I could see, listened thoughtfully, then nodded to mother and smiled at me and said 'Yes, of course, you are right. What can we do?'

The bank of the River Elbe was not far from where we lived. In a hurry one could reach it in less than fifteen minutes. Along the bank were nice shady parks, most of them established during the Weimar period. After having walked through them, one arrived at a short promenade called Övelgönne which had several restaurants in whose gardens it was very pleasant to sit in summer and watch the ships gliding past. Up to the first day of the 1939 war there was much music and dancing. Övelgönne was a pearl of a place and on a nice day we often went down there for a stroll.

A pier bridge led to a floating landing stage where the river boats called, tying their thick ropes for a stop around the iron props. They operated like buses to a frequent timetable and were cheap and convenient to use between Hamburg and Altona as well as to other places up and down and on both banks of the river.

With the Nazis taking a slow but firm grip on all things cultural in German life, jazz had officially been declared un-German and down-town nigger music. As with all restrictions, however, reactions to this one soon took place. After all, many people, especially the younger ones, did like jazz. Louis Armstrong was a household name and most of us youngsters knew the melody, and some of us even the English words, of 'Tiger Rag'. I too, though I did not have much of a musical ear, liked some of it and indeed found it a bit odd that it should be officially forbidden.

A group of youngsters between sixteen or seventeen came together on summer evenings on the pier bridge close to the railings and played jazz. As they were not disturbing anyone, no one seemed to mind. On the contrary, many people seemed to like it for they stood around the musicians, tapped their feet and moved their bodies to the rhythm of the jazz.

However, and it was not really a surprise, this idyllic interlude soon ran into trouble, for the Hitler Youth had got wind of this morale-under-mining performance and decided to do something about it. At first a couple or so Hitler Youth Streife (roamers) went down to the river and tried to convince the performers to stop this un-German activity. But as there was no real law against it, the restriction had only been announced by the Hitler Youth, they met with little success. The music went on as before. The group was determined enough to carry on but found that the Hitler Youth was equally determined.

Then a senior leader, who had something to do with furthering German culture amongst the young, took events into his own hands. His name was Heinz Vollmer. His reputation was one of arrogance and few liked him. To prove that he had courage, he always came down on his own almost every weekend and wore his full Hitler Youth uniform, jackboots and all. But then one lovely Saturday evening, probably getting fed-up with getting nowhere, he foolishly overstepped his limit. He strutted up the pier, grabbed one of the home-made instruments and threw it into the river. Well, that was it. He just stood there, looking arrogantly at the players as if to say, 'I know all of you as you know me. And surely none would lift a finger against a well-known Hitler Youth leader.' And they didn't, at least not at that time. They waited a week or two and then prepared to set a trap. They were in no doubt that Vollmer, whom they regarded with some contempt – after all, who else would become a leader in the Hitler Youth? – would walk right into it. Then the Saturday evening of action arrived. Everything was well planned and well prepared. But this time the whole thing was slightly different, none of the usual jazz players were on the pier. They were standing further back at the far end of the promenade from where they had an uninterrupted view. Their playing places had been taken by friends, another jazz group who came from Hamburg and were not known in this part of town. To play safe, they had also arranged for several older friends to stroll up and down the pier and on the promenade, just in case witnesses were required.

And then, sure enough, as he did on almost every Saturday evening, Vollmer arrived on his bicycle to strut up the pier in his brown uniform, to do his bit for Führer and Fatherland. It really should have surprised him a little, that this time he could not recognise any of the jazz players. Later one or two of the 'independent witnesses' remembered having heard him say so. Only Vollmer, being so full of his own importance, could not remember.

Dusk was already setting on this fine summer evening when he went straight into action and attempted to grab another instrument, no doubt with the intention of throwing it into the river. This was the signal which set off the rest of the now rapidly following steps. Up to now, so it seemed, everything had gone like clockwork. Instead of Vollmer being able to grab a jazz instrument, the jazz players grabbed him. It only took them a few seconds to relieve him of his well-polished jackboots – they landed in the river. Next his trousers and underpants came down and one of the jazzmen observed that Vollmer, coming out on an important mission of this kind on a Saturday evening, could at least have washed himself properly down below. A pair of scissors was at hand to cut off the lower part of his brown shirt to where his navel was. As they were at it with the scissors, they gave his military hairstyle an extra criss-cross trim. One of them then produced a thin willow stick to make a few marks on Vollmer's fat bottom so that he could remember his Övelgönne interlude for some time afterwards by looking into the mirror.

As it so happened, a large number of condoms had collected and floated against the wall of the quay-side, which came out of the sewage outflow from further up the river. One of the jazzmen climbed down the iron ladder to collect a large handful of them, which he then stuffed into Vollmer's mouth to the point when his cheeks started to bulge. It never became known whether he actually swallowed one. As a final act they tied condoms round his ears, popped one or two on his toes, tied another tightly around his sensitive parts, and then threw him into the river and ran. All this had taken only a few minutes.

Later when the police asked for witnesses, several of the 'respectable' citizens volunteered. They all protested that they had been unable to do anything about the assault, because they were too frightened of being thrown into the river. Had they recognised any of the jazz players, had they seen them before? No, they had not, they all seemed to have been strangers to Övelgönne, indeed, on the whole they were unable to assist the police with their enquiries.

They then described to the police what had actually happened – and later also told others who wanted to hear. After his plunge, Vollmer had quickly swum to the shore, had crossed the beach and with his hands covering his front, had climbed up the few steps to the promenade where many onlookers had gathered. The witnesses had to apologise several times to the police officer, that they could not help laughing when relating this 'sad' happening, he would have to understand that the spectacle of Vollmer approaching the promenade in the gathering dusk had just been too hilarious for words.

Uniforms usually cover a lot of shortcomings. They can prop up and completely change an otherwise pitiful figure into an almost admirable one. Vollmer had a fat bum and a potbelly and when he appeared on the promenade, though dripping wet of course, he was still in a way correctly dressed in his brown uniform, that was from his tie under the chin down to his navel. The witnesses reported that condoms were kind of hanging out of his ears and that he was almost sick when he spat and pulled them out of his mouth. He had then walked over to his bicycle, when a police constable arrived and offered him a cloak for cover.

I doubt that the original jazzmen ever came back to the pier to play music again. Many people thought it was a shame, but then it was late in the season and the incoming bad weather would have stopped it anyway. I do not know whether after that Heinz Vollmer ever went down to the river and showed his face at Övelgönne. Maybe he learned his lesson. When I told my parents about the incident, they could not stop laughing. Mother had tears in her eyes and father showed no sympathy for anyone wearing a brown shirt.

At about that time a terrible tragedy was brought home to us all. It concerned my friend and class mate Siegfried Weisskamm whom I had already known from before our school days, when our mothers had taken us to the park where we had played together. Siegfried lived in a nicer part of the town than we did. There were hardly any factories in his area and shady trees stood along the pavements. The tenements had front gardens and Siegfried and his younger sister Veronika lived in a spacious flat with a balcony, from which you could watch the trams go by. They also had a bathroom where one of the taps was for hot water. He often came to our place to play with me as I went to his. Mother liked him because he was always so well behaved and never forgot to say 'please' and 'thank you', as I sometimes did. His father was not a working man and wore a good suit when going to work; he had polished manners not as straightforward as those of my father, and he had an educated way of speaking. If I remember correctly he worked as a salesman for a big Hamburg firm and was often away from home. Siegfried's mother was petite, her hair was dark and always set in the newest fashion. She was well dressed and very friendly towards me.

Then one day Siegfried did not come to school. There was talk straight away that something strange and sad had happened to him. Being known as my friend, people asked me about Siegfried, had I seen him lately and questions like that. But I hadn't and neither did I know where he was nor what had happened to him. Mother gave me strict instructions not to go to his place to find out but neither did she tell me what all this secret about Siegfried was.

A few days later our class teacher when coming into the room, did not shout at us as he usually did, but asked us quietly to sit down and listen to what he had to say. Siegfried, our good friend, he said, would not come to school any more because he had died. He then asked us to sit quietly for a minute, not to talk nor do anything but to think of Siegfried as a tribute. When one of us asked what had happened to Siegfried, how he had died, he told us that we should ask our parents who would probably tell us more. I straight away asked mother when I came home. Yes, she had known that there had been an accident from which Siegfried had died. A gas tap had been left open in their flat and he, together with sister Veronika, and their mother, had been found dead, after neighbours had smelled gas and had broken the door down before the police had arrived.

When father came home from work I told him that my friend Siegfried had died from an accident. He laughed a forced laugh and said something about what one could call an accident. 'Did you know that Siegfried had been a Jew?' No, I hadn't and neither did I really know what a Jew was. He explained that Jews in our country were people like us. If one went back in history one would find that their path of life had been very difficult, being scattered all over the world since Roman times, and that they had a different religion from ours. Whenever we had religion in class, Siegfried and a few others were allowed to leave the room and I had always thought that it was because he was probably a Catholic as were the others.

Of course I was very sad over Siegried's death. He had been a good friend of mine, as had his sister Veronika. But it did not make sense to me what his being Jewish had to do with his death. As father was usually very forthcoming in explaining whatever I asked him, he became now very reticent on this issue and merely said that the Nazis did not like the Jews, that this had probably something to do with his death and that I must not mention this to anyone. All this left me bewildered. Why would the Nazis want Siegfried to die? I knew in my heart that he never had done any harm to anyone.

I do realise now but did not then, that because of my age, firing questions and demanding answers to issues I could not understand, must have been a trying problem for my parents. The Nazis were making wide inroads into all aspects of life everywhere. Wherever people were at work in factories, offices or shops, Nazi informers were known to be around, weaving their nets and making their monthly or so reports on those they worked with. Father had to keep that in mind, for the sake of keeping the family together, he could not afford to fall foul of these people.

Probably to make me see for myself and knock some sense into my young inexperienced mind, he took me one evening to the Gewerkschafts-haus (Trade Union Building) in Hamburg to show me what had happened there. It was just before the trade unions were amalgamated into the Arbeitsfront and a few days after the Nazis had raided the building in search of evidence, saying that trade unions were acting as enemies of their country and were receiving money from Moscow. I think that the coining of the term 'Moscow Gold', largely thought up by Göbbels, originated from there.

We stood under the tall trees in front of the building and when I saw the smashed door and the broken windows, it all looked very frightening. Father said that it had been organised and well-orchestrated, as it had happened all over the country at the same time. He explained that the trade unions were the organisations of the working people through which they collectively defended themselves against the ruthless power of capital, as operated through the so-called 'free' market. And this was what the Nazis, being big business's most effective tool, were hell-bent on destroying. When I told him that we had learnt at school that the Nazis were the workers' party, that they even officially called themselves that, and it therefore did not make sense for them to smash workers' organisations, he pointed out that calling yourself something is one thing, reality is quite another. Father must have realised that at that time I had become very much more critical of what he was telling me, that the influence of school and Hitler Youth had created a rift between us. It must have hurt him very much as he loved me deeply, as I of course loved him.

The direct pressures on teachers to teach the line of Nazi ideology in almost every sphere and aspect showed itself outwardly in a gradual replacement of history books and a methodical introduction of portraits of the Führer and paintings of battle scenes and such like. Schools became little more than Nazi training institutes, where German youth were prepared for their eventual role in the ensuing war. Only Catholic schools and private ones, affordable to the rich, retained a relative independence. The Concordat, an early agreement between the Vatican and the Hitler Government, not only provided a mantle of international respectability for the Nazis, but also ensured that Catholic schools did not teach anything challenging the authority of the Nazi state. The only real chance therefore, as I see it now, for me to have entered the adult world with a critical mind, capable of thinking independently and searching for the truth, lay with my parents. But that last chance was as good as eliminated by a catastrophic blow which hit right into our street and the heart of our lives.

To a larger or lesser degree the majority of the population was aware that concentration camps had been set up all over the country. Those of my generation who claimed after the war that they knew nothing about them, were in my view avoiding the truth. But the time to protest against the camps had long since passed, for anybody speaking out would have ended up in one themselves. Whenever the camps were mentioned with party people present, it was usually explained that it had been the British who had first introduced them into South Africa during the Boer War. I assume that quite a large minority at least had a fair idea of what was going on inside them. My parents for instance did. But I suspect that few of them, except those on the political left, had given much thought to the deeper political implications of the camps.

As it happened, we soon learned more about these camps when one of our neighbours, who had been an active trade union secretary down at the ship works, became the first tangible victim in our very midst. I do not know whether Herr Eycken was a member of a political party but I had heard his name mentioned by my father, who was well acquainted with him and whose steadfast character I had heard him praise. Herr Eycken was ever ready to help people in our streets with thorny problems they themselves were unable to deal with.

It happened one early morning around three o'clock when everyone in the tenement was asleep. I only heard about it when mother got me up for school and, seeing her disturbed, I asked her what the matter was. She told me she had heard from neighbours that two cars had pulled up outside Eycken's tenement a few houses away from us and three men, one a policeman in uniform, one a civilian and the third in brown uniform, had ascended the stairs to the Eycken flat and had knocked loudly and repeatedly. When Herr Eycken had come to the door, he was told to get dressed, to put a few necessities into a suitcase and follow them down to the car. When Frau Eycken intervened at the door, she was told not to worry as her husband would soon be back after a necessary routine check. Well, as it materialised, he wasn't. Much later when I was already in the army, someone told me that he had died of pneumonia in a camp.

The family was now without an income and soon in dire financial trouble. At first Frau Eycken found it even difficult to receive information about where her husband had been taken, and there were very few people who dared to be seen helping her. My mother, who usually was very courageous, was now frightened to openly talk to her, and few of us boys were prepared to play with the two Eycken sons, as they now carried the stigma of 'sons of a traitor'. The family moved away to a poorer part of the town and I do not know what happened to them.

Needless to say my parents were thoroughly shaken. 'How can that happen in our very midst, that they come in the night and take one of us away from right under our noses and none of us can do anything about it?' father kept saying. I personally liked Herr Eycken. He had always been friendly to me, had gone out of his way when he saw me in the street to say something funny to make me laugh. Deep down I simply could not believe that he could be a traitor or whatever. On the other hand, having been taught in the Hitler Youth that it was necessary to take people into custody for security reasons, I could and would not believe, as my parents did, that our government would do something wrong, something illegal.

And when all this boiled over one evening into a bitter quarrel with father, he ordered me to sit down with mother and himself at the table. Though he had always encouraged me to state openly without fear what was on my mind, this time he shouted at me to shut up and listen to him without interruption. When I looked at mother for help but seeing her stern face and realising that she was totally on father's side, I did what I was told. 'Now, Junge,' he said, 'times are very hard and difficult for all of us.' Whenever he called me 'Junge' (boy) I knew that he had something serious on his mind and I had better look out. 'When I tell you that I want the very best for you in every respect, then you will believe me, won't you?'

'Of course, Papa,' I nodded. But when I wanted to add something, he cut me short, saying 'No, this time I will do the talking and you the listening.

Afterwards you can have as much say as you want.' That, I was well aware, was father at his logical best and I loved him for it.' I am a worker and have to keep my family, that is mother and you, with my wage which I bring home every Thursday. There are many things in life which I would love to provide you with, things which rich people can easily afford to give their children, but I cannot do that for the simple reason that my wages are too low, that they are barely enough to cover the absolute necessities to support our lives. Now then, whenever prices in the shops and rents go up and I try to better my wages accordingly, my employer, all employers, say "No!". They usually add, and I know pretty well beforehand that they will, that times are bad and that they simply cannot afford to pay us more. They claim that they are not a charity and that first and foremost as an industry and a business they must balance their books. If I am too greedy, they warn me, I, whose income is a fraction of theirs, then I will price myself out of my job. Tails, I lose, heads, they win, that is the reality of the situation, if I accept the basis of their argument.

'They also warn me that there are many people outside the gate who would love to do my job – and probably for less wages. So that's the situation, and before you come up with any of your Hitler Youth ideas, you had better remember that every single bite you eat, every piece of cloth you wear, every present you expect for Christmas or your birthday, comes out of this weekly wage of mine. Having told you all this, I hope that you have enough intelligence to understand why I joined with other like-minded workers who are all in the same boat in the trade union movement and why any right-wing government, which is a government that governs on behalf of the rich, will always be hell-bent to at least restrict and if possible smash any effective workers' organisation.

'As you well know from Haller's and other factories around here, workers down their tools and go on strike. They have no other weapon to defend their living standard, and if we lose the right to strike, which the Nazis have more or less robbed us of, we will be nothing but helpless slaves in a vicious capitalist system. Our "betters" of course will try to tell us that instead of using the strike weapon we should use the ballot box. But that is clever talk on their part for they know very well that the ballot box will be unfailingly influenced by the media, totally owned by a handful of super millionaires who will pump out what suits them best.

'Now they have opened up concentration camps. They use them as a warning threat to all who are even potentially against their whole set of policies. That's why they have come in the night and have taken Eycken away, right out of our midst, to frighten us all, and if you go out now and tell any of the little Nazis what I just have told you, they would come and take me too. What would happen then to mother and you, for I would be unable to help you any more.'

He had spoken so clearly, so emotionally, what he had said had come from his heart as well as from his brain and I could see that he was close to tears, and my heart went out to him. I got up, slung my arms around his neck and told him that I loved him very much when he pulled me on to his lap with mother joining us. We sat there for a while without saying anything. We were a close, good family. I promised him that I would never, never report on him, whatever he said, however much it might anger me. But to split on him – never! And I knew that he was sure of that. But what a horrible strain it put on all of us.

Then the order came through from the Hitler Youth that everyone had to wear a proper uniform brown shirt. When I passed it on to my parents, father just laughed. 'You know how a bull hates a red rag when it is being waved in front of him. Well, that is what a brown rag does to me. The very last thing I would do in my life is to give money to buy a brown shirt for my son.'

'But what shall I tell them when I turn up at the next meeting without one?'

'Tell them that my wages are too low to pay even for family necessities. Just tell them that I have no money, they will have no option but to accept that.'

At the next meeting, after we had lined up in military column and our leader strode along in front for inspection, he noticed several of us, standing in the middle out of sight and wearing our ordinary clothes. As expected, he at first shouted at us: 'Did I not tell you to turn up in proper uniforms, where are your brown shirts?' We were ordered to step out in front for all to see. And as it so happened, without having pre-arranged anything, we all had exactly the same excuse: 'my parents have no money to pay for one.' Well, that was that, though he moaned a little bit at first, it then happened as father had predicted, he could do nothing about it. At the next meeting we un-brownshirted ones had to step forward again and each of us was given a parcel, which we were told not to open but to hand to our parents at home.

When mother did so, she said: 'Oh look, Fritz, two sturdy brown shirts for the boy.' There was also a note in it, saying 'with the compliments of the Party.' 'Well, good,' said mother, 'then the boy has two good shirts which saves me buying material and sewing them.'

'How do you make that out, he can only wear them to the meetings, he cannot play in the street with them.'

Mother pondered a bit. 'That's right, then he can wear them at home where no one can see it but we and instead of rubbing his elbows through his own shirts, he can rub them through the brown shirts to his heart's delight and we needn't even tell him off.'

At first this was a bit much for father to swallow, having to look at his son sitting opposite him in a brown shirt in his own home. But mother's practical logic prevailed and from then on I wore a brown shirt in the evening – and right under father's nose. How he must have hated it! The advent of the Nazis had changed habits and attitudes even in our close-knit family.

Being about twelve years old then and having no chance of making comparisons, it was near impossible for me to assess the political developments taking place in our country and how they affected our lives. With all my love for my father, he was to me politically an old square, unable to fit into the round hole of understanding the modern ideas brought to us by the genius of Adolf Hitler. It was not only my own father whom I judged like that but his whole generation, especially working people. The middle classes were far more attuned to Nazi ideology. That was why my father became less and less able to guide me the way he wanted me to go.

Then came a little hiccup of sorts which gave father an opportunity to have a go at me and my presumptions. At first I did not recognise the significance of the event. But then, after father's intervention, it made some sense and sank in a little.

One of my cousins, after having left school at fourteen, went into service with a wealthy family in a near-by town. Her job was that of dusting, cleaning, shopping, peeling potatoes and helping generally with daily duties. It was also the time when Hoover vacuum cleaners had come into more general use and this family acquired one. Oh, was my cousin Marga over the moon, telling all and sundry what a wonderful cleaning machine such a Hoover was. Though a bit noisy, it was easy to use, so very efficient and she could now do the job of cleaning in half the usual time. She now looked forward to going to work every morning and even felt important, considering perhaps that she would now be entitled to a small pay rise as a machine operator. But then a couple of weeks or so later she was in for a nasty shock: together with a wonderful character reference for being a good worker, loyal, always punctual and obedient, she got the sack.

When my uncle, her father, suggested she ask the lady of the house why after such a good reference she had lost her job, Marga was told that it was the result of labour-saving and improved efficiency, in this case the introduction of a Hoover into the household. Well, that was that then, and it provided an excellent illustration of father's point, which otherwise nobody seemed to understand. Could I not see that this small incident, unimportant as it might seem, was proof of how the system of capitalism really worked in practice? He knew that his brother-in-law had always voted for right-wing, capitalist-supporting parties, and now that his daughter had to pay the price for what he had all the time been voting for, he could not even understand it.

Each Hitler Youth troop had a Heim (home) where we met for our Diensts (meetings) which took place at least once a week and often also on Sundays. A Heim had to have at least one decent-sized room in which we could all congregate together. Sometimes it was in a disused factory, an old barn or in a cellar which most houses or tenements in Germany have. Sometimes it was in an odd room in a private house which the owner, probably wanting to be in good standing with the party, provided for us at no expense.

We always decorated our Heim ourselves. The white-washing of the walls was great fun and a large swastika flag, draped against one of them, was the centre point of attraction. We hung pictures of Hitler and the other Party 'Greats' on the others. We made use of large posters, all politically motivated and whenever we managed to procure one, we hung an old sword, a rifle, a pistol or a steel helmet around paintings of battle scenes and wrote quotations of Hitler's *Mein Kampf* in black against the white wall. Tables, benches and chairs were never difficult to get hold of. And when we then sat together in the evenings, sang our songs and listened to talks, we knew that we had created our own atmosphere, the atmosphere of the young, the coming German generation. Had not the Führer himself written in *Mein Kampf* that 'Germany's future belongs to its youth?' When I wanted to impress father by mentioning that momentous quotation, he merely responded by saying 'Yes, all that you spout is that the grass is green.'

For any ordinary Dienst we met outside our Heim and milled playfully around until the appointed time when one of our lower-ranked leaders shouted a sharp command, to which we had to line up in column. He then strutted down in front of us, making sure that we were all clean and properly dressed and that we were standing in a straight line. No doubt he felt himself important for having the power to make us stand stiffly to attention. Then he shouted 'zählen' (count) after which all those standing in the front row had to call out the numbers: one-two-three, and so on to the last one who had to calculate the end result and report the number present.

While all this happened, the real troop leader stood slightly away from us as if all this was of no concern to him, until the lower-ranked leader turned away from us and strutted up to him. Two steps away he stopped sharply in military fashion, clicking his iron-studded heels together with a loud bang and raising his arm into the air, and reported the assembled number present. The troop leader thanked him, they shook hands, again clicked their heels together and shot their arm in the air. Then the troop leader turned to us and shouted 'Heil Hitler, troop so and so, a three time Sieg Heil for our Führer Adolf Hitler – Sieg', which he did three times, to which we each time answered with 'heil' with a loud bellow.

His command 'dismissed into the Heim' then followed. We all trooped in, stood behind the benches and only sat down when he told us to. Not being allowed to speak until spoken to and having to sit like rods with our hands on our upper legs, all our natural boyish exuberance had by now evaporated. In most cases a short lecture on the week's political and other events was followed by an 'open' discussion. The word discussion is perhaps a bit overstated, for if any of us had thoughts and ideas of his own, he would not have been so foolish as to voice them, but merely tried to mechanistically express in a loud voice what he thought our leader wanted to hear, because it was politically correct.

Each one of us had been issued with a Hitler Youth song booklet from which we had to learn the words of so many songs. Most of them related to Führer, Volk and Fatherland as well as to blood and honour and dying. Many dealt with going east into our future, of the great battles of the 1870/71 War, as well as the historic ones, while a considerable number, so nasty tongues claimed, had been stolen from the Bolsheviks of the Russian Revolution and translated into German. The words did not count all that much with us, in most cases we did not understand their meaning anyway, but when we were sitting in our Heim or marching in formation through the streets of our town the melodies did matter. There were so many attractive ones, at least we thought so. Some about the peasant wars were especially melodic and very appealing in their simplicity, and lent themselves to our beating drums and probably expressed the dreadful sufferings of the people caught up in it all.

The general standards of discipline were harsh, perhaps understandably so. To occupy three quarters of Europe and hold it down for several years was a most gigantic task by any standards, and could only be undertaken by German youth who were prepared and ready for it in every sense, who were not only disciplined in the extreme but who on the whole believed fervently in what they were doing.

It was probably natural in the circumstances, that I did not want to believe what my father said, namely that our Hitler Youth semi-military training, together with our expressed racist upbringing, created a belief of racial superiority, which was a preparation for the task which lay ahead of us. He made the point that the imperial nations – the Spanish, Portuguese, Dutch, French, British and Belgians – could never have accomplished the subjection of millions of people without their own young having been effectively brainwashed into believing in their own racial superiority.

We were often reminded in the Hitler Youth and later in the army that the task of our leaders was firstly to bring us down to earth by destroying all individuality, so as to build us up again in the image of the Nazi ideology. Looking back now with the advantage of hindsight, I believe that that task was carried through very successfully. For by the time I was about thirteen or fourteen, I, and I think almost all of us, accepted uncritically what was handed down to us from state and government. How dreadful it must have been for my father to helplessly watch me sliding down that disastrous path. It was fear of the concentration camp and the threat of unemployment which lay behind the failure to neutralise the Nazi influence over the younger generation.

As with everything in life, there were exceptions to the rule, of whom we had one in our class. Towards the end of the war I heard that Walter Römer had taken his own life and though I never found out the reasons nor circumstances, it did not surprise me. Walter had a lively and enquiring mind. He was probably far more sensitive than the rest of us rougher lot, as he quickly burst into tears when upset by something going wrong. His schoolwork was well above average. He showed much more interest in literature than in sport and was good friends with everyone around him, including me. His trouble was that he stuck out like a sore thumb by being the only one in our class of about forty who was not a member of the Hitler Youth. Our class teacher Herr Hinck was of course aware of it, as was the whole class, but never once, at least not in front of the class, did he bring that subject up nor try to convince Römer to join.

Father had told me that all institutions, places of work, shops, offices etc. had at least one party representative, whose job it was to spy and report on people and everything going on. He was sure that this kind of thing happened in most other countries, however much polish and gloss their leaders tried to put on their 'free' and democratic image. But in other countries it was mainly done by their paid secret service whose job it was to report on every potential threat to the established order, while in Germany it was carried out rather more openly and clumsily by party hacks.

As with everything political, I argued with my father for the very reason that he had said it. Though not admitting it to him, I knew very well that he was right when he suggested that we had a Nazi spy amongst our teaching staff. Everyone else knew that this spy was our biology teacher Karl Sieg. Jokes were made about him and his connections, but no one wanted to go as far as to make a serious accusation. The Nazis were known to punish anyone who crossed their path.

What must have niggled teacher Sieg was that it was Walter Römer who prevented him from reporting a one-hundred per cent Hitler Youth membership. I do not know whether he ever made individual approaches to Römer, but from time to time, at the very least once a year, he came into our class and, of course knowing the score beforehand, said 'Hands up those who are not in the Hitler Youth'.

All of us being well aware of what was about to follow, and loving any interruption of the teaching process, already started to giggle in anticipation, when Römer, blushing badly from either embarrassment or anger, slowly raised his hand as if saying under his breath, 'Oh no, not that again!' ' Why not?' Sieg wanted to know, to which he received no answer. Did he not believe in the great cause of national socialism, did he have no respect at least, no admiration for our Führer? Did he not want to support him for what he was doing for Germany, for us all? But the more and louder he spoke, the more stubborn Römer became. When he ordered him to stand up and answer his questions, the most that came from Römer's lips was 'no' or 'I don't know', which as an answer to Sieg's questions sometimes did not make the slightest sense. All that it did was make Sieg, shouting and dancing around in fury, look the ridiculous figure he was.

Then he became calm again, much too calm to be trusted from Römer's point of view. He pursed his lips in his own curious manner which he often did when he thought that he was on to a winner. Standing now straight in front of Römer, he fixed his stare on him for a few long seconds which made us all realise that something important was about to happen. There was not a sound amongst us anywhere, no shuffle, no cough, one could have heard a pin drop. 'Tell me, is it your own decision not to join the Hitler Youth, don't you want to be part of the most important youth organisation the world has ever witnessed – or is someone influencing you not to join or even preventing you from doing so? Surely you must have discussed it with your parents. What do they say to all this?'

Well, this was it. We were all fully aware now that the questioning had reached its climax. How was Walter going to pull his head out of this tightening noose? Surely, the bringing in of his parents had put the entire situation on to a very different, a much more dangerous plane. And besides, the longer this harassment of Römer lasted, the shorter became our teaching hour. And no one, except Herr Hinck perhaps apart from Römer, regretted that.

Up to then our class teacher had quietly sat behind his desk, scribbling something on a bit of paper, but had not said one word though it was clear that he was annoyed about this whole performance, and seemed to be struggling with his conscience whether to intervene or not. But now with the drawing in of Römer's parents, it suddenly looked as if finally he had had enough. He raised himself with a jerk from his crouching position, took one stern look over the scene before him, and slowly strode over to Sieg who was leaning against the wall close to Römer's seat. He quietly and firmly addressed Sieg as Karl, and asked him bluntly to 'please leave the lad alone.' Could he not see that he was close to tears, that it was patently unfair to question him like this in front of the whole class, that he looked choked and must be almost physically incapable of thinking clearly and saying anything sensible?

No doubt, this intervention annoyed Sieg, and he insisted that this was a serious matter, that he was not doing it for himself but on behalf of the Führer, who had recently in a great speech called on German youth to organise for the tasks ahead. But Hinck cut him short by shutting his eyes and, characteristically, waving his right hand in front of his face. He reminded Sieg that there was a time and place for everything, but in the end it was he, Hinck, who had to teach forty boys and was responsible to the rector for covering the curriculum. He could therefore not allow the teaching process to be brought to a halt because of the questioning of one boy.

Sieg had no answer to this. Sadly shaking his head, he walked to the door while Römer just sat there, looking bewildered as well as exhausted. But when Sieg looked back at him, probably thinking that he had come close to having broken him mentally, he stopped and made one final attempt, using a totally different approach this time.

'Walter,' he said, for the first time calling him by his Christian name, and in an unusually soft-speaking voice, 'I promise not to press you any more, all I ask you is to think it over in a rational manner. You see, all your friends in class have become members and they have done so of their own free will. Surely, so many cannot have been wrong in their choice while you are the only one who is right. Remember, they are all determined to help the Führer. I am telling you with the best will in the world that it simply is no good for you as the only one in class not to show that effort nor, and I admit it, is it good for me whose great honour it would be, to report back that this class stands one hundred per cent behind our Führer – nor can it be for your parents . . .'

With this Hinck moved into action again. For a second time he approached Sieg, 'Karl, please,' he said in a much harsher voice, brushed past him, opened the door with a firm grip, held it wide open and beckoned him unmistakably to leave. Sieg turned to us, raised his arm and said loudly 'Heil Hitler, class' to which we responded 'Heil Hitler, Herr Sieg.' I don't think that Walter Römer joined in that Heil Hitler chorus, in fact, I could not remember having heard him say that greeting once.

Herr Hinck then came back straight away to pick up the pieces, trying to carry on from where Sieg's entry at the beginning of the hour had interrupted him. He made it easy for Römer by asking him a simple question for which Walter was visibly grateful and we all respected Hinck for it. But though he tried to carry on as if nothing had happened, it did not work any more, the steam had completely gone out of his teaching and everyone was greatly relieved when the bell rang for the break. We streamed down the wide stairs with the rest of the school to the dusty playground at the back. It was probably more instinctive than calculated that almost all of us wanted to show Walter that, Hitler Youth or no Hitler Youth, we were on his side, still very much his friends and there was no one who had anything good to say about teacher Sieg.

I suppose that though it might be true that working class boys show little love for their teachers, Herr Hinck was considered by most of us as a decent man who tried his best to drum knowledge and understanding into our thick heads. He was strict with us, sometimes, I think, perhaps too much so. Those who had not done what they were told had to go to the front of the class, bend down and receive three of the best. As I understood it at the time, caning boys, which in state schools had been forbidden during Weimar days, had been fully reintroduced after the Nazis came to power. My parents, though in principle they did not agree with caning, never officially objected to it, whereas one set of parents in our class did, as a result of which their son was never punished in this way.

Herr Hinck was in his middle fifties. He had been born in the Dithmarschen area in Holstein to the north, not far from the Danish border, where people had the reputation of being stubborn. Coupled with his intelligence, this had a positive effect. Though he was a member of the Nazi teachers' trade union section of the Arbeitsfront, as I believe all teachers had to be, and carried a swastika badge on the lapel of his jacket, I would not have described him as a Nazi in the accepted sense. Like all teachers, he had to stick to the rather restricted framework of the curriculum, laid down by the Ministry of Education. It was said that those who did not placed themselves in the political firing line and were eased out of their profession. So the pressure was on, as in one way or another it was really on everyone in the Reich.

One of our teachers, a Herr Lindemann, was well liked by all who knew him, including his pupils, but he rather abruptly left the school. Rumour had it that he had fallen foul of Karl Sieg about something said in the common room and had to leave the teaching profession as a result. I did ask Herr Hinck once what had happened, but he seemed annoyed and uneasy at my question, and even blushed a little, telling me he did not know. I was well aware that he was not telling me the truth and he knew that I knew, as it was common knowledge that the two had been good friends for many years and that together with their wives they had been on holidays together.

Without being able to put my finger on it, I sensed that there were many contradictions entangling our lives. Brainwashed as I must have been, I nevertheless realised that this had something to do with the discrepancy between Nazi ideology and the way things always seemed to be going wrong. It bothered me a great deal, especially after quarrels with my father, but I stubbornly refused to accept that what really had gone wrong was probably the Nazi ideology.

Where before I would have asked father to help me to undo any knot of non-understanding, I increasingly resisted this because I knew only too well what his reaction would be. His explanation would have been the exact opposite of what I had learnt in the Hitler Youth, after which we would end up in a useless and hurtful quarrel. There was something in me which made me refuse to look squarely at the truth. I do think now that it had possibly something to do with my categorical refusal to question my own self-created belief in the greatness of our Führer. Father pointed out that those who are brainwashed are naturally the last to realise their condition, but I quickly countered by saying that in fact I did realise it, to only then become aware that I had contradicted myself. To my surprise father did not attempt to score a point out of this but reminded me quietly that, given the horrible circumstances of the times we were living in, it was perhaps better that way, as otherwise Nazism would mentally break me. Such was the confusion inside my young mind in a society that was in deep mental turmoil.

Our normal school week consisted of five six-hour days, Monday to Friday and four hours on Saturdays. Discipline was strict and any misconduct was punished by caning. The pressure to learn was strong, our teacher often complained that he had not enough time to teach us all that the curriculum had laid down. It must have been in 1937/38 when the Staatsjugendtag (state youth day) was introduced by the Ministry of Education. From that time on, every Saturday was lost to the school curriculum and given over to the Hitler Youth. We did not go to school any more on that day but had to attend Dienst with the Hitler Youth instead. Of course we kids liked it but our teachers as well as my parents did not. Father protested, though not to the authority, that the introduction of the Staatsjugendtag was nothing but an intensification of brainwashing with Nazi ideology, all part of a preparation for waging war.

At the beginning, the Hitler Youth Dienst lasted only until lunch time but with war looming, it took up the entire Saturday. We were told to bring a pack of sandwiches and a field bottle with drink. This was to be taken on a march, train journey or lorry ride to a convenient place away from town where we were taught military commands, moving around the countryside, and how best to attack strongholds. For the latter purpose we were divided up into two groups, the blues and the reds, each of us wearing a blue or a red string around our upper arm. One group then had to defend a given position while the other had to attack it. When the whistle was blown for the start, the attacking group went on the move after which contact with the defenders was quickly made. There was much noise, sometimes bloody noses, twisted arms, loud hurrah shouting and shrieks of pain. The point of the battle was to pull off strings from the enemies arms, who were then officially dead and had to leave the battlefield. The group with the most armstrings left were the declared winners.

In the beginning I hated this kind of fighting but with time I got used to it. Human beings, given enough time, seem to get used to anything and then accept it as something natural. In any case, it developed the latent aggressiveness in us which, I am sure, had something to do with the Wehrmacht's early successes in the coming war. Even though sometimes I would have preferred to play with my friends in the street, than trooping off to a routine Hitler Youth Dienst, I loved all the outdoor activities. During my more than six years in the movement, I went to summer camp at least once every year. Most of the camps were not far from our base within an easy radius of between fifty and one hundred kilometres. A number were farther afield, one of them in an old castle in the wooded

mountains of Thuringia, another far along the Baltic coast in a large barn
close to the Polish border, which we looked on as something like an enemy
front line. All the others were tent camps put up in lovely places in woods
or on meadows, along rivers or next to lakes. It was largely through the
Hitler Youth that I learned how varied and beautiful Germany, my
Germany was, which in turn instilled an unconditional love for my
Fatherland, coupled with an almost holy preparedness to defend it under
all circumstances and by all means, even to the point of laying down my
life.

Up to then I had never known what a real holiday was. Father's wage
was much too low for such extravagances. Often I heard it said at home
that holidays like so many other good things in life are only for the rich
and not for the likes of us. I never gave it serious thought, that there were
rich and poor people, and I am sure now that thinking on those lines was
highly discouraged by those in charge of our education. Father said that
anything which could threaten the status quo, meaning the rule of the rich
over the poor, was taboo.

The money we were asked to contribute to Hitler Youth camping
activities was very little. Mother said that it was almost less than the cost
of feeding me at home. If there were some parents who claimed that they
were unable to scrape the money together – and father to my embarrassment, as a matter of principle was always one of them – the Hitler Youth,
backed of course by the Party, was generous in making up for what was
missing. That ensured that every single one of us was able to join the
camp. Those who did not go had to provide a really watertight excuse.

The trip to the camp itself was always a large part of the fun. There was
so much to see and the importance of the places we passed was explained
to us. Sometimes we travelled on the backs of lorries and at other times by
train. Each one had to wear uniform so that there were no visible
differences between us. After arriving at the destination railway station,
we had to shoulder our pack and march off in column. A wimple (small
triangle swastika flag) and sometimes a drum made up the head and
along we went singing. We never walked in an ordinary manner except
when we were on some paths, but always marched in step. It was
drummed into us that we were the young soldiers of the Führer and
Fatherland. As most roads in Germany at that time were cobbled, the
marching was sometimes painful.

The tents in most cases had already been put up by a Vorkommando
(advance troop). Usually they were large round ones, pointed at the top
with a thick pole in the middle next to which one was able to stand up.
Straw, generously provided by the nearest farmer, covered the ground on
to which we put our canvas and blankets. And with about twenty of us
with our feet towards the pole and an oil light flickering unsteadily down
on us, singing quiet melodic songs before sleep, the atmosphere was a

very happy one. I loved all that and especially when it rained at night, and I listened to the drumming sound of the rain falling on the canvas above.

The tents were usually arranged in a large tidy circle in the centre of which was the Tingstätte, an old Germanic word for meeting place, with ample space for a bonfire, around which the entire camp assembled in the evenings for singing, talks, recitals, discussions and all sorts of happenings. There were always accordions and a large number of mouth organs, which with good strong singing voices, produced musical offerings of a sometimes surprisingly good quality. The tents of our leaders, as well as those for kitchen, storage etc. were outside our common circle. The lavatories – we called them Donnerbalken (thunderbeams) – consisted of long wooden structures above a deep trench, hidden in the woods or shrubs by sheets of tarpaulin. A long pipe or hose from the nearest farm provided the water for our kitchen and our washing facilities.

Absolute cleanliness was compulsory. To be found dirty was a major crime which demanded the harshest of punishments which usually started off with a stiff dose of military square bashing. The unclean culprit then had to dress up in full uniform including a heavy pack on his back and was chased around on rough ground, running, jumping and crawling to the point of near-exhaustion. With that ordeal over, he was marched into the assembled circle of the camp, was undressed and thrown into cold water, brushed down with a very rough stable brush, handled by one of the strongest and most probably sadistic lads, dressed up as Neptune. The lesson worked in almost all cases, for after that experience, the culprit saw to it that there was no one cleaner in the whole camp than himself.

Early each morning at six the trumpeter blew the morning call. That was the official start of the day and within minutes the camp turned into a beehive. We had an hour to do all the personal things necessary, like washing our underwear, towels and other belongings. Boots had to be polished, only our leaders wore jackboots, and we also had to get our tents tidied up for later inspection. The tent leader whose place was next to the entrance was responsible for that.

Few of us owned watches, that's why we relied totally on our trumpeter as the timekeeper for our daily routine. Trumpeting three times meant 'attention' after which everyone had to be quiet and listen to the shouted announcement. The call for breakfast came at seven. With our mess tins, mugs and cutlery – spot-checks were often made as to their cleanliness – we lined up outside the field kitchen and received our rations from the cook. The latter, male or female, was the only person in camp not a member of the Hitler Youth. He or she had to have a cook's certificate and was therefore already elderly in our eyes, probably in their early twenties. The food – though we usually moaned about it, calling it Stuhlgang der Seele (bowel movement of the soul) – was on the whole well-cooked, nourishing and plentiful. One could have as many helpings as one liked.

Except for our leaders who had tables and benches, there were no special eating areas for us. Like real soldiers, depending on the weather, we had to make do inside or outside our tents, on the ground or on anything suitable which we could find to sit on.

We were given three meals daily, porridge in the mornings, the main cooked meal at midday and bread, cheese and sausages, as well as local fruit, in the evenings. For coffee, we brewed roasted barley, which we drank without sugar or milk. Midday meal over, the rest hour started. Only leaders gave themselves permission to move around, while the rest had to lie down, until the silence was broken by the trumpeter rallying us for the next stage of camp activities.

All entrances to the camp were guarded around the clock and the wooden barrier only lifted after the guards had carried out strict checking procedures. One guard only was on duty during the hours of daylight and two during the night. Guard duty, we were told, was a special honour. I often wondered why, because I hated it so much and found it extremely boring. It is of interest perhaps that I never lost that intense distaste for it throughout my later years as a soldier in Russia.

The mornings were mostly occupied with sport and games. All of us had to be able to swim and those who could not were taught how to. Sometimes this 'teaching' was done in a dangerous and rough manner, on the basis of sink or swim. After the theory was explained, the victim was thrown into the deep end, thereby given the opportunity of proving or disproving that humans, like animals, have a natural ability to keep themselves above water. When the disproof factor became all too obvious, a couple of the strongest swimmers rescued the unfortunate victim, who was held upside down, shaken out, and left in peace until the next day. If my memory serves me correctly, there was not one camp of the many I have attended which did not end up with all boys being able to swim. However, in one of the camps, a Hitler Junge (that's what we were called) was drowned, after which this barbaric custom was forbidden and proper regulations introduced.

We played football, handball and other ball games, and sometimes, special sports coaches were invited and stayed in the camps for several days. There were many competitions in all branches of athletics. Usually a mini-marathon was arranged, running to the next village and back. The winner was raised above our heads in triumph to receive a specially baked cake as a trophy. We learned about boxing, wrestling and gymnastics. All the equipment and things needed for it were generously provided by the Hitler Youth.

But there was also a far more serious side to it, which our athletics were supportive of. Every afternoon, several hours were set aside for military education and training. We learned how to throw hand grenades, to dig ourselves into protective earth, and dig trenches, foxholes and earth bunkers. We were taught how to attack strongholds, making proper use of cover, and move round the countryside unseen.

When father pointed out that this was designed to prepare us for war, I saw nothing wrong with that. Neither could I see that killing people was unchristian or wrong. It was only several years later after I had become a soldier, that I realised that what we had learnt in the Hitler Youth had helped reduce army training time, and that more specialised training for warfare and killing could be accelerated as a result.

We also had much theoretical education about past and modern warfare in the form of lectures and discussions, often with the help of battle positions drawn in a sandbox. Von Clausewitz and von Schlieffen, the 'great' German master tacticians, were often quoted. We liked it when young officers from the Army, Navy or Luftwaffe came to talk to us. Not yet having taken part in any actions of war themselves, they aroused our keen interest in the technology of war. They described the 'beauty' of the latest Panzers, Messerschmitts and U-Boats.

At times ex-soldiers from the 1914/18 war were dug up from some-where. By their very definition they were heroes to us. Why someone who had been forced to take part in a war, and most soldiers of the war had been conscripts, should automatically become a hero, was never explained to us and neither did we ask questions. They told us about the great battles they had taken part in at the Marne, the Somme, at Verdun and in Flanders. One of them told us that it was the greatest honour for any soldier to die in battle for his country. He came a bit unstuck, because one of us innocents, sitting in the back row on the grass piped up, and asked him whether he was sorry not to have received that honour. An embarrassing silence was the result, after which our innocent was ordered to report to the leader's tent for half-an-hour's special square bashing. When I watched the old soldier walking away from the meeting with our leaders fawning on him, he looked a bit dented and I thought of my father, who always tried to make me understand that talk of this kind was undiluted nonsense, and only passed on to us youngsters to mentally prepare us for becoming docile cannon fodder.

Once a clergyman from a near-by village came to talk to us. I forget what he said exactly, but it was all about courageous soldiers fighting for their Fatherland, God in heaven, the Führer in Berlin and Jesus Christ in our souls. We listened politely, but I don't think that anyone really took him seriously.

We often went on long marches over hard and rough ground which was painful to feet and legs. None of us then felt like singing until some eager one from the front shouted, 'ein Lied' (a song), announced the title, then counted three-four, after which we bawled in a tired and rowdyish manner. Our leaders, walking up and down at the side of our column, saw to it that no one slackened and that we marched in step like a real company of soldiers. All this was done to raise our endurance level. It did happen that some of us weaker ones collapsed under the strain, but little or no sympathy was shown.

While marching on unsuspectingly and turning our own thoughts over in our minds, speaking to each other was forbidden, and thinking how long this suffering was to go on, a loud warning command came suddenly from one of our leaders, shouting something like, 'enemy plane flying in low from the left' or 'enemy machine gun firing from the right' or 'troop of enemy infantry approaching from the front', to which we had to respond by throwing ourselves into ditches or dashing into bushes or other shelters out of sight.

Our flags and wimples, of which we had quite a number, were kept under cover in holders and clips next to our main gate. A flag, it was impressed on us, was much more than just a piece of cloth. It was a symbol of our nation and country, and of our honour, for which many of our fathers and forefathers had heroically given their lives. It was therefore our holy duty to protect the flag, if necessary to our last breath. In our Heim was a large framed print of the sea battle of Skagerak (Jutland) showing a drowning naval soldier hanging on to a naval flag, above the raging waves with the inscription 'fulfilling his last duty'. When one of us once jokingly remarked that if it had been him, he would have grabbed a large floating bit of wood close to him, instead of pointlessly trying to raise a soaked flag out of the water, he was shouted at by our leader and sent home because he had besmirched German honour.

One night my friend and I were standing on guard duty at the main gate, which had flags on each side. I think it was somewhere between midnight and two o'clock when two of our leaders joined us, and behaved towards us in an unusually friendly fashion. One of them coaxed us away from where the flags were fixed, saying 'come with me and have a sweet.' Though we found it a bit odd, we went with him, took a sweet and talked to him in a relaxed manner. But when I heard a noise and looked back, I saw the other one taking one of our flags out of its holder and running away with it into the dark.

'Schirmer, Schirmer' (that was his name), I shouted, 'come back with that flag, please come back!' While normally, especially in camp, I would have addressed him by his rank, I now called him by his name, partly because he had gone to the same school as me. But he took no notice of my shouting, just kept running until he disappeared out of sight. To have run after him was hopeless, as he could run much faster than I could. At first my friend and I thought that it was a part of a sick joke, but when we told the other leader that Schirmer had run away with one of our flags, he pointed out that we had been at fault in taking sweets and not guarding camp property properly.

'But if we have done wrong in taking sweets from you, have you not done wrong as one of our leaders, in offering us one?' At this he started shouting, told me to stand to attention when speaking to him, and ordered me to report to our camp leader that a flag we were guarding had been stolen.

'What do you mean by "stolen", you know as well as I do that Schirmer has taken it. In that case Schirmer is a thief and if I report it to the camp leader now, you should come with me, honour the truth and back me up.' But he repeated the order, turned and walked away, leaving us standing there in misery, thoroughly bewildered and not knowing what to do. However, we decided that we had best go and wake up the camp leader.

Rather shaken as well as frightened, I took my long guard's spear and stalked to his tent, while my friend stayed guarding the rest of the flags. I called 'Camp leader, camp leader', to which there was no reply. I did it again – nothing happened. Then I went back to my friend, asking him what he thought we should do. 'Well,' he suggested, 'you had better go and wake him up, otherwise, if we leave it to the morning, we will be in even deeper trouble than we are already in.' So back I went and did as he suggested. I saw him lying on his bed, seemingly fast asleep and hoped that he would wake up because of my presence. Normally we boys were not allowed to enter his tent and I felt very uneasy about it all. I quietly repeated 'Camp leader, camp leader', to which there was no response. Then I gently touched him and he jumped up as if stung by a scorpion. Straight away he started to shout at me, asking me what the devil I was doing in his tent. He even called me by name in spite of not being able to see me, which later made me realise that he must have known all along, had not really been asleep and had actually waited for me to play out this ridiculous pantomime. I reported that leader Schirmer had taken one of our flags and had run into the woods with it.

'How dare you accuse Schirmer of stealing!'

'I am not accusing anyone, all I am doing is reporting to you the fact that it was he who took the flag, that I and my friend saw him doing it, and that we could do nothing about it because he is taller and stronger than we are.' He then shouted at me to get out of his tent, saying he would see me in the morning.

After coming back from guard duty, I did not sleep that night, I was so worried about what would happen to us next morning. After the trumpeter's call, I went straight to Schirmer's tent and waited for him to come out. When he appeared, I stood to attention and said to him: 'I report that at so and so time early this morning when I was on guard duty at the main gate, you took our flag and ran away with it into the woods. I recognised you clearly and would swear to it on oath.'

'Are you mad, accusing me of theft, how dare you?'

'No, I do not accuse you of anything, all I am doing is to report the truth and you know very well what the truth is. You gave us a lecture yourself last winter about how important it is for Hitler boys to be truthful, one of our basic Hitler Youth commandments. And I am telling the truth now.' I could see that he was rattled because he looked nervously around, making sure that no one was listening. But then he ordered me to go away and wait and see what was coming to me.

Everyone had breakfast. Only my friend and I did not, as we were both extremely worried. Then came what we had feared and expected: the trumpeter blew three times to announce that we, the two guards, had to appear at morning parade in full uniform with complete packs on our backs. After the camp had lined up, we two were ordered to stand to attention in front of the leaders. Then the camp leader announced that we two had brought disgrace on all by having accepted sweets while on duty and as a consequence lost one of our flags, which it had been our duty to guard. When we both tried to protest, he ordered us to shut up and only speak when spoken to. He commanded us to lie on our bellies and drag ourselves forward on our elbows along the whole line of the assembled camp. Next we were ordered to stay in the tent for the rest of the day, only permitted to go to the lavatory or washplace under guard. We were thus dismissed, marched to our tent, accompanied by the giggling of several of the assembled boys.

Later the others joined us in the tent and made us both furious by accusing us of having let the side down. All we really wanted after this was to leave the camp and go home. But we knew that was impossible, for we did not even have money for the fare. For the remaining time in camp we both acted and responded sullenly and though some of our leaders, after a day or so, tried to make it appear as if everything had been forgiven, we made it clear that it was not for them to forgive us – but for us to forgive them.

I never spoke to Schirmer again. When later in the war I heard that he had been killed on the Eastern Front, I was of course sorry, but I was still unable to wipe from my memory the foul trick he played on me, which I had no chance to redress. I was not prepared to forgive him and even now, sixty years later, I still have not forgotten what happened in that Hitler Youth camp. Judge me, reader, but such is human nature, at least mine.

Shortly after this had taken place, the Gauleiter of Schleswig Holstein came to visit our camp with a number of underlings and reporters. He behaved in a very friendly fashion towards us, inspected our tents and talked to us. As it so happened I almost ran into him when I came back from the washplace. He answered my 'Heil Hitler, Herr Gauleiter' and asked me whether I liked life in the camp. Behind him stood one of our leaders and when he heard the Gauleiter's question and probably noticed my stubborn face, he stared at me, raised his lips, made large eyes and, probably unnoticeable to those around him, shook his head. Of course, I knew what he meant but answered the Gauleiter that I did like camp life, but did not like the unjust treatment I had been the victim of a few days ago. He asked me what had happened, and I told him the whole story and how we had been made to look silly and ridiculous in front of the whole camp. We did not think that we had done anything wrong and were sure that we had been set up by some of our leaders. He listened carefully, not once interrupting, only saying once or twice 'Go on'.

'Have you come to the end?' he asked. And when I answered in the affirmative, he turned towards the leader who had tried to shut me up and asked whether what I had said was true. By now a large number of boys had collected around us and the leader, having been put on the spot, felt obviously embarrassed and first stuttered something which made little sense. The Gauleiter must have noticed his uneasiness, for he went for him in a more direct manner :'Yay or nay, is it true what this Hitler boy has said or is it not?' And our leader, blushing all over, had no choice but to answer, 'Yes, Herr Gauleiter, on the whole it is true.'

The Gauleiter then again turned to me, put his hand on to my head and said that after what I had told him, he did not think that I had done anything wrong and promised that he would discuss the case later with the camp leader. I was sure that he was true to his word because from then on none of our leaders mentioned the flag incident ever again and treated us with kid gloves. I didn't like that either, as it made me feel that I was no longer a proper and full member of the camp. But all that was compensated for by the knowledge that we had at least achieved some sort of justice.

Although I was a member of the Hitler Youth for more than six years and fully committed to the Führer's cause, I never came close to any promotion. I stayed Hitler Junge, the lowest rank, and I think to this very day that having spoken to the Gauleiter, having told him that I had been treated unjustly by my leaders, had somehow slipped into my record to my disadvantage – or perhaps advantage, depending on the way one looks at it.

In camp as well as at school and in ordinary Hitler Youth Dienste in our Heims, we were heavily subjected to racist teaching. The all-underlying 'truth', so the teaching went, was that we, the German people, though not said in so many words, as it possibly would have sounded too biblical, were God's chosen people. The word for it was 'Herrenrasse' (master race). For those who had to teach this theory, there must have been so many obvious contradictions, that a logical formulation was as good as impossible.

In Germany alone, so we were taught, there existed about half a dozen races – and it was obvious that the majority of people looked anything but Nordic. From this arose the question: were we a race, a nation, a people, or what? And the answer was always a load of nonsense. Most of the Nordic or Aryan types were to be found in the northern part of our country, in the area stretching along the southern shores of the Baltic towards Poland. But with the word Poland, we were lumbered with the difficulty that though the people near the Baltic were tall, blond, blue-eyed and good looking, they had quite a few pints of Slavic blood in their veins. Their cheek bones were slightly more pronounced than ours.

In the rest of Germany all sorts of curious mixtures had developed over the centuries which at some time in the future would have to be sorted out. In the south in Bavaria and more so in the mountainous regions of the Alps, lived the Dinaric people, who were generally short, squat, had large protruding bellies, thick upper legs and large heads, flat at the back. So they were anything but Nordic, and what were we to make of that?

For teaching purposes a kind of league table was set up for us, stuck against the wall in our class room which created even more confusion in our minds, because the more we looked at it, the less we understood it. We all stared at it as a kind of duty but no one dared to admit that it made little sense to him. Needless to say, we the Nordic Germans were top of the first division, followed after a large margin by Swedes, Norwegians, Finns, Icelanders and Danes. As their countries were no threat to us, except perhaps in a strategic sense, and they never achieved anything very significant, their following us in the league table did not bother us all that much. Then came the Dutch and the English, who in fact were not all that bad racially, rather like second-rate cousins, had they not absorbed so much Malayan, Jewish and other darkish bloods from their colonial conquests. They were followed by the Scottish, the Flemish and the Irish who, though they might not really be aware of it, because of their distinctly lower intelligence, all had a touch, but only a touch, of Germanic blood. Next in line were the French. They were not too bad. After all, they had brought the best out of us at Verdun and other great battlefields in the Great War. Of late, sadly for them, they had allowed too much useless North African blood to filter into their blood streams.

The second division was headed by the Italians. That position looked a bit better than at the bottom of division one. With them everything was a bit embarrassing because at that time, under their great leader Benito Mussolini, they had established themselves as our potential ally in the, to us, important Mediterranean region. We had to be a bit polite and under-standing towards them which, however, did not stop us spreading discreet jokes about their characteristic 'successes', like swallowing heaps of macaroni and flogging mouse traps wherever they went. The Spanish came a close second followed by suchlikes as the Greeks, Poles, Czechs, Bulgarians, Yugoslavs and other riff-raff with most unspeakable names. At the very bottom of this division were the Americans. The only good thing about them was that they had a considerable number of Germans in their midst. They were such a hopeless mix-up that they really could not be regarded as a nation.

Then came the third division, and what a joke that was. The Turks were the leaders. I think they had been put there on account of having been our ally in the war when they had defeated the British at Gallipoli. The Chinese came next, after all, far back in history they had had something like a civilisation, which one had to recognise. Then came the Egyptians who, after a good start, had somehow lost their way and did not quite know whether they were coming or going. At the time when the tables had been set up, the Japanese held a very lowly position, they were known as crafty copycats. But since they looked like becoming our allies and especially as our Führer had called them the 'Prussians of the East', they had been promoted to a position of honourable Aryans and were now sitting quite comfortably on the reserve benches.

As to the fourth division we could not really care who came first, second or last. It was a laughable mish-mash of Gypsies, Red Indians, Malaysians, Jews, Blacks, Arabs, Aborigines, Eskimos and Maories.

We had a rather unfortunate friend in our class who had the nicest of natures, was friends with everyone, always understanding of other people's problems and ever ready to help anyone. Apart from being short, plump and hopeless in anything athletic, he had an unpronounceable name, unpronounceable that is to us Germans. It was always a hilarious expectation when a new teacher came to our class and started calling the names from the register, he came to Guido's. (I have changed his name, as he might still be alive.) The teacher made a face, as if he could not believe what he was reading, until we all broke out into uncontrollable laughter, which even affected Guido, who then politely gave the correct pronunciation of his name.

He had to carry the added difficulty that his father was a high-ranking local Nazi, who in a speech had made an electrifying call to German youth to keep our race clean from outside poisonous influences. Everyone in class was sympathetically aware that Guido could not help his looks nor the strange antics of his father. But whenever racial features and other peculiarities were mentioned, by which our super-race could be identified, everyone's eyes diverted to Guido and then to Herr Hinck, almost challenging him to explain why in that case Guido, the son of a Jew-baiting top Nazi, could possibly look like that and get away with being called a German.

Almost everyone in our class at one time or another must have felt bothered by the pronounced racial divisions dominating so many facets of our society. I myself was much concerned when around the age of fourteen my hair began to darken and my nose seemed a little bit too long for a real Aryan. When I pointed out to mother that she was blond but that father was much darker, she simply laughed at my anxiety, telling me not to be so silly, taking seriously what the Nazi idiots were coming out with. She pointed out that she had married father because he was the kindest and most intelligent man she had ever met, and that she had found his dark, wavy hair very attractive. It greatly reassured me because I loved them both so much. For us, the mere thought that anyone even with a hint of Jewish features could have crept in among our ancestors was a worrying anxiety.

Once our class teacher Herr Hinck was put on the spot during one of his involved race lectures. At the best of times, he was clearly unsure of himself and seemed unconvinced by his own arguments. One bright spark asked him which of the German races he thought the Führer belonged to. Well, the cat was surely out of the bag, and some half-suppressed giggles came from the back of the class as Hinck painfully attempted to get his brain into action. I don't really know why, but I was convinced that I loved our Führer and that he was the greatest man on earth. But the thought alone of him being anywhere near the Nordic ideal was a bit much even for me to swallow, and I knew that Hinck must have been in the same boat, which made me feel a pang of pity for him.

What made this question more important and topical was the release of Charlie Chaplin's film *The Great Dictator* in America. Of course it was forbidden in Germany but knowledge about its content, and even some pictures, had somehow become public knowledge. Whenever Charlie Chaplin was mentioned, and he was a household name, thoughts about that funny little man with a short moustache inevitably invited com-parisons, which were probably the reason for the giggles in our class at the mention of Hitler.

Herr Hinck gave this hot potato of a question much laboured thought, which under the circumstances it undoubtedly demanded. He explained that there were several races present in Germany, and in the way that most of us had a good mixture of healthy bloods, so had our Führer. Adolf Hitler was the last person to want anything special for himself – he was one of us, and that was the great thing about him. Apart from his obvious Nordic qualities, such as determination, wisdom, consideration and truthfulness, there was little doubt that the Dinaric influence – the Führer having been born in Austria – was shown by his daring and fearless attitude. Well, who could argue with this masterly assessment, and in the circumstances, who would dare do so? Hinck must have felt relieved and proud of his quick thinking, which had saved him from slipping on a very oily patch.

At school and of course also in the Hitler Youth, we were always told that we had many reasons to be proud of German achievements in science, music, literature and industry. There was an old saying 'an deutschem Wesen soll die Welt genesen' ('through German character, the world will righten itself'), and we younger ones believed it. That many of the greatest composers were German was probably a fact which even father accepted. But my father pointed out that few Metelmanns had an ear for music, and for us to elevate ourselves on the laurels of Beethoven, Schubert and others was too ridiculous for words. He stressed that Beethoven had given his great gift to humanity and not to a narrow inward-looking German section of it.

For us schoolchildren, the most important aspect of German culture was films. I remember the films *Hitler Junge Quex, SA Mann Brandt, Jud Süss, Gruppe Bosemöller* and others, each of them stressing the goodness and straightforward honesty of Germans, as against the untrustworthiness of political opponents of the Nazis, the Jews and our military enemies of the Great War. Whenever one of these films was shown in one of our town's cinemas, our whole school marched in column to it which we liked as it cut our school day. On the next morning we usually 'discussed' the film, always from a strong nationalistic point of view, then write an essay in which we stressed the superior quality of us Germans. We knew, of course, that type of essay would give us good marks. While putting it on a bit, many of us really believed that what we had written was true.

Across the road from where we lived was an SA Sturm Lokal, an ordinary pub, where an SA Sturm, the equivalent of a military company of about 150 men, had its meeting place, its Heim. The pub had a back room large enough to accommodate all 150 men, and this room was kept in reserve for the SA to use. To agree to his pub becoming an SA one must have been a difficult decision for any landlord to make. An outright refusal, without a watertight reason, would have been politically very unwise to say the least. To have the SA on his premises increased a landlord's takings considerably. The counter-effect was of course obvious: it kept many of his former customers away. Once the SA had moved into the pub across the road, father and many of his friends would not have been seen dead in it.

At least once a week and on most Sunday mornings, the Sturm met at its Sturm Lokal for their official Dienst. As it was now 'their' pub, and there was a beer discount, many good beer-swelling stormtroopers congregated there privately throughout the week. Only the foolhardy amongst the local residents would have complained about the noise late at night. I could see from our bedroom window everything that happened in the pub. Most troopers arrived long before the appointed time of the Dienst, in jackboots, brown trousers, brown shirts and caps. When the senior Trupp Führer – there were three of them in a Sturm – shouted 'all out' in the bar room, the troopers, many of them already the worse for drink, came jostling out, lining up in military formation three deep, on the cobblestones of the street. There was not much road traffic in those days, while in any case no driver who knew what was good for him would have dared to complain about brown-shirted rowdies interfering with the traffic, unless perhaps they were the SS.

The three Trupp leaders then stood on the pavement until the straightened lines had been counted. That done, the senior officer then went inside to fetch the Sturm Führer, after which both came strutting out together. One could see from their whole demeanour how important they considered themselves to be. Not one sound came from the Sturm, who stood to attention while this was going on.

The senior Trupp leader reported and gave the Sturm Führer an exchange of salutes, after which the two of them, the Trupp leader always a step behind his superior, walked the line for inspection. Sometimes an undone button on a brown shirt was criticised, sometimes a straggly haircut, but in most cases it was done in good spirit, in a comradely fashion. After all they were all volunteers, no one was forced to join the SA. While this was in progress, the troopers stood like rods, not blinking an eyelid, and only shouted a stupid response to a stupid question from one of the officers. I know all this because when I was eighteen years old, I automatically transferred to the SA, and I behaved exactly in the same manner.

After the above ceremony, the official Dienst started. The troopers stood at ease while general announcements were made and certain things and events discussed. Usually a march through town followed. As with the Hitler Youth, they marched through working class districts only, never through middle class suburban areas. When I asked father why that was, he told me that it was a warning reminder to the poor not to entertain dangerous ideas about changing the status quo. I did not understand what he meant, for at school and in the Hitler Youth we were repeatedly told that there were no longer any differences between rich and poor in Germany. We were all the same now because our Führer had made us a classless society. Father merely laughed when I came out with that gem. 'Yes,' he said sarcastically, 'the millionaire in his mansion and the docker in his rabbit hatch are all the same now because the Führer has made them so.' He took me then sometimes by my shoulders, looked me straight in the eyes and said, 'dear, oh dear Henry, can you really not see through that cobweb of deception, and realise you are being fooled by these lying rascals?'

The Sturm leader, his name was Herr Bonni, who in Weimar days had already made a name for himself as a doorkeeper at a Reeperbahn brothel, strutted in front of the column, chest out, belly in, while the Trupp leaders marched alongside, keeping a watchful eye on the marchers and shouting the names of the songs to be sung. The nailed jackboots made a loud clacking sound on the stones and everyone marched well in step. They sang mostly military songs from one of the wars, or occasionally political songs. Some had a strong anti-Jewish content. There was one, and we sang it in the Hitler Youth as well, with the words, 'yes, if Jewish blood drips off our knives, then things will go that much better.' The marchers grinned at each other as if they were really proud of themselves.

They seldom carried a flag in front on ordinary marches like these. But they did so on more important occasions, and the passers-by were then expected to greet the flag by giving the Hitler salute. To us this was often a hilarious sight, watching an old lady for instance, loaded with shopping bags, trying to do the almost impossible. To many like my parents it was embarrassing and humiliating. If they saw the marchers approaching with their swastika flag, they either disappeared into a convenient doorway or side street, or turned round quickly, behaving as if they had forgotten something.

In the last row of the Sturm marched two or three Fegers (sweepers), whose job it was to jump out of the column and pounce on anybody not greeting the flag. In the early Nazi period some dared not to greet the flag in this way, but as time went on, very few had the courage to resist. If it was a male resister, the Fegers dragged the culprit forward in a rough manner, using abusive language but giving him the chance to correct his 'oversight', by admitting he was 'sorry'.

After about an hour's march, the SA arrived back at their Sturm Lokal, where they relaxed with large glasses of beer, listening to lectures or such like. Drinking went on until late in the night and there was much noise, and sometimes unpleasant scenes involving drunken troopers. On the following morning one could see the landlord, Herr Ewald, come out with a bucket and brush to sweep vomit into the gutter and pick up broken glass and other rubbish. Many people moaned about it. My parents did, but I never heard of anyone who had the courage to complain to the police, who as everyone knew, were very close to the SA.

Just down the road from us lived a Herr Schmidt, a typical worker at the shipyards on the other side of the river. He was about fifty. He lived in a small flat with his wife and two sons, who were several years older than I was. I knew Herr Schmidt quite well as most of us children knew most of the adults in our part of the town. But though he hardly knew me, he responded always in a friendly manner whenever our paths crossed.

It all happened on a lovely summer evening when a group of us children were playing in the street and a column of SA, carrying the swastika flag in front, came marching along. The next thing we noticed was a scuffle, when we saw a man lying on the pavement with a couple of SA men running away to rejoin the marching troop. We all rushed over to the man, who we then recognised as Herr Schmidt. He had blood on his face, there seemed something wrong with his teeth and he appeared embarrassed if not confused, when he at first unsuccessfully tried to raise himself from the pavement. I touched him and said something like 'Herr Schmidt, Herr Schmidt, are you all right, what is the matter?'

'Give me a hand, please', and we gave him our support to get him back on his feet. He was a big man and heavy. He held his face and said 'My God, my God' followed by something like, 'the brown bastards running wild.' He dusted himself down and hobbled unsteadily to the door of his tenement hardly more than a dozen steps away. We could still see the marching SA column further down the street, with their military songs still in our ears. Some glanced back to where we were, giving the impression that they were well pleased with themselves for what they had done to Herr Schmidt.

There were people walking on the pavements nearby, as it was a lovely evening, many of the windows of the five-storey tenements were open and people, as was the custom in our working class district, were leaning out with their elbows on the sills to watch life in the street. But no one came down to help Herr Schmidt, no one wanted to know nor be seen by the SA to express sympathy for him. Only several days later was I asked by people if I knew what had happened to him. But their enquiry, it seemed to me, came more from curiosity than sympathy.

This incident happened around 1934 and as it bothered me, I rushed up to my parents to tell them. They looked aghast at me and then at each other. Had I recognised any of the brownshirts?, father wanted to know. But I hadn't. Then he said more to mother than to me 'Well, what can we do? – we are so powerless against these brutes. It's so sad because the SA on the whole are working class, our own. They act on behalf of the rich against their own kind.'

But it was in the summer of 1934 when suddenly a political bombshell exploded which almost tore the SA to pieces and made it a very different organisation. It all blew up one night in Bavaria, Berlin, Bremen and later reached into every SA Sturm in the country. The top man of the SA was Stabs Chef Ernst Röhm, a large man with the features of a fairground boxer. He was a personal friend of Hitler's, one of the few who called him by his Christian name. After the failed Nazi putsch in 1923 he had to flee to Bolivia, where he worked as a military adviser, setting up and organising a third-rate copy of an army on German lines. But when his friend Adolf was appointed German Chancellor, Ernst Röhm came back and took over the SA.

At first there were only rumours about what had happened in Bavaria. Killings on a large scale amongst the top SA ranks were mentioned. Father heard about it, laughed and said that he really was not surprised and in some ways it was the best news he had heard for a long time. But mother took him to task, asking him never to say things like that again in front of me.

For a day or so after the rumours, nothing official was announced. By that time the entire German propaganda machine was controlled by the Nazis, and there were few people in our part of town who owned a radio powerful enough to pick up a foreign radio station. When the banner headlines finally appeared on the front pages of the papers, accusing the SA leaders of 'betrayal', this was received with some scepticism by the population. However, people had learnt to keep their thoughts to themselves and their noses out of such a dangerous quagmire.

It was no secret to any German adult with some understanding of life that Röhm, and not only he, was a practising homosexual, and that Göring was a drug addict. But as homosexuality was a punishable offence under paragraph 175 of German law, people had to be doubly careful about what they were saying, as it was dangerous to get into the black book of the brown ones, as the saying went. However, many jokes about Röhm, as well as degrading stories about SA leaders and blond Venus-type youths were making the rounds. Also, everyone was convinced that they were true.

In Germany a homosexual was, and I think still is, called 'ein warmer Bruder' (a warm brother). At this time an American film *The Cold Kitchen Maid* was being shown in the cinema, and sniggerers renamed it, 'the cold kitchen maid and the warm Röhm.' In spite of this, Ernst Röhm had an unshakeable reputation of being one of the staunchest supporters of the Führer. People said that if anyone would, he would lay down his life for Adolf Hitler. To many it was therefore almost unbelievable that he was a wily traitor making plans to assassinate his good friend Adolf.

Being very curious about such an important event of this kind, I asked father what he thought lay behind it. However, with me growing older and being strongly influenced by the Hitler Youth, he became more cautious about criticising what he called 'the brown pest'. He constantly warned me against telling anyone what he was telling me, although he knew that I never would knowingly do that.

The root of the Röhm affair lay in Hitler's bondage to those who had appointed him to the Chancellorship. The German establishment, of which the army was an important part, had not done that for nothing. They were still determined to rule, even though they had to do it through friend Adolf. But now they wanted payment in the shape of the head of Röhm. Father argued that the name National Socialist German Workers Party had drawn many sincere working people, including the unemployed, into its ranks, who genuinely wanted a socialist future. Many had even come from the Communist Party, and the SA had swelled to a membership of almost three million.

It was well known but never openly stated that over the years the SA Sturms had acquired weapons, some of which were kept in their homes, while others were in secure hiding places all over the country. The SA had loyally helped Hitler to establish himself politically, by removing his opponents from streets and meeting halls. The Führer had ridden to the very top on their backs and they were sure that he would be eternally grateful to them. But as it now turned out, their beloved Führer had an extremely short memory. He also had other ideas. Now he had become Prime Minister, his problems had become entirely different, both internally and internationally, and he no longer needed the help of the SA. Now he needed the support of the army, the industrialists and others of the right-wing establishment. In any case the comfortable middle classes had never liked the brutish behaviour of that brown mob, and it became clearer and clearer to the top Nazis that the SA had become more of a liability than an asset.

The army, the powerful Ruhr barons and all the other reactionary elements in political life demanded that Hitler get rid of or at least tame the Röhm-led SA. The Führer simply had no choice: he was well aware that his rather brain-restricted Nazi lot would never be able to run the complicated German state machine on their own. So the Führer got his orders and together with Göring and Göbbels planned to strike. The final decision was made not far from Bonn at Godesberg in the famous Hotel Dreesen above the Rhine. From there the trio flew down to Munich where they were met by reliable SS and Gestapo units, who accompanied them in cars and lorries to the small spa of Wiessee only a short drive away. The SA was holding its annual Congress there, with almost its entire leadership very conveniently tucked away in hotels and guest houses.

What then happened was quick and brutal. Arrests and shootings were carried out without delay. Hitler himself, father said, did the rounds with the assassins and at times had to make the personal decision as to whether this or that SA leader was to live or die. Hotel staff and others were present, and it must have been through them that the ghastly details of what happened had leaked out. Several of the well-known names were found in bed with young blond stormtroopers. By all accounts, they could not believe what was happening to them, thought that it must all have been a mistake, as they recognised trusted comrades amongst their executioners.

When after a considerable delay, press information was released, there was of course much praise for the Führer, his wisdom, foresight and decisiveness, by which once again he saved the Fatherland from turmoil. Ernst Röhm himself, father said, offered no resistance, only asked whether all this was a sick joke when he was locked up in a local cell. A loaded pistol was put on the small cell table next to him as a last 'friendly' gesture perhaps from 'a former friend', no doubt with the hope that Ernst would save him the embarrassment of doing the job himself. But Ernst, perhaps really not knowing what it was all about, refused to play ball. Father shrugged his shoulders and grinningly said that as I could see, there was no honour amongst criminals, even when they needed it most. Röhm was said to have challenged his executioners to tell Adolf that if he had the courage to condemn him to death, then to come and shoot him himself. Of course, friend Adolf didn't, someone else had to do it for him, who could then safely claim 'not guilty' for having acted under strict orders from above.

Feeling that I could not let father get away with all this, I asked him how come that he had the inside knowledge, as of course nothing of this kind had been reported in the press. He cut me short and told me that I must not ask him such questions but must trust that he would never lie to me. And in spite of all my Hitler Youth inspirations, I was nevertheless wholeheartedly prepared to give him my trust.

After this heavy blood-letting, the SA was not abolished. There was probably no need for that any more and the upheaval had to be kept to a minimum. The brown stormtroopers still kept strutting through the towns, still singing their bawdy songs about German greatness and 'Jewish blood dripping off their knives.' They still carried their swastikas in front of their columns and still forced the passers-by to salute them. But it was all too evident that the steam had gone out of them. History had moved on, had overtaken them and they were of no importance any more. The German State after the early Nazi turmoils had straightened itself out, and was back in the hands of the establishment, never mind what kind of noises the Nazis made on the sidelines. A relative nonetity, an SA leader from Hanover with the name of Victor Lutze, was appointed by Hitler as the new Stabs Chef.

It was in the late summer after Hitler's ascendancy, when a kind of international breakthrough occurred with the signing of the Concordat between Germany and the Vatican. Hitler's Vice Chancellor Franz von Papen, unofficially representing about forty per cent of Germany's Catholic population, mainly living in the south and west, together with Eugenio Pacelli, who was Nuncio to Berlin and later became Pope Pius XII, were said to be the prime movers behind it. The Catholic Church on the strength of that treaty secured the continuity of the clergy-led Catholic schools for the whole of the country, while the direct Nazi advantage from it stayed rather vague.

Of far more importance, according to the line given to us in the Hitler Youth, was the signing of the Anglo-German Naval Agreement, which allowed the building of Germany's Navy to thirty-five per cent of British tonnage. Hitler made a great deal of this agreement in a speech, saying that this was proof of Germany's desire for peace. What the wily British had in mind was not easy to assess, as they seemed to gain little from the agreement. Our strength anyway was well below that thirty-five per cent limit, but we smiled the crooked smile of the rascal, when we heard that the French were much displeased with the British move, and that there was now talk in Paris of 'perfidious Albion'.

The Führer, we all clearly realised, could not refuse such an offer. Versailles' chains around our ankles and wrists were loosened by that agreement and as most people knew, a long-prepared naval building programme could now be set more openly into motion. It gave a great impulse to German industry and showed itself very strongly in the shipyards of Hamburg where we lived. The battleship *Bismarck* was started, so was the battle cruiser *Prinz Eugene* if I remember rightly. Contracts were handed out for building torpedo, U-Boats and other vessels. As to the U-Boats, even we could not help wondering what the British thought Hitler might ultimately do with them.

It is understandable that many of the formerly unemployed shipyard workers hailed Hitler as their saviour. I knew many of them, as they lived in our part of the town. It gave the Nazis a great political lift in Hamburg, where the slogan 'Hamburg bleibt rot' (Hamburg stays red) had been very much in fashion amongst working people, and where previously the Nazis had been unable to make much headway.

Father was angry and sad about this development, bemoaning the short-sightedness of the German workers. Could they not see that building battleships and U-Boats meant preparation for war, and this was not the way for a civilised society to solve its deep-seated economic and social problems. Looking at me, he said to my mother that it would be the young ones of my generation who would pay the price for this deception, that one day we would be put into uniform and made to fight and kill, all to keep this iniquitous system in being. And when years later I heard at the Russian Front that tens of thousands of innocent people had died in Hamburg like rats during one air raid alone, and when coming home later from the war and seeing the ruins, I thought of what my father had predicted.

CHAPTER V
Learning from Günter

It was around 1935/36 when I was thirteen or fourteen years old when something happened which I now realise had a considerable impact on my life. In itself, it seemed rather unimportant. A new boy had come into our class. His father had been a civil servant in Berlin from where he had been transferred to our town, which brought Günter into our class. His mother was a Berliner, who like Cockneys in London had the reputation for quick-wittedness. Günter very much had her temperament.

From the word go, the day when he arrived and was introduced, it was clear that he differed from the rest of us in many ways. While most of us made somewhat heavy work achieving reasonable school results, Günter took everything in his stride, and after he had been with us for one year, he was top of the class. Without being aggressive, he was very argumentative, took on everyone and argued about everything possible. His general knowledge was well above average, his logic sharp as a knife, and there was nothing he did not show interest in.

He had one weakness though, which amongst us youngsters was a weighty one: he was bad at sport. Being slightly smaller than average and of slightly plumpish appearance, he was never selected for any class or school team. Watching him taking part in any athletic competition, it was a foregone conclusion that he would end up last and a sight tinged with barely hidden pleasure by many. Schadenfreude is the German word for that. He had a brother Kurt who was two or three years older who was also at our school.

About seven or eight years later his brother was killed somewhere in Russia, while Günter, I was told after the war, had been executed on the Eastern Front. It was said that he had been condemned for Zersetzung der Wehrkraft (undermining defence power), an accusation which at the time could not have been more serious. The sentence, there was no appeal, was usually carried out within twenty-four hours, meaning at once. When I heard about it, my memory switched back to the many discussions and arguments we had. I was extremely sad and angry about his death, but I was not surprised, given his rebellious nature.

After his arrival in class he appeared to be a real loner and showed no

111

interest in making friends. After a few weeks or so he rather unexpectedly began to seek my friendship. At first I was not quite sure whether I liked the idea, as my general preference for friends lay with those who were good at sport. But then, rather selfishly perhaps, thinking of Günter's excellent school work, when he suggested that we should do our homework together, one day at his place and the next at mine, the idea of befriending him began to appeal and I responded readily. It took some time before I began to appreciate him as a person, and we became real friends which lasted until separated by going off to serve in the army.

The German school day started early at eight and finished at two in the afternoon, which gave us plenty of time for homework and play. Living only ten minutes apart, we met after lunch and did at least an hour of concentrated work together. And when my school results improved dramatically, my parents quite rightly put it down to Günter's influence and gave all possible encouragement to our friendship. I also got on well with his parents, especially with his mother who had a very happy disposition. His father was a quiet type. Günter said that he was a deep thinker, a great reader of classics and interested in philosophy.

Günter had a bicycle, whereas I did not, which put a restriction on our being together more often. I think it was this more than anything which made my parents present me with a bike on the following Christmas. As our flat was small and bicycles were a favourite target for thieves, mine had to be carried up and down the four flights of stairs in our tenement. Then we found that our corridor was much too narrow to let it stand against the wall, so father fixed a pulley under the ceiling where it was winched out of the way. It did not look very nice to anyone entering our flat but it was very practical.

The time had arrived when I was beginning to spread my individual wings. In summer Günter and I made many trips to the lovely countryside surrounding our town. We cycled through the forests, the rolling farmlands further north, into the Lüneburg Heath and to the lakes in Holstein. When we wanted to cross the River Elbe, we had to negotiate a part of Hamburg to reach the famous Elbtunnel next to the international bridge where the ocean liners tied up. Huge tunnel lifts, of which there were five or six on each side of the river, transported horsecarts, lorries and shipyard workers, many of them on bikes. The use of the tunnel was free.

As soon as we got out of the tunnel building on the other side, we discovered that the entire area was heavily industrialised. All the big ship works like the Deutsche Werft, Blohm & Voss and the Howaldt Werke had their yards there. Small powerful steam locomotives shunted strings of rail wagons along the road from yard to yard and back to the railway connecting points. Smoke, dirt, grease and noise were everywhere and constituted the main characteristic of the entire area. There was little greenery and the few trees that there were, were laden with layers of pollution. For us in spite of that, it was a fascinating place. Every yard and workplace was surprisingly accessible. We simply pushed our bikes into them amidst the loud hammering, grinding and flying sparks from the welding and moved close to the giant cranes and house-high scaffolding which surrounded the hulls of the ships. We only moved on when some miserable foreman or yardmaster decided that we were a nuisance and gave us our marching orders.

We then continued our trek and after a kilometre or two, left the industrial area behind, crossed the flatlands until we arrived at the wooded Harburg or Black Mountains as they were also called. We passed the village of Hausbruch from where we reached the top of the low ridge to find a view through the trees, from which we looked back towards the river, with our own town stretching along the high bank on the other side. We sat down in the woods, unpacked our picnics provided by our mothers, watched the wildlife, climbed trees and swam in a local pond. Having cycled so many kilometres, we were then too tired to take the same long route back all the way through the tunnel and Hamburg, but spent some of our pocket money and took the much shorter route by ferry across the river and back to our town.

On both sides of the Chaussee, on the riverside sometimes halfway down the bank and on the other, the wooded flat side, stood impressive large villas, generously set back in their own parks, often fenced off with high wrought-iron spiked fences or stone walls with broken glass on top. Sometimes there were dogs to scare away potential intruders like us. Never having really given deep thought to it before, I was surprised and somewhat thrown out of gear, when Günter claimed that all this place was insulting to human dignity. Until now I had only noticed the beauty of these properties, had admired them and by implication those who were living in them. I had never bothered my brain about the social relations which had brought all this about.

Günter reminded me that just a few kilometres away from here were masses of poor people living in ugly streets, often in unhygienic and degrading conditions. 'How is it,' he wanted to know, 'that no one seriously asks how those who have lots of money have come by it in the first place? Why should they have the unchallenged right to grab the best places for themselves, build imposing villas and palaces on them, call it their own and keep the likes of us away from it by imposing spiked fences?'

And when we later pushed our bikes down to the river's edge, lay on the sands and drew figures on its packed surface, he became pensive and wanted to talk with me about rich and poor, and why the former had so much economic and other power over the latter. Were we not wrong to unthinkingly accept the given situation as if it were God's law, handed down from heaven and therefore to last for ever and ever? Were we not on this earth to change things for the better, of which the first step surely should be to challenge all that exists, particularly the differences between rich and poor?

I just lay there lazily, looking at the slowly moving water of the river and the ships graciously gliding by, and said nothing because I really did not know what to say. 'Now come on,' he said, 'we Germans are supposed to be a nation of poets and thinkers and you make a face as if I just asked you a question in a language you do not know.' Being pressed like that did not exactly make me think more clearly and when I mumbled something about this just being life and quite natural, he cut me short, saying that I was expressing a docile and unintelligent attitude, accepted uncritically as if it was holy writ. He pointed out that I surely could not but agree that there was so much injustice in our lives, so much brutality, physical and mental, and an all-pervading poverty of mind, largely due to an education system set up to perpetuate the interests of the rich. All this was a bit much for me to swallow and I could not really grasp what he was driving at. We had a number of these kinds of exchanges over the months which mainly originated from him, and to which I reacted feebly. But much later after the war, I remembered what my father had tried to tell me about the dangers of challenging the privileges of the rich, and then thought about the many argumentative arrows which Günter had aimed at me, and wondered whether it had not been this kind of enquiring and critical mind which in the end led him into deep trouble and execution.

When I told father about Günter's strange ideas, he put on that wry smile of his with that cheeky glint in his eyes which so often annoyed me and said: 'Well, well, is that what your friend Günter said?' He then urged me not to dismiss his way of thinking but to think more deeply about it myself; and be prepared to throw my Hitler Youth prejudices to the wind. 'One thing I can tell you and surely you know it yourself: your friend Günter is not stupid. I have a feeling that he, being your own age, can probably do more than I to open your mind, to expose you to a dose of objective intelligent thinking.'

Günter, there was no doubt, was much more of a realist than I was. He made it his job to stop my imaginations and dreams from running away with me. When for instance I talked about the wide world and how exciting it must be in far-away places, he questioned my illusion that a far-away place with a romantic sounding name should be more beautiful and exciting than one close by. To underline the point he quoted Goethe, 'Warum in die Ferne schweifen, sieh das Gute liegt so nah?' (Why dream about far-away places and miss the beauty on your doorstep?) He told me that he had read about dreadful living conditions of masses of people, in rich places like New York and other American cities, and that in Latin America, Asia and Africa, continents we like to swoon about, there were millions of orphans starving to death because no profits could be made out of them. He looked at life with very different eyes from me: he had his feet firmly on the ground, while I was riding around on clouds with pink spectacles on my nose.

You should have your own thoughts, make your own assessments, he sometimes angrily shouted at me and not soak up all the lies which priests and Nazis try to pump into you, and yet he loved Germany but only as a place where he happened to have been born. He wanted to have nothing to do with what he called the ghoulish patriotic nonsense, which countless generations had dragged around with them. The notion to fight and kill, for instance, and to die for one's country was to him the height of madness. He stressed that if people in other countries were being fed with the same nonsense, then it was no wonder that the generation of our fathers had been led like sheep to slaughter on the 'heroic' battlefields of the Somme, Verdun, Passchendaele and Tannenberg.

When saying all these things to me, he was of course fully aware that he was out of step with what we were being taught in the Hitler Youth and at school. But he had already learnt to be careful. I remember him making questioning remarks of this kind in class, which he then never followed through or stood up for in further discussion. But he did with me, but only when we were on our own.

On some occasions like on the Saturday before Totensonntag (Remembrance Day) the whole school went to church. As usual Günter and I sat together. As hardly any of us had had a meaningful religious upbringing at home, we were not really interested in what was going on around us. We found it all a bit of hocus pocus and very boring. So we looked around and admired the beauty of the ceiling and the coloured windows and quietly discussed how the craftsmen of their day had been able to build such architectural marvels with their then relatively primitive tools.

But we found we were in trouble because our teacher had watched us waving our arms about and paying no attention to the service and told us off afterwards. Günter as a response quite craftily brought in the Hitler Youth for our defence, stating that we had learnt there that Christianity was a system of misery, designed and used to make masses of ordinary people docile, so that the rich rulers could fleece them to their hearts' delight. He elaborated that we had learnt that this had been going on since the collapse of the Roman Empire and that he therefore saw no reason why we had been marched into this church in the first place. The mention of the Hitler Youth was enough for Herr Hinck and he let us off without further ado. We walked away giggling and Günter said: 'There you are, he is a typical product of Christian upbringing, blowing hot bubbles, telling us off and as soon I mention the Hitler Youth, he puts his tail between his legs and simply walks away.'

It must have been in the summer of 1934 when the Nazi Party held a big rally in the large exhibition hall not far from the river in our town. The big draw of the event was that Prince August Wilhelm (known as Auwi to his friends), the fourth son of the Kaiser, was going to speak to the faithful brownshirts. As Günter and I had never seen a real prince in our lives, we decided to go and have a look at him. The event had been well-advertised in newspapers and on posters all over town. For days before SA men could be seen standing in groups at railway stations and other busy places handing out leaflets. On the day itself, well before starting time, the Sturms met at their Sturm Lokale from where they marched in columns to the Exhibition Hall, taking in as many working class side streets as possible. One brownshirt marched alongside the column on the pavement with a megaphone announcing the venue of the event.

Many onlookers had already gathered outside the large wrought-iron gates to the exhibition grounds where Günter and I joined them. A couple of SA men came along and ordered us to step back behind the lines on each side, to allow plenty of space for the VIPs to walk on. Though there was some suppressed grumbling in the back about the uncouth way the SA men gave their orders, we all obeyed like lambs. Certainly no one, and probably wisely so, showed any inclination to argue with the brownshirts.

We did not have to wait long for the official convoy of cars to arrive, led by several brownshirts on BMW motorbikes. By now we had pushed our way through and were standing right in front of the crowd from where we had an uninterrupted view. Three or four high-ranking SA leaders had already arrived from inside the grounds and stood waiting by the kerb. A large black Mercedes with a Hohenzollern emblem on the mudguard came to a smooth halt in a central position, where a large carpet had been unrolled on the rough gravel. Only after some SA and other security men had jumped out of their accompanying car and had taken up encircling positions, was the back door of the Mercedes opened from the outside.

The talking had now completely stopped amongst the crowd behind us. All that was left to us now was to gape open-mouthed at the open Mercedes door or rather into the dark hole behind it. There were two or three people in the back compartment, one of them, we were sure, the prince of the royal blood. But none of them came out, they carried on with their animated, even laughing conversation, as if whatever was happening outside was of no concern to them.

All of a sudden there was movement. One long leg in SA breeches, stuck in a shiny brown jackboot, came dangling out and clanked heavily with its sole on to the kerb. But that was all for the moment, nothing else happened and everyone stared at what we thought was the royal leg. The laughing conversation inside the car had still not come to an end. The high-ranking reception outside appeared decidedly lost as if not quite knowing what to do, and looked like sad victims of a sick joke, having been ordered to appear but forgotten to be collected. From behind us came giggles, with a gruff voice remarking that he had never viewed a kerb pantomime before and certainly not a royal one. But all went quiet again when the brown-shirt in front of us tried to pinpoint the person who had made the remark – looking back I only saw innocent-looking faces.

Then there was movement, tentative at first, but with the distinct promise of something more exciting to come. From the inside a hand reached out for the top above the open door, and then out came Prince Auwi in all his royal glory, standing on the edge of the carpet and looking around in what seemed unexpected wonderment. But just at that moment, when the leader of the reception committee was about to swing into action, getting his arm ready to shoot into the air for a Hitler salute, the prince turned and bent back towards the dark hole again. He said something to those left inside, after which an arm reached out with the prince's SA cap. A quick swinging plonk and it was on his head, and there he stood, now ready to deal with all-comers and everything.

If I remember correctly, his rank was that of SA Standartenführer, roughly equal to army general. Now he had to endure the clicking of steel-studded heels of the jackboots, arms shooting up in front of his nose, military handshakes and loud pronouncements of meaningless names. Though unlike the others he did not click his heels, the prince's arm too had to go up as a matter of formal Nazi protocol. But he did it in a leisurely way, just like the Führer, by bending his elbow and arriving with his hand not higher than his right ear. He was taller and slimmer than those standing around him. His face was gaunt and he gave the impression that all this charading around was a bit too much for him.

I think that at that time he was somewhere in his mid-forties though his whole bearing was that of a much older man. Several shiny medals and coloured ribbons dangled from the left breast pocket of his brown shirt. Stuck to his chest was a strange-looking shiny star the size of a large egg, which royal houses of Europe had exchanged with each other, for obscure services rendered. His entire behaviour, his demeanour, seemed strange as if he had got out of the wrong side of a train and had landed amongst a crowd of ruffians whom he had no choice but to get along with.

His gait was slow and measured, almost as if he was stalking, while those around him walked with a distinct swagger, trying to hustle each other out of the way so as to walk close to him. He seemed to have difficulty in either hearing or understanding the working class accent because whenever any of them said something to him, he had to bend down slightly to catch the words. There was not one smile on his face, not one slight sign of any enthusiasm for what he was engaged in. In fact he looked thoroughly fed-up with it all.

The group walked slowly towards the large main gate while the prince gave several dutiful waves with his hand towards us gaping peasants on either side. Apart from a small group of brown-shirted girls waving small paper swastika flags and giggling, there was hardly a response, just sour grins and mumblings. Everything seemed so mechanical, without any conviction, a dishonest display of unity between the old and the new which had fallen decidedly flat. As the group moved through the gates into the grounds, loud clacking commands were shouted towards an SA Sturm whom the Prince had been invited to inspect. After that they all disappeared up a few steps and out of sight into the Exhibition Hall in which the thousands were waiting. From there we heard loud clapping and shouting followed by trumpets, flutes and small drums, the German way. Then all became quiet.

By now the crowd had dispersed and Günter and I made our way home. As we always did after we had seen or experienced something together of this kind, we discussed our thoughts about it. I was more inclined to accept everything uncritically, accepting the conventional wisdom handed down from above, whereas Günter showed his more questioning approach by straight away making scathing comments on what we had just seen.

'Don't you think that there was something very odd, something fundamentally contradictory if not idiotic about this entire circus of a royal prince surrounded by pot-bellied creeping brownshirts?' And when I, as I often did, hedged about, not really knowing how to respond and searching for an easy way out by throwing the question back at him, asking what he meant, he became angry with me and swore that I was acting like a backward political simpleton. 'It might not be the right one, but the very least you ought to have surely is an opinion, your own and not one which others have already formed for your consumption. Can't you see it, the Nazis claim to be socialist and very radical at that. What do they therefore want with the fourth son of the Kaiser in their ranks? And what does he think he is doing in the midst of that lot, insisting that he has blue aristocratic blood in his veins and joining a party of rowdies, even accepting their rank as Standartenführer? He is a member of one of the richest families in the land, owns vast tracts of it, has invested millions in industry and banking. Can you think of one reason why he should join a political party whose acclaimed aim is to create a socialist society? We have both read Hitler's *Mein Kampf* and his aim of creating socialism in Germany is clearly stated there.'

He went on and suggested that either the prince had got it all wrong, or the Nazis did not know what they were doing. Or indeed could it be that they both knew what they were up to and that we, the ordinary people, did not know what we were doing by looking up to the one and blindly following the other?

His direct attack on me, knowing how confused I was on all this, made me well up in anger. 'But what makes you so sure that you are right, do you think that you have got a monopoly on understanding such involved and complicated issues? But I see no reason why I should feel ashamed of following the Führer's ideology, because I stand four-square behind my country, which by the way is also yours. Do you think that I am following the brownshirts blindly? I have carefully read the twenty-five points of their programme and have listened to many of our Führer's speeches, thought deeply about it all, agree with it and really don't like you laughing about it as if it were a load of rubbish.'

Well, that was it. This time I had given it to him, whereas I mostly let him get away with his line of argument. He went very quiet at this outburst of mine, and we walked along in complete silence. His head was down, he stared in front of him at the pavement and I knew that I had hurt him, and was beginning to feel sorry. Suddenly and to me quite un- expectedly, he put his arm around me with his hand on my shoulder. His voice and whole demeanour had become very serious.

'Look at me, Henry, let me see your eyes. I haven't been laughing at you as you said, the matter is far too serious for that. We are friends, aren't we, so why should we quarrel? But as friends we should always be honest with each other, should openly say what is on our minds and do it in the knowledge that we would not pass it on to unsympathetic ears. We might not agree on everything, and certainly I am not claiming that my view is the correct one, but neither can you say that yours is either. In the last analysis none of us can know about what is going on in high places, in the end all we can do is surmise. But to do that effectively we must look critically at the facts as they present themselves to us. We must weigh them up and think about their meanings, what made them what they are and what lies behind them. I am well aware that you trust the Führer, you have said so often enough and I accept that you are sincere in your belief. But please believe me, I too am sincere when I openly tell you that with the best will in the world, I simply cannot trust that man and all he stands for. I think he is nothing but a big conman, a tool of others and though cunning, not all that clever. If he was a wise man, he would not shout in the way he does. He might believe that he is the Almighty, but in reality he is walking on a long lead held by very powerful groups of men, whose aim is to keep what they have. And if they see the necessity to drive us all into a war to satisfy their selfish ends, and millions die as a result of it, they will not hesitate to do it. You have told me that your father does not trust him either and as you also consider your father to be an intelligent man, does it not make you think about these issues more deeply? Unlike in Russia where in 1917 the revolution swept away all the former top people, in Germany by and large, they remained in their positions after the November Revolution. What's more, they kept most of the strings of ownership and control in their hands, the two things which mean real power. And against all that, our flimsy talk about living in a democracy means exactly nothing.'

What could I say after all this? I could see the logic of what he had said but refused to see it in the light of present reality. Yes, I admitted that the prince and the Nazis were strange bedfellows. I realised myself that what I had said sounded pretty hollow and I felt uncomfortable in my own position. But when he said, 'Is that all that you have to say on this?', I got angry again, so much of me was in turmoil, I felt pulled from one side to the other. I pointed out to him that the Führer himself had written in *Mein Kampf* that the Nazi aim was to abolish class struggle in Germany simply by abolishing classes. Could it not be that Auwi had seen the light and thought in those terms, namely that we are all Germans, never mind what fancy family background he came from, that we should reject the Marxist teaching of the class struggle, as it was contrary to the German character?

'Henry, have you gone completely mad, spouting such idiotic nonsense? If the Führer really had that in mind, do you think that the Ruhr barons would have propped him up with money as they did ? If that was the case, before he could even raise his arm in his own heil salute, they would have him out on his ear and he would be glad to be back in Vienna painting houses again.'

The summer evening was warm and pleasant, but after this exchange an unhappiness came over me. Yes, I wanted my way, I did not want to cave in to Günter every time, but I thought that if we went on like this, I would lose him as a friend. After both of us were quiet for a while, he went on: 'Anyway as to the Führer's classless society, who do you think lives in those large beautiful villas we have just passed, our classless brothers? Doesn't it strike you as odd that none of their children are going to our school, if they become ill, do you think they are taken to the same hospital ward they take us to? Oh, Henry, why are you so blind and cannot see what is in front of your eyes?'

By now I had completely lost my ability to argue rationally and because I did not know what to say any more, I said nothing. We had arrived at his tenement and I looked up at its grey and uninteresting façade and thought about the grim housing conditions so many millions of working people had to endure. Deep down I knew that he was right, but having my own pride, I did not tell him what I thought. So we just patted each other on our upper arms as we always did when we parted, said 'until tomorrow', and I went on my way home deeply enmeshed in thought about what had happened that evening. I was sure that the last thing I wanted was to fall out with my friend Günter.

Next day at school we mentioned to our teacher what we had seen, and Günter asked him outright what he thought about Auwi the SA prince. I could see in Hinck's face that he had smelled a rat in the question. It seemed clear to me that, though he had an opinion on the issue, possibly a strong one, he did not want to be drawn into the trap. All he mumbled was that the prince, like everyone else in our country, had the right to join anything of his choice. After school I went to Günter's place to do some homework and he showed me the front page of a newspaper which showed a large photo of Auwi stepping out of his car and being greeted by a large joyous crowd of onlookers. 'Can you see how people are being fooled and bamboozled again? All we did was stand there and gape at that funny performance. At most we could have been called curious or inquisitive but certainly not joyous. Doesn't it prove that the newspapers are in it too?'

It was a little later in the year or early in the next, that the party, not only the SA, organised a public rally in the same hall which, I believe, was at that time one of the largest indoor arenas in the northern part of our country. A party bigwig, Dr. Robert Ley, had been billed as the main speaker. As a well known and popular orchestra with a choir was due to entertain the crowd for an hour or so before the start of the rally, Günter and I decided to go and listen.

All those who had joined the Nazi Party at an early date and had taken part in the political struggles against the Weimar Republic, were called 'alte Kämpfer' (old fighters). To be one of them had now become a much sought-after honour as it opened so many doors to privileged government positions. There was a joke about that 'honour' which pointed out that while the number of people were generally becoming less as they got older, the Nazi 'alte Kämpfer' were growing more in numbers.

When we arrived at the hall, we found that all the places in the front had already been taken, so we had to go to the back. The music and the singing was beautiful, especially as we were invited to participate. This led Günter to remark that the Nazis were past masters at pulling in the crowds. He was sure that without the music, only half of the people present, certainly the young, would have bothered to come. Though it was a bit uncomfortable, we had managed to climb on to some beams of the roof-supports from where we had a commanding view, looking over thousands of heads in front of us, towards the large and well-lit stage. We were disappointed when the music finally stopped and the musicians and singers walked off, preparing us for what we were sure would be the boring part of the evening.

The main entrance door was further to our left and while there was plenty of noise within the hall, we could hear loud 'heil' shouting from the outside. That was the signal that Dr. Ley and his entourage had arrived. We had not long to wait before they appeared. Being a bit too far back, we were at first unable to recognise any of them, and could only make out the bobbing brown uniform caps moving along through the narrow cleared passage, which led from the door straight to the stage. At first we could make little sense of it, but then we realised that hilarious laughter was coming from the crowd close to the passage and necks began to crane from all around the hall to see what was the reason for the laughter. It was only when the group reached the elevated stage, which was draped with swastika flags, that we realised that something very funny indeed was happening.

When the first of the group had reached the four or five steps leading up to the stage, the laughter grew louder. And then we too were able to see the reason for it and laughed with everyone else. These leading Nazis, or most of them, were drunk as lords, so much so in fact, that they seemed to be incapable of climbing the steps. There was no hand rail which they could hold on to and when the first of them somehow managed to get to the top, and stretched out a hand for a pull-up, we recognised that the person to be pulled up was Dr. Robert Ley. But as it happened, the helping pull had been a bit too strong for him, for when he reached the last step, he stumbled and fell flat on his face. He knocked his nose on the floor, his cap fell off his head, and that was it, he was lying there now on the stage for all to see. To us, the crowd, standing back in the half-dark of the hall, everything was clearly visible as the entire stage was well lit. The laughter in the hall turned into a roar; no circus performance of clowns could have been more effective.

Only about a half of Ley's followers, four or five, had reached the stage, while the rest of them were still in confusion, pushing and shoving at the bottom of the steps. One of them, having almost made it, came down with a crash and had to be helped from the hall. The mood of the crowd now changed, there were insulting whistles and loud shouting, together with all sorts of animal noises. Günter and I were in danger of falling off our beams with uncontrollable laughter. He shouted across to me above the din that this was really great, well worth having come for and much more revealing and interesting than the music and singing before. It was a real, first-class pantomime.

After a few more minutes when they had all more-or-less managed to reach the stage, a sober but low-ranking member of the party tried to help Ley up, whom the rest seemed to have forgotten. He was half up, looking through the jackboots surrounding him, when he was shouted at by the drunken high-rankers to leave the stage, which he attempted to do. It took some time for Ley to get back on to his feet, but once he felt the solid boards under him, he made an unsure dash to a row of chairs at the back, plonked himself heavily on one, and was visibly relieved to have regained relative safety. Now these leading party members were all assembled, what a picture to behold! The glaring lights were still fully on and there was a row of drunken top Nazis sitting on a row of chairs for all to see and judge.

But what was going to happen now? No one seemed to have any idea. The official organisers were sitting below on the first row of chairs and because one of them had been ordered off the stage, no other dared to take events into his hands. They just kept whispering and looking at each other and all the time there was the rostrum and the microphone on it, waiting to be used. Now came the period when the early pandemonium turned into something much more effective and much more telling. Silence, a deep silence had descended on the hall. It was like an ominous warning from the crowd. One could hardly hear a sound apart from a slight shuffle and the occasional cough. Not one word was spoken. From where we were sitting in the beams we could see how the smaller ones in the crowd stood on their toes, being lifted by their neighbours to be able to see better, and all eyes were on the stage. There was a sort of expectation in the air, for everyone realised that this could not be the end of the performance, something had to happen, something had to give. Looking around below, I could see many a smirking smile on so many faces, almost expressing those forbidden words, 'you brown bastards, serves you right . . .'

The lower ranks sitting on the chairs in front of the stage were getting restless and worried, turning their heads towards each other as if to say, 'what the hell are we going to do now?' Then, suddenly, the ice broke. One of the drunkards on the stage somehow struggled out of his chair, managed to walk unsteadily over to where Ley sat, and said a few words to him. Both nodded their heads and seemed to have agreed on a plan, which resulted in the one who had got up reaching the rostrum. The silence of the crowd was now absolute, no one wanted to miss anything, there was an air of eager expectation. But we still had to wait, for nothing then happened. The lonely figure just stood there, both hands holding firmly on to the rostrum. Then disaster struck again. Probably not knowing what to do next, he had started fiddling with some of the switches in front of him, presumably to test the microphone. And before he could even say 'Heil Hitler', he had managed to switch off the stage lights and was now standing like a nebulous shadow in the semi-darkness. But that was enough for the crowd. The silence was abandoned and an incredible pandemonium broke out with a very added sting in the tail. For this time, after the initial whistles had faded, a concentrated chorus of 'shame, shame, shame', in which almost everyone took part, rose throughout the large hall into the very rafters. With it came an almost tangible anger, people had had enough, they had come for a rally to listen to speeches, and all they felt now was that they were being insulted.

Then one of the other top-rankers came from behind to help the first out of his misery. Together they tried to find the right switch, while lots of cracking and clicking could be heard from the loudspeakers in the hall. The mumbled conversation of the two could also be heard, including their swearing and expressions of helplessness. However, after much ado they finally succeeded, the lights went on and the helper struggled back to his chair.

By the way and manner in which the main would-be speaker now raised his head and looked from one side of the hall to the other, it became clear that he was begging for silence and ready to speak. 'Heil Hitler' he said, and one could clearly detect the drunken slur in his voice. 'Dear citizens, party members and friends . . .' For a time that was all, he had already lost his thread, that is if he ever had one, and could not think of what to say next. A couple or so of unconnected words like 'pleasure' and 'honour' came unconvincingly from the loudspeakers, followed by a slightly more coherent introduction about what a loyal paladin of our Führer Dr. Ley was. He then stretched out an inviting hand towards the row behind him where Ley was struggling to rise from the chair, walking with unsure but quick, short steps to the rostrum and almost bumping into his introducer, who had quickly taken the opportunity to dive out of the way towards the relative safety of his chair.

Ley then went through the large side pocket of his uniform jacket, at first through one, then through the other, his unsure hands went to his breast pockets, all the time keeping in bodily touch with the rostrum. But his whole body language then expressed that there was nothing. And when with approaching desperation he looked back towards his cronies, they looked behind his chair and on to the floorboards around and responded with a shaking of their heads. After that there was no space for Ley to sink further. He was forced to do the only honourable thing left to him. He owned up. He grabbed the leads of the microphone and his voice started to boom from the loudspeakers. 'Kameraden' (comrades), he said, which was a totally inappropriate address under the circumstances, 'I cannot but sincerely apologise to all of you in the hall and hope that you will understand.' At this, and he must have heard it too, we heard subdued animal noises like the miaowing of a cat from the back and the wuff-wuff of a dog. He went on: 'Unfortunately when we discussed the general planning procedures for this evening, we had, as you all so embarrassingly must be aware, a few drops too many to drink.' To this someone shouted from the far side, 'not drops, mate, bottles!' 'All right' said Ley, 'don't let us quibble and call it bottles then. The fact is that while we were still in the hotel lounge, we hardly felt the effect, at least I did not. But when we came out for our cars and hit the fresh air, I suddenly lost my sense of balance.' The same voice from the back seemed to shout again 'not sense of balance, mate, just sense.' Ley went on to say, 'I want to state to you right here and now that I am deeply ashamed and very sorry for the shambles you have witnessed. The responsibility is mine and mine alone. I hope that you can find it in your hearts to forgive me. Thank you all, Heil Hitler.' With this he turned round, just managed to get back to his chair without hitting the floor and then sat there as if he now had committed his absolution, and was no longer responsible for what was to happen next.

Well, so far so good. A slight murmur developed throughout the crowd which could have come either from ridicule or an attempted under-standing. But everyone knew and understood that after all that had happened, the issue could not just die there without further explanation. Something else surely had to come. For the crowd to simply go home and leave it at that, would have added ridicule to insult. A shuffling, a subdued noise went round the hall like a layer of electricity which was almost tangible. Looking around from the vantage of my high position in the beams, I could see a great deal of frustration on the faces of the crowd, with everyone staring towards the stage expecting some sort of action. Without it, I was sure, an explosion would have been imminent. The built-up high tension simply had to be released.

Then I noticed feverish activity in the seated rows in front of the stage. They had gone into a frantic conference with each other, resulting in calling for the stewards. They did not do so by shouting, which was the usual custom in the SA, but by merely waving their hands, as if any quick movement or noise could set off a bang. The stewards understood and walked into the aisles, preventing any possible movement in the hall. The crowd realised the significance of this, changing their potentially explosive mood into one of uncertainty, sliding into passive acceptance. It all ended in flabby depression, an indecisive retreat out of which nothing came but polite clapping, which moved half-heartedly through the crowd. Whether this was from fear or to show an appreciation for Ley's courage in admitting that he had let the side down, I was unable to judge.

As there still was no action at the back of the stage, several of the organisers came together below the rostrum, quietly talked amongst themselves, after which one of them went to the microphone, asked for silence by waving his hand and announced that he was going to address us on the current political situation. As he was totally unprepared for this, everyone in the hall sensed that he did not really know what to say. He huffed and puffed a bit, and brought out a few garbled sentences which nobody listened to. From the back came wolf whistles which in effect were telling the heroic speaker to shut up. At this, the stewards in the gangways pushed into the crowd, looking for more potential whistlers and preventing any further trouble.

Next we heard crashes from the sides. The main doors had been flung open and the crowd below us began to shift. Like a movement into a funnel, a surge of irritated people were sucked past us into the dark night outside. And all the time the poor fall guy at the rostrum kept bla-bla-ing like a sick sheep. Günter and I clambered down from our beams and joined the crowd outside. There was much laughter and head-shaking in a general atmosphere of disbelief at what they had just witnessed. I heard very few voices daring to express outright condemnation. And those who did probably, looked nervously around to make absolutely sure that no brown ears were listening.

Almost all of the crowd were working people with very few women amongst them. The so-called 'better' classes, except perhaps in their capacity as works managers, did not go to this kind of rough lower-class rally. As Ley was the head of the Deutsche Arbeitsfront, it might well have been that pressure had been exerted on factory and other branch members to attend this rally. There were clumps of people standing around, obviously discussing what had happened. Though neither Günter nor I wore our brown shirts, it struck us that whenever we came close to such a group, being naturally curious to hear what our elders had to say, they either stopped talking or told us to make ourselves invisible.

On the way home Günter of course wanted nothing else but to discuss the event. At first we could not stop laughing about what we had seen and heard, reminding each other about this and that, about how stupid Ley had looked, hardly being aware in his alcoholic stupor who he was. 'It's unbelievable, totally incredible,' Günter kept repeating several times, 'no one in his or her right mind will believe us when we tell them.' Apart from a number of Hitler Youth rallies, this one had been the first real adult one either of us had attended.

But then our loose-laughing discussion changed to a more serious one. 'If these self-proclaimed guardians of our nation's honour and conscience are like that, what can we expect from everybody else?' he challenged me. Of course I was well aware of his intention, he knew that I was bound to react, that this incident must have thrown my rigid Nazi line out of balance and that he was now holding a trump card against so much of what I pretended to stand for. Knowing what was now going to come from him, my brain worked feverishly. I didn't want to admit that Nazism as such was thoroughly rotten and tried to steer the conversation towards showing that this was an isolated and for the brown movement, rather unfortunate event.

But he kept on pressing me, wanted to know how after this I could possibly still defend this brown lot any more. 'Yes, but . . .' I tried to stop his avalanching onslaught on me, 'this was Ley. At the best of times he has the reputation of a drinker and I do readily admit to you that his per-formance was a very disgraceful one. But don't forget, there are others too, Göring, Göbbels, Hess and of course the Führer himself who are all honourable men and who, no doubt, would condemn Ley for his behaviour this evening.'

'Yes, condemn Ley as we do. That is possible. But I bet you that they would only do so for the reason that he has let the side down, for the last thing they want is to see their own reputation dented because of that drunkard's behaviour. Henry, why for heaven's sake do you try to fool yourself, their condemnation would not be from a moral, principled stand but simply because he had been caught with his trousers down. Why for their own good they don't get rid of him, put him out to grass, I cannot see for the life of me. Your Adolf and some of the others might not be drunkards, and that is not really the worst accusation one can level at Ley

126

and nor is that the point I am trying to make. The thread that ties them all together is their mediocrity, each single one of them. Read up on any of them if you can – although most information on them has been destroyed – most of them were failures in civilian and professional life. Ley was nothing more than a jumped-up chemist. The fact that they were failures is one of the main reasons why they have joined that idiotic party. No other political party who cared for their reputation would have allowed the people now at the top of the Nazi Party to have joined them. Anyone, Henry, who has some sense and political understanding can see that, why not you? Is it perhaps that you don't want to, that you simply are too thick-headed to admit that you could possibly be wrong?'

With this I had had enough because this time he had touched me personally and I felt my temper rising to the point that I felt like thumping him. We shouted at each other and eyeing him in the dark, I knew, being more athletic than he, I could easily have floored him. He had insulted the Führer in whom I totally believed and was now pressing me beyond the point of endurance and would not let go. As I had already agreed with him that the rally had been utterly disgraceful, I was no longer capable of rationally defending myself. But then he probably saw it too, realised that he was tormenting me and certainly being the wiser of us two, handed me an olive branch. He touched me in a friendly way, offered me his hand and said, 'friendship, Henry, first and foremost our friendship, I know that I have used strong words which touched you personally and which I should not have said. But our friendship can only go on and blossom if we both say to each other what our brains and hearts dictate, without fear of the consequences.' I readily accepted the offer with much relief because I did not want to lose him as a friend. I grabbed him, pushed him around in a playful manner and all was well again between us.

We both went home, he up to his tenement and I on my ten-minute walk. On the way I thought a lot about what he had been trying to tell me. Deep down somehow I felt that he was right. But then I forgot about it all again. The all-dominating influence coming from school and the Hitler Youth swamped all tentative attempts to think independently and to analyse events unrolling in front of my eyes. Allowing my memory to spin back now, more than half a century later, I am sure that it was Günter's urge to bite into things which he believed in and not let go which led him to be executed. Such was the grip which Nazism had over the German people.

When I got home I was still upset. I told mother about what Günter and I had experienced, that Nazi Ley had been disgustingly drunk and that Günter and I had quarrelled about it all and had almost come to blows. She called father into the kitchen and told him and they were both very understanding. Father in his dealings with me, I think, had become much wiser of late. He had probably learnt that the way to convince me was not to clash head-on. After I told him about Günter's version of what happened, he lovingly pulled my head towards his so that we were cheek by cheek. I loved him so much and by now felt almost like crying. Then we three sat round the table and they both encouraged me to talk it over with them, as they wanted to help me and not merely score points against my Nazi way of thinking. Father made it clear that he was of course much more sympathetic to Günter's way of thinking than mine, but he pointed out that as I rated Günter's intelligence so highly, did it not make me think about the correctness of his political analysis?

I told him that I suspected Günter's father of having influenced his son as well as his brother Kurt, who behaved irreverently at school when we all stood to attention singing the National Anthem. At this father pulled me up short and warned me never to mention Günter's father in relation to this. He reminded me of what had happened to our neighbour Herr Eycken and that loose talking about Günter's father could be very catastrophic for him and his family. But then he came back to Günter and said that though he was probably not more intelligent than I, that it nevertheless seemed to him that he was making better use of his intelligence. He asked me whether I thought it was Günter, whom I suspected of following his father's beliefs, who was brainwashed, or was it I, who did not? This set me thinking again and I felt I was being sucked into a big cage of confusion, out of which there was no escape. Father must have realised that I was moving into my usual hedgehog position and said, 'I tell you what, I have met Günter's father once or twice, we have talked about you and Günter and we are both happy that you are friends, that you go and see events together and discuss them. I think that his father and I see the world through the same kind of eyes. You must understand that fathers always will try to influence their children, I feel I would not do my duty if I didn't. I want to be honest with you, from what I hear about Günter, I must admit that I envy his father for having managed to make his son see matters of history and politics along the same lines as he does. It is obvious I have not succeeded in this, but my love for you has not diminished in any way. However, there is another way of looking at it. I am a realist, not a dreamer, and considering the political circumstances at present prevailing in our country, I can foresee dangers for Günter. And even though I am convinced that you are wrong in your political analysis, in a strange contradictory way, I am glad about it, as your path might be much smoother than his. But now go to bed, you had a tough day and you look tired.'

I had listened carefully to what he had said and deep inside there was a strong glimmer of recognition that he was right. But there was also that barren stubbornness in me which did not give me the strength to admit it to him or myself. Maybe the Nazi brainwashing had already gone too deep for that, but the conflict did create a wild clash in me and I burst into tears, rushing around the table and slinging my arm around his neck and sobbing uncontrollably. Mother joined us and the three of us held each other. No one spoke a word for some time and then I tore myself away, went to bed and slept deeply in the knowledge that our love for each other was deeper than any disagreement about politics.

CHAPTER VI

Living with Nazism

In our tenement were fourteen flats which were occupied by the same number of families, some of whom took lodgers. Our next-door neighbours were Herr and Frau von Essen, a childless couple of about the same age as my parents. One evening a week, usually on a Saturday, they either came over to us or my parents went over to their flat, where they played cards. They were always kind to me, showed great interest in what I was up to and I liked them. As 'von' before a German name suggests aristocratic origin, more often than not stemming from an impoverished landowning family east of the River Elbe, Herr von Essen, though an unemployed toolmaker with similar political views to my parents', showed considerable pride in what my father called 'breadless heritage'. If someone addressed him merely with Herr Essen, he always politely corrected the person with 'von Essen, if you please.'

His whole way of speaking, as well as his accent, pointed to a better education than my parents'. He apologised at times, saying that he did not want to show off, but that he simply could not help speaking in that way, as his parents had brought him up in that fashion. Apart from official High German, both my parents spoke Plattdeutsch, which was the main language of the countryside and the poor areas of the towns. The von Essens, though they understood Plattdeutsch, never spoke it. We children were not allowed to speak it in school, unless it was treated in the curriculum. Several respected and well-liked authors such as Fritz Renter wrote their entire works in that language. But we children almost exclusively spoke it in the street when we were playing. It flowed so much more easily from our tongues than the more distinctive High German, and seemed to us a much more friendly and personal language.

My parents subscribed to the local paper *Hamburger Anzeiger*, which was delivered to our door every evening except Sundays. I believe that it was a left-wing paper during the period of the Weimar republic, but together with all other newspapers, changed over to supporting Hitler after his rise to power. My father read and discussed extracts from the paper with me, but from the age of about ten I began to read the newspaper for myself. I knew that both my parents were delighted by this eagerness at such early age. They kept reminding me that I must not swallow everything I read in it uncritically and that I must try to separate the bits which were factual from those which reflected the opinion of the editor. Father often tested me on this by reading out either articles or passages and asking me whether I thought them to be facts or opinions. He pointed out that the opinions of the editor reflected the wishes of the owner, who in all cases was a rich person with very different economic interests from working people.

Herr von Essen, whose dole money was probably considerably less than my father's low wage, came every night to collect the *Anzeiger*. He then stayed for a while to discuss current affairs with father. During the period of the Weimar Republic, political discussion was completely uninhibited and I was witness to the many lively debates which took place in our flat, always without fear or any sense of inhibition. The emergence of the Third Reich changed all that, free discussion was no longer possible, and I realise now what a sad shadow Hitler's rise to power cast over our home life and relations with friends and family.

Almost everything said in our kitchen was exactly the opposite of what I was being taught in the Hitler Youth. It bothered me a great deal as I did not know any more what and whom to believe. Naturally I loved my parents deeply and respected Herr von Essen's intelligence and integrity. I wanted my loved ones to be right. But I also loved my Fatherland and firmly believed that our Führer was in the process of giving us back our honour and dignity which the Versailles Dictate had so cruelly taken from us. I realised that I was being torn in two and found it so hard to understand why my parents of all people could not support what the genius of our Führer was doing for us, for Deutschland.

It was about that time that Father had got hold of an old radio set. By now an increasing number of my school friends had a radio at home, and when I heard them in the morning talking about what they had been listening to on the previous evening, I wanted to take part in their discussions and laugh with them about some of the programmes. But now at last the time had come! I could hardly believe my eyes when father came home one afternoon, put a box on to the table and asked me to have a look at what was inside. We had a radio! Suddenly, there it was, we had all heard it, first a kind of faint crackle followed by words and then music, real music for the first time in our kitchen, in our home. We all smiled in utter happiness.

Needless to say, the reception range was limited, although there were larger and far more expensive radios available in the shops but only a very few working class families were able to afford them. I remember the trade names of Telefunken and Blaupunkt which produced, so we were told, outstanding German quality work which was in great demand the world over as the export figures proved. A neighbour of ours, a factory worker,

Herr Krüger, who lived alone in a small flat with his son Karl Heinz, a playmate of mine, had such a Blaupunkt. It was a most beautiful large set with an integrated record player and produced a wonderful sound.

Father had known Herr Krüger over many years. I think that they had been actively involved together in the trade union movement. He then told my mother that he had borrowed money to buy that set and considered it a great advantage that an ordinary worker could do such a thing. But when he then also said that he credited Adolf Hitler with that achievement and that for that reason he had now changed his mind and supported the Nazi Party, it was too much for father to swallow. 'To change his political ideas like a shirt,' he said 'because he is able to buy a radio with borrowed money, shows what kind of man he is, a miserable turncoat.' From then on whenever he met him in the street, he cut him, which was embarrassing to me because his son was my friend.

Compared with Herr Krüger's Blaupunkt, our radio looked very ordinary and our range of reception was nothing as compared to his. Only during the hours of darkness were we able to tune in to foreign stations. At that time it did not really bother us much, as it was not forbidden. To go forward in time, we still had that same set in 1939 when the war started and Hitler announced on the first of September that 'since the early hours of this morning we have been shooting back across the Polish border.' From that day onward it was forbidden to listen to foreign radio stations. The penalty for breaking that order or even for spreading foreign news was death. 'How much lower can one sink?' father wanted to know, 'what an admission of weakness for any government and what a show of contempt for its own people to forbid them to listen to anything which has not gone through Göbbels' sieve.'

But after it had become dark we switched the lights off – why we did that I don't know for when our curtains were drawn no one could see us anyway – we all three huddled around the radio out of which a slight glimmer of light shone, fiddled with the knobs, only whispered to each other and cocked our ears for the faintest of sounds of foreign stations reporting in German. Sometimes we heard steps coming up the communal staircase, switched off at once and waited like thieves in the night for their passing. Though we still outwardly disagreed on most political issues, when we listened like this together for which the penalty was death, I felt very close to father. On one occasion like this he must have felt the same for he put his arm around my shoulder and said, 'whatever the Nazis are doing to us, you are still very much my son.' I was very proud when he said that but deep inside, I felt horrible confusion.

Though Göbbels was not a member of the government when Hitler came to power, the Ministry of Propaganda and People's Information, as it was officially called, was set up shortly afterwards. From then all news was presented from a Nazi point of view, which effectively directed the thinking of the German public. However, right up to the war it was possible to buy foreign newspapers, if only of a limited range. But these were only available in the city centres. It would have been useless to try to sell them in our working class part of the town, as no one would have been able to afford them and secondly, no one was able to read them.

Most articles or reports in our *Hamburger Anzeiger* concerned themselves with local or national issues. Foreign news, except in a very general sense, was rare. If the paper went into more detail, it dovetailed the news in such a way that, given the line of comparison, all things German appeared in a superior light. We did read about Sir Oswald Mosley and his blackshirts, how they courageously marched through London, shouting anti-Jewish slogans and urging their own government to make Britain fit and clean for British people to live in, and calling for a better understanding with Germany.

Another British name repeatedly mentioned in our media was Mr. Montague Norman, the Governor of the Bank of England. He visited Germany on numerous occasions and was said to be a personal friend of Dr. Hjalmar Schacht, financial wizard and President of the Reichsbank. Montague Norman was presented as one of the most valuable friends Germany had abroad. Father reckoned that he provided the main channel for the considerable influx of British investment into German rearmament. 'Where profit is king, national borders between the main capitalist country means very little,' father remarked. To him the wallet was the capitalist's country. One of the main slogans of the Nazi regime was that our country was 'the bulwark against bolshevism', and if I remember correctly, it was credited to Mr. Norman.

At some time in the middle thirties one of the largest halls in Germany, if not the largest, had been constructed in the Rothenburgsort area of Hamburg. A year or so later, I believe, Hitler came to Hamburg and gave one of his big speeches in the Hanseatenhalle. I went there for that occasion and, needless to say, not with my father but with the Hitler Youth. What was a bit unusual about that event was that none of us was ordered to attend, as we had been for previous Führer visits. To go or not to go was simply left to the individual. Nazi ideology had taken such root and was so firmly embedded in the minds of the young, that there was no longer a need to pressurise any of them when it came to hearing their beloved Führer.

And when the great day came, all of us went. We met at the Altona main railway station where it was announced that the rail fare was to be paid by the party. The short journey took us to Hamburg Main Station, from where we marched in column to Rothenburgsort which was about half an hour away. In those days people in the cities were accustomed to marching and singing brown columns, all part of Nazi advertising as father called it. The boy in front, marching on his own, carried the Hitler

Youth swastika flag which was slightly different from the usual one, having a wide, white horizontal strip in the centre. Behind him marched a couple of pipers and drummers followed by us, the peasant soldiers or Hitler's Grenadiers as we sometimes called ourselves.

On a march like this, not really more than a walk, our leaders roamed around us like wolves and seldom marched in column. They walked on the pavements, sometimes arrogantly brushing aside pedestrians, ordering us to sing and at times shouted at those who had become sloppy and were marching out of step. Talking amongst ourselves was forbidden. The title of the song was then shouted through from the front to the rear and when the rearguard one had understood it, he shouted 'durch' (through). Then the one on the right in the leading row shouted in line with our stepping 'two, three', after which we started singing with full throat. As we all knew the words, our singing was always effective and melodic. Passers-by looked at us admiringly and smiled, making us feel proud.

It was already dark and a pleasant evening when we reached our destination, the Hanseatenhalle. Many people were already milling around outside, some in ordinary clothes, nearly all men, and most dressed in brown. Marching and singing columns were constantly arriving and within the hall everything was well organised. Most people were well disciplined and obeyed the instructions of the stewards, who were all big fellows and in brown. Close to the main stage was a large roped-off area into which we the Hitler Youth were directed. We had arrived in good time as we usually did on big occasions like this, but that did not bother us as there was so much to see, listen to and laugh about. A Nazi Frauenschaft (female party section) group was entertaining us with songs accompanied by a large SA orchestra. They played folk songs as well as popular classics.

From time to time there were announcements from the stage, all given in a friendly almost festive manner, and more and more people were continuously streaming in, slowly filling the hall. Many were smoking and, looking up, I watched the smoke curling around the large lamps as if attracted by its light, giving a dream-like impression. Large swastika flags were everywhere, hanging down from the beams, arranged against the walls, draped around the supporting pillars and all along the stage. Flags and banners were not cheap, showing that the Nazi Party had access to money. To us, Nazism had very effectively created a warm atmosphere of unity and togetherness.

Then someone announced that the Führer had arrived outside the hall. It was said that he liked to come a little late on purpose, perhaps to heighten the expectation of the waiting crowd. Fanfares from close to the main door sent their piercing cries into the hall followed by the snarling rolling of the drums. This was it, we knew, the evening was now going to begin in earnest. We heard commands being shouted, names were introduced, weapons presented, heels clicked and all seemed to go off with great military exactness. And now came what we had been waiting for for over an hour. The Führer had stepped in. It was a great feeling, we were now under the same roof as he. Someone next to me was convinced that he actually felt an electric charge coming from the Führer, and for a split moment, I thought that I felt the same.

A wide carpeted gangway had been kept free from the door to the steps by the stage, lined on both sides by SA and SS along which Adolf Hitler now stepped. In those days he still wore his brown uniform, which on the very first day of war he changed into field-grey, promising not to take it off until final victory. Several subdued jokes on this promise were of course making the rounds, about the eventual smelly condition of the uniform.

A small group of about five or six, in brown or black uniforms, were walking with him. All we could see, however, was the bobbing of the heads and the almost continuously raised hand of the Führer. Around him was much 'heil' shouting, with hands shooting up into the air while further back and around us, eager faces and stretched necks were trying to get an early glimpse of the greatest man on earth. At least that's what most of us youngsters thought. Right in front of the stage was a large empty area and once the Führer had reached it, he was fully in our view. A prettily dressed little girl was ushered towards him by a woman in brown. Hitler took off his cap, wedged it under his armpit, brushed his hair back with a slight swipe of his hand, took the flowers, touched her head saying something to her, to which she freely responded. There was a slight smile on his face.

I had seen Adolf Hitler before but not from that close and this time in spite of my great joy, my first impression was a bit disappointing. But I quickly brushed that fleeting thought aside as not being true. He was much smaller than I thought he was and in my mind I had to agree with father, that everything around him was always very cleverly stage-managed. At all official events no tall person was ever seen standing or walking close to him. All this notwithstanding, I was now shouting my 'heil, heil' with everyone else. By now the Führer had climbed up the four or five steps to the row of chairs at the back of the stage, turned round, acknowledged the shouting all around and sat down. There was very little expression on his face and I wondered whether he might perhaps be nervous. Further towards us close to the edge of the stage stood the slightly elevated rostrum.

Then Hamburg's Gauleiter Karl Kaufmann walked to the microphone next to the rostrum and beckoned us all by the movement of his hand to quieten down. He had to do that several times as no one seemed to take any notice of him. But when he had almost succeeded, he made the mistake of turning round to where the Führer was as if to say, 'see how popular you are with the people of Hamburg', after which the shouting started once again and he had to resume his quietening-down gestures. Karl Kaufmann then made his introductory speech in which he said that it was totally unnecessary to introduce the Führer to us. He knew that we all loved him and went on to suggest that tonight no one in his or her senses would want to listen to a long tirade from Karl Kaufmann but had come to hear what Adolf Hitler, our beloved Führer, had to say. With that he beckoned to the rear and handed over to Hitler, who then stepped up to the rostrum.

The applause was tremendous. It was as if all hell had broken loose, as if we had all gone mad. We had completely forgotten who and where we were. Everyone seemed to have only one thought, one single wish: to show loyalty and love to the Führer, who was now standing firmly on the rostrum. The 'heil' shouting slowly receded after several minutes, when Hitler pushed a palm of his hand tentatively in front of him. That was how he indicated he was ready to speak to us, but it was only when he made an unmistakable sign of impatience, that the noise died down. And suddenly, no one probably really realised it, there was deep silence all over the large hall. Hardly a suppressed cough could be heard anywhere.

However, with all eyes now fixed on him, the great man had chosen to let us wait a little. Where he had shown impatience before, he now seemed to be in no hurry. It was almost a bit eerie. Was it because he intended to punish us for having been naughty? But one thing was certain: he was totally in command of himself and the situation. He looked in front of him as if looking at a bit of paper. He raised his arms slightly to grip the elevated sides of the rostrum and looked patiently to the right, the centre and then to the left. Next he looked right down in front of him where we were, his Hitler Youth. But still, not a word, neither from him nor from anyone else. Under the circumstances who amongst the crowd would have dared to speak anyway?

But then it came, slowly at first, rolling the vocals, 'Deutsche Volksgenossen and Genossinnen' (German male and female comrades), the beginning of the first formal sentences. I am not sure any more exactly what followed, probably that he had come to Hamburg, our great city, having joyously accepted the invitation of our Karl Kaufmann. His Austrian accent, so very different from ours, sounded very pronounced. But that did not disturb us, he was as good a German, if not better, than all of us. We all knew of course that he had been born in 1889 in the small Austrian town of Braunau on the River Inn just across the border from Bavaria. In the Great War he had fought with distinction as a volunteer in the Bavarian Regiment List, in appreciation of which he had received the Iron Cross First Class, which he was now wearing.

In the beginning of the speech there were few interruptions because so much of what he was saying was known and expected routine. All over the hall were loudspeakers. None were too close to us in front and though at times we had difficulty in understanding what he was saying, we had the privilege to listen to the natural tone of his voice. His hair was still very much in place. But after a while, after he had got excited or genuinely angry about something and started to bang the rostrum, that famous strand of hair slipped down to his eyebrow. And after that came what we had all been waiting for, no holds were barred, the real speech-making had begun.

I have forgotten now what the main content of the speech was, but I remember him swearing about Jews, communists, plutocrats and other wily traitors, whose opportunities to freely milk the good German people had now come to an end. The applause was tremendous. Everyone looked happy, had their arms in the air, shouting 'heil, heil' as loud as they could. The speech must have lasted for more than an hour, having been inter-rupted a number of times. Whenever that happened, the Führer showed no impatience but looked around the hall as if judging the effect he was having on the crowd. When he came to the end, he finished with some sort of threatening sentence, raised his hand in his usual salute and quickly stepped down and back to his seat. The roar was terrific. Those sitting next to him stood up to cheer him by clapping their hands in a measured way, beaming all over their faces until Gauleiter Kaufmann strode up to the rostrum, thanked the Führer on behalf of us all and declared the rally closed.

That was when the National Anthem was played, a combination of the Deutschland and the Horst Wessel songs. Horst Wessel, as all those hostile to the Nazis knew, had been a Berlin pimp before he had joined the SA, and had died in a fight in the gutter where father thought he rightly belonged. All now stood up including the Führer and one could see them singing. With that over, he and his cronies, again to tremendous applause, walked out the same way as they had come in, and only then the thousands began to stream out. We too went home the same way as we had come. On the train, guided by our leaders, we animatedly discussed the great event and found that we had very little to say about the actual speech, it was all about the performance as such. Thinking about it now, sixty years later, none of us had really come to listen, just to take part in a big event, in a tremendous rally.

When I got home father was reading to mother from a book. When I wanted to tell them about my Hitler evening, mother simply cut me short and said, 'No, not tonight, Junge, it is late and tomorrow is another day. By then you will have cooled down a bit and will be less excited.' Father just sat there, looked at me over his glasses and smiled. He knew and understood his son only too well.

On another occasion, I arrived at school to find an atmosphere of great excitement. Something extraordinary and of great importance had happened, we were told. Under the Führer's orders, German troops had marched into the German Rhineland and had thereby torn asunder another shackle of the Versailles chain. Our whole school was called together for announcement of the news. The Gemeinschaftsempfang (common reception) was held in the Aula where Herr Duggen, the rector, himself delivered a speech on the issue. After the rector's introduction we listened to the Führer's speech on the radio. At the best of times the sounds from the loudspeakers were rather scratchy and with his Austrian accent, we found it all rather difficult to understand. Anyway, we knew the facts by now. But there was one thing which we did understand: the horrible ghost of Clemenceau expressed in the Dictate of Versailles, by which we were forbidden to have any of our soldiers between the French border and a line fifty kilometres east of the River Rhine, was now dead as a result of the decision and action of our great Führer, Adolf Hitler. From the moment he had come into office, and even before that, he had promised to make Germany free again and he was in the process of doing it right now. The new Germany was coming of age and the world had better look out.

We always loved a meeting like this for it shortened the school day. But this time there was really something else, it was as if we felt it in our bones, we knew that something very special, something very important had happened. And it whetted our appetite for more to come. When we streamed out of the Aula, the excitement could be seen on all our faces. When I came home to tell mother that we had had no lessons that day but instead had listened to the Führer, she showed annoyance and only a very negative appreciation of the news of the German occupation of the Rhineland. She implored me not to go for father on his coming home with this dreadful story. She reminded me how father hated everything connected with the military, because he knew the human suffering involved through being a soldier.

When he did come home, I did what mother had asked. I did not say a word about it but behaved in such a challenging way, that he walked right into my trap. He asked me what I was grinning about and suggested that it was probably that ghastly Rhineland story which he had heard about at work. Mother saw trouble coming and tried to stand between us. But father very gently eased her to the side, came close to me, held me by my shoulders and said that he understood why I was so caught up in Germany's renewed rise to military power, but asked me to try to understand how he felt about it, having experienced the tragedy of the war in France. It pained him deeply to see a new generation of soldiers being led along the same route as his generation had been. The Rhineland occupation had not led to war yet but he was sure that it would be the first step towards it.

All the time he was speaking to me, mother hovered behind us, pleading with her eyes and by gestures for me to let father speak and not to interrupt him. He went on to say that he fully understood how difficult it was for me at my young age not to fall for all the military razzmatazz. The Rhineland occupation, he was sure, was much more than simply that, it was the testing of the water, watching what France and Britain would do, and depending on that, more occupations would follow. He told me that he was deeply disappointed that our former enemies were letting Hitler get away with it, for which in the end humanity would pay the price. 'In 1914,' he said, 'it was dangerous to talk about peace. If you did, people said that you were a traitor. Today the same thing is happening all over again. It is sheer tragedy.'

My father's attitude was largely explained by what had happened to him and his friends in the First World War. Though he possessed three or four medals, he had put them away in a small wooden box in a chest of drawers, which he showed to me a couple of times, but never wore. It made me sad to hear him say that they were nothing but emblems of human stupidity, brutality and arrogance rooted in ignorance. I would have been so proud of him had he appeared on Totensonntag (Remembrance Day) and worn them, so that the people in our street could have seen them.

He told me that he had not forgotten his many dead comrades and more so the circumstances in which their lives had been taken from them. He always used this form of speech, instead of the official version which was that they had given their lives for their Fatherland. Neither did he view them as heroes as our nationalists wanted us to see them, but as victims who had been led like lambs to slaughter, not even knowing what they were supposed to be dying for.

'Afterwards when we laid them out,' he said, 'we prayed and sang as their cold bodies were lowered into French soil. Sometimes when we had too many corpses, we put two together or five or ten or even a hundred into one grave. They all had parents somewhere, wives or children who were later informed by official letter that their loved ones had given their lives for Kaiser and Fatherland. We were sad then, sincerely sad because they had been our friends, our comrades, not like those who today march to the memorial as a kind of a show. When we came home on leave, we visited some of the relatives who showed us the letters they had received from our commanding officer. Of course we did not say anything to them. But all the letters contained the same words that their son, husband or father had died a hero and had been one of the finest soldiers of the regiment.'

There had been a joke about it, saying that if a German soldier was lucky enough to survive a battle, he might get the Iron Cross, of the lowest order of course, but if he did not and all the parts of his body could be found and put together into a bag, he might get the wooden cross, provided enough wood was lying around. He told me about a comrade of his who, like everyone including himself, had been terrified at climbing up what they called the 'ladder of death', to make a hurrah attack. This comrade had soiled his trousers through terror, and had fallen backwards into the trench the moment he had reached the parapet, with a bullet through his head. My father stressed that he certainly did not want to speak badly about him, quite the contrary. He was only telling me this so that I could realise what stupid, hypocritical lies surrounded everything associated with that war. What annoyed him more than anything was the role of the regimental clergy who used the name of Jesus, the prince of peace, to justify this criminal mass slaughter of the innocents.

My father's reaction to the invasion of the Rhineland was typical of his attitude to war. But soon after the invasion, an event occurred which distracted all of us from a preoccupation with war and gave a sorely needed boost to Nazi respectability, both at home and abroad. It was announced that the ex-King of England, now Herzog (Duke) von Windsor and his Herzogin were to visit Germany in a private capacity. The Nazis, with Göbbels' sharp appreciation of good propaganda, made the most of this unexpected and rare opportunity. The reception in Berlin was shown in the cinemas on the weekly newsreel, die Wochenschauen. The friendliness towards them was tremendous. Hitler greeted them personally and then invited them for a visit to his Berghof on the Obersalzberg near Berchtesgaden. Wherever the royal couple went, they were warmly greeted by masses of people who had been thoroughly prepared for the visit by long and glowing articles in the newspapers. The couple were shown around many places, met lowly factory workers, talked and had lunch with them in their spotless canteens.

They also attended a rally of swastika-waving Hitler Youth where the Duke made a statement, quickly picked up by all who were only too eager to make use of it, saying that German youth was indeed very fortunate to live at such a momentous time, in such a great society. This statement, needless to say, was the main theme of our next Hitler Youth meeting. It not only made us feel proud but boosted our morale and determination to tread even more firmly on the path marked out by Adolf Hitler. Whatever the outside world's criticism of us, and we had heard quite a bit about that, the Herzog von Windsor had wiped all that away with one swoop. It confirmed to us that our Nazi society was something to be proud of. After all who could doubt the truth of what a man of his standing, a former King of England, was saying?

Another event of very great importance at this time was the 1936 Olympic Games. Naturally I would have loved to have gone to Berlin, but I was not yet fourteen years old and my parents could not afford to pay for such a trip. I knew of a group of young men from down our street who went to the Olympics on the back of a lorry. They had managed to get tickets, had slept in tents in the woods and had had the time of their lives, as they said, never to be forgotten.

I think it was on the second day of the games that Jesse Owens, the legendary black American athlete, ran in the final of the hundred metres and swept all competition before him. On the next day he also received gold medals for the two hundred metres, the relay and the long jump, a feat no athlete had ever achieved before. It was said that earlier on that day Hitler had personally congratulated a couple of German and other white winners of events and there was much speculation as to whether he would stay and congratulate Jesse Owens as well. It was said that he actually watched him win but then left the stadium abruptly, no doubt to avoid the dilemma of having to congratulate a black man on his success. Many eyebrows were raised and even I felt that had been a mean gesture. But as to Owens, no party directive nor the behaviour of our Führer could have prevented him from becoming the darling of an over-enthusiastic German crowd.

During the games, the euphoria especially amongst us young people was tremendous. Our work at school was much neglected as all we could think about were the games. A medal league table was set up every day in most newspapers which showed the points every team had reached. All of us at school, in the streets and in the Hitler Youth, followed its changing fortunes with great patriotic interest. Right from the start the German team did well. There was disappointment during the first week that the Americans were more successful in track events than we were and occupied the top position in the table. However the gods of sport were clearly with us, for during the second week the scales of success began to tip our way. In the more technical disciplines, like fencing, rowing and equestrian events, the German team was better prepared than the American and so step by step, point by point, we edged past them. For us youngsters it was a nail-biting experience to the very last day. But it all worked out all right and at the last count we, Germany, were the winners by a few points. A wave of unbridled patriotism swept the youth of our country. To pretend that participating was more important than winning was not necessary any more. We had won!

We learned at school that having won the Olympics was proof of our national and racial superiority over others and many believed that it was thanks to our national-socialist ideology and of course to our Führer, that we had achieved this fantastic triumph. When father heard me coming out with this, a crooked smile lit his face which told me that he felt sure of having caught me out once again. He said he would have given a whole week's wages to have travelled to Berlin to watch our great Führer, preferably in long johns, run the 100 metres against Jesse Owens. Even I had to laugh at the mere thought of such a spectacle and for a couple of minutes or so forgot my adoration of our Führer. But out of respect for him, I did not repeat the joke to anyone else.

One day I came home from the pictures where I had watched a U-Boat film called *Morgenrot* (*Red Dawn*). It showed a German submarine hit by a torpedo lying on the bottom of the sea bed, its mariners drowning one by one. It was a real tear-jerker. The theme song was also called 'Morgenrot' and was about soldiers who had to die. The melody was beautiful, at least to my ears and I liked it. It depicted soldiers who were willing to die for the Fatherland, as if it were something great, something holy.

Mother, hearing me singing it over and over again, asked me what the stupid song was. When I told her it was not stupid but heroic and good, she asked whether I really thought that dying, especially while one was still young and healthy, was a good thing and whether I really would like to sacrifice my life for the Fatherland, the Führer or anyone else. After all, she pointed out, it had been her who had given me life in the first place. Well, I really had not thought about it in that way and after turning it over in my mind, I said: 'You know, it need not necessarily be me. But if we ever did get into a situation in which we had to fight a war whether it be in a U-Boat or fighting on a battlefield, some soldiers simply would have to die, give their lives for the Fatherland, so that others can live in freedom. Is it not said in the Bible that there is no greater sacrifice than laying down one's life for others?'

'So you would give your life which after all I have given you, for others? For which others? Please tell me what you mean.'

'Well for Deutschland, don't you know the quotation which we have learnt in the Hitler Youth "Deutschland muss leben und wenn wir sterben müssen (Germany must live even if we do have to die)."'

'But once you are dead, you won't be aware of anything any more. Deutschland then, which you make sound so holy and which to me is nothing but a geographical entity, will then mean nothing to you. And who do you think you will really help by that stupid sacrifice of yours? Moreover what do you think it would mean to father and me if we got a letter from France or Russia telling us that you had died on the battlefield as a hero? And please do not think that dying on the battlefield is a nice and heroic thing. They might tell you such stupid rubbish in the Hitler Youth about dying with a song on your lips and a painless little bullet hole just where your heart is. But if you would only listen to father, he will tell you that in most cases dying on the battlefield is very different from what the patriotic youngsters think it is. Soldiers are torn to pieces with their guts hanging out, screaming with pain.'

'But then, mother, I would have died for you and for father to protect you against our enemies.'

'But I have no enemies and I don't want to have any. The only enemy I can think of is your Hitler and most of the other top Nazis, though I have no intention of trying to kill them. I want to be friendly with all people, be they German, French, English or Russian.

143

'I can't think of any reason while whole nations should think of others as their enemies. But enough of this now. You are my child and the very last thing I want is that you should die for me. I want you to look after yourself and be good and considerate to other people, never mind in which country they happen to live. Now go out and play football, I think I can hear your friends calling you and for heaven's sake stop singing that stupid song, "Morgenrot".'

Mother was very unlike father. Where he confronted me squarely and bombarded me with logic and fact, mother was far more effective in convincing me to see things her way. She opened her heart to me and appealed from the loving side of the argument, which brought it back to an essential human meaning, robbing me of all my wordy defences. That's why I never liked arguing with her. Mother died after the horrendous bombing of Hamburg, when my parents lost everything they had ever possessed. She would have forgiven anyone for their misdeeds, perhaps even Bomber Harris, but he ended her life before she could do that.

I must have been sixteen or seventeen years old just before the war started, when one day mother asked me to sit down with her because she wanted to discuss something serious with me, which very much troubled her.

'Soon when you are eighteen years old, you will be called up to the army and I hope that by that time there won't be a war. I know that you, like most of your friends, have all these big ideas in your head about Fatherland, Führer, glory and such like, and as your father cannot manage to get them out of you, I will not even attempt to do so.' I just sat there, and as the best line of defence said nothing, thinking 'why is she telling me all this?' She hesitated slightly as if searching for the right words, and then in her quiet way said something about the military state of ours having in so many ways put barriers between parents and their children, that she now had to be careful to use the right words in conversation with her own son. I muttered something about not seeing it in that light at all, becoming impatient with her. Naturally the last thing I wanted was to hurt her, but I nevertheless became annoyed with her beating about the bush, and asked her outright to please come out with what she wanted to ask or tell me.

Well, she had heard about several youngsters in the neighbourhood, who were under eighteen and had volunteered for the SS, with their parents completely unable to do anything about it. 'But what has it got to do with me, Mutti? I have no intention of joining the SS, but even if I did, what would be so very wrong with that?'

I could see that she was visibly upset. 'Please, Henry, do not ask me this question. Believe me, I could give you a straight and very telling answer. But as things stand, and that's what I mean by barriers between parents and children, it is better to leave it at that, and in any case we need not talk about it further, as you have now promised not to join the SS.'

'No, Mutti, I have promised no such thing, all I have said is that I have no intention of volunteering for the SS. I hadn't really thought about it until you brought it up. But later when I am eighteen and will be called up anyway, what would be so terrible if I join the SS, instead of the ordinary Wehrmacht? The SS on the whole seems superior to the ordinary Wehrmacht. One has to be something special to join the SS.'

'Please, Henry, please, please, please, for my sake, don't join the SS – please.' I noticed that she was close to tears, so I promised in a half-hearted manner that I would not join, just to keep the peace, but I urged her to give me at least one good reason. To simply ask me not to volunteer for the SS was not good enough. Was it the name, was it the uniform, was it that they saluted not in the ordinary but in the Hitler way, what was it?

'Well, I will tell you and you must promise me, not ever to pass this on to anyone. Father and I know of a number of people who have been taken to concentration camps as if they were criminals, which we know they are not. They have broken no law. The whole reason they have been sent there is because they do not agree with the policies of our present Government. Or do you think that is a crime?'

'And if it is really as you say, what has it got to do with the SS?'

'The SS, Henry, is guarding the camps.' Never having given it a thought before, I asked her how she knew all this, but she refused to tell me. She then got up rather abruptly and I feared she would burst into tears. 'You have now given me your promise and that is all I want.' I too got up, held her tightly and just nodded. But I thought about it for the rest of the day and it bothered me a great deal. But being so young, then came the Hitler Youth again, the marches, the flags, the drums and the singing, with which I so easily pushed all these disturbing thoughts on to the back burner, and mother and I never mentioned that conversation again. The trouble was that I could tell no one, could not discuss the issue even with father, though I am sure that he knew about it all along, and anyway as it so happened, I did not volunteer for the SS and only joined a Panzer division of the Wehrmacht when I was called up at the age of eighteen.

Father told me one day that his friend Otti Prautsch, had been somewhat careless at work, saying that we should be striving for peace and not preparing for war. As a result, he had a visit a few days later from several brown-shirted young hooligans. As soon as he opened the door, they had simply barged into his sitting room. Shouting loudly, so that all his neighbours could hear, they warned him in the presence of his wife and daughter, that if he did not mend his ways, they would take him away for a stint of what they called reeducation in a concentration camp. Then they had left. Otti had become very worried about it all, had become ill and his boss had sent him to the industrial doctor for examination. But the doctor was well known for being an ardent Nazi, so Otti could not even tell him about the probable reason for his illness and had to go on suffering in silence.

'Look at me,' father said, taking me by the shoulders as he often did when emotion got the better of him, 'I know that at heart you are a good boy. You cannot help that you have been born into this terrible period in which the brown pest has taken hold of you, and if they found out what I am telling you now, they would deal with me at least in the same way as they have done with Otti – and perhaps even worse. That is the cold reality of the freedom they have left us with. Can you not see that it cannot be right to threaten fine ordinary working people like Otti in this way?'

This was too much for me, I simply did not know how to respond to that and I started to cry. I very much liked his friend Otti, who often came to see us and who, I was absolutely sure, was a good man. I hated the idea that he and his family were being treated in this way, but I also loved Germany, my Germany which I did not like to be undermined by anyone in any way. It was all so awful, so confusing, so difficult to understand. Father realised it, and apologised for having talked so harshly, patted me on the back and eased my heartache by telling me that he loved me.

I think it was a typical German custom to celebrate political events, birthdays of leaders and national holidays with 'Flaggen heraus' ('out with the flags'). People fitted brackets to the lower wooden part of their windows into which they stuck short flagpoles. The flags were usually about 150 by 100 centimetres, some larger, not many smaller. Before Hitler's coming to power, there had been a great variety of flags. Each political party had its own, most of them were tricolours. The conservatives' was black-white-red while the socialists' showed black-red-gold and the communists' the hammer and sickle in the top right corner of red cloth. Some ex-soldiers even hung out their regimental flags, the more war-torn the better. By just walking through the streets on celebration days you could see which parties the tenants supported. I am sure that within large working class tenements, many political arguments if not personal enmities must have arisen from this.

Father never hung one out. I know that during the Weimar days some of his friends had urged him to do so, because it would give encouragement to like-minded others. But he did not like this way of posturing, thought that it was somewhat vulgar to hang one's political belief out of the window and that it was not fair to his family. When the Nazis came to power, the whole situation changed drastically. From 1934 onwards it demanded much personal courage to hang out any flag other than that of the swastika. The last people sticking to their individual preferences were the militarists with their regimental flags, and a few of the right-wing nationalists like *Stahlheim* (Steel Helmet). After a while these too disappeared and only swastika flags were from then on seen fluttering in the Nazi breeze.

Josef Göbbels, always wide awake to opportunities, made the most of this flag-hanging custom. Usually a day or so before important dates in

146

the national calendar, newspapers carried the front page reminder 'Flaggen heraus'. Ignoring for the moment the politically dark side of it all, so many flags full of strong colours fluttering in the breeze created a festive atmosphere in the often drab and grey working class streets, which to my eyes was beautiful.

I cannot judge whether Germans at that time gave more significance to their flags than other nations, but I am sure that my generation, and I think that of my father's too, was brought up with the notion that a flag, especially a national one, was more than just a piece of cloth, but was something holy. We learned a number of songs about brave soldiers dying in defence of their flags and to their last moment considering the saving of the flag as an honour. The main, the signature tune of the Hitler Youth started:

> *Unsere Fahne flattert uns voran,*
> *unsere Fahne ist die neue Zeit,*
> *unsere Fahne ist mehr als die Ewigkeit,*
> *unsere Fahne ist mehr als der Tod*

> *(Our flag flutters in front of us,*
> *our flag is the new time,*
> *our flag means more than eternity,*
> *our flag is more than death.)*

If I remember correctly, only two family heads of fourteen living in our tenement were members of the Nazi Party at the time when that party came to office in 1933. The rest were considered at best non-enthusiastic apoliticals. The ground floor flats were occupied by two shopkeepers and their families, one a grocer, the other a chemist. As flags sticking out of their windows would have obstructed the pavement, swastika Führer posters or something of that kind were exhibited in their shop windows. No more than three or four flags decorated our grey tenement façade during the early Nazi period. From then on the numbers increased gradually, with every new one putting pressure on the rest to follow suit. Below us lived a postman, a Herr Haack who had finally succumbed to hanging a flag out. I heard him say one day to my father: 'Well Fritz you know how it is and what I think about it all, but I have a family to support, my job is with the government which I want to keep and also there is the question of promotion.'

Towards the middle thirties there were only three or four families left without a flag, which the Nazis attached great importance to. I kept pleading with my father to hang out a flag too, as I very much wanted to see one fluttering from our window. Some of my playmates remarked on the Metelmanns not showing one, which made me feel awkward. As I wanted to say nothing against my father, I explained it away by saying that flags were expensive and that father was bringing home a low wage. But then on one fine summer evening, looking up from the street, I could hardly believe my eyes. From our corner window, lustily fluttering in the breeze, hung a swastika flag, not one of the largest, but of decent size. Much excited I rushed up the four flights of stairs to meet mother at the door, who sheepishly grinned, pleading with me not to upset father by mentioning the flag. But how could I say nothing, I was vibrating with unconcealed joy? I walked into the front room and found father sitting by the window in a most filthy mood. He looked at me in a certain way expressing a look of defeat but which always made me love him. There was no doubt that this time he had been beaten, thoroughly beaten, and with that very divided feeling of loyalty and love I asked him how it had all come about.

'That damned August Stiebert,' he said, 'I have known all along that he had it in for me. If he is stupid enough to join the brownshirts and hang out their flag, that is his business, but why does he have to interfere with me, poke his stupid nose into my business?' I wondered how Stiebert had managed it. I liked him, our neighbour on the same floor with his large family, who was always friendly to me. He held a job as a labourer across the river at one of the ship works, where he drove an electric loader and felt himself important, as if he were managing director. According to father he had been one of those loud-mouthed social democrats who had spouted lots of empty words during the Weimar days.

Then it slowly came out why we had a flag hanging from our window. Quite out of the blue, Stiebert had knocked on the door and told father that, as a token of friendship, he was going to give his flag to us, having bought a larger one for himself. According to mother he handed father his flag, saying something like, 'Fritz I know you as a good German, front-line soldier, the Somme, Verdun, the mud, being wounded for the Fatherland. You are also the quiet type, modern politics don't seem to be your line. But that doesn't matter to me, that is entirely your business, after all, we live in a free country and we are all different in our own way. I am totally sure that deep down you love our Führer like the rest of us Germans. So I have decided to give you my old flag, and will give you a hand with fixing the bracket straight away.' As it so happened, he had brought a screwdriver and screws with him.

Mother told me afterwards that she, having quickly seen the funny side of it, would have loved to have taken a photo of father, standing in the door frame as if struck by lightning, holding the stick with the swastika flag as if he were on parade and not quite knowing whether to smile or knock Stiebert over the head with it. The latter, not even waiting for an answer, all the time nattering and laughing in his friendly manner, squeezed past father into the front room, opened the window and started hammering and screwing away. Well, what could father do or say except whimper: 'Thank you, August, that is really nice of you, but are you sure that you don't want any money for it?' But Stiebert declined, saying that he was doing it for the Führer and for Deutschland and of course for a good friend and neighbour. He then asked father to give him a hand with the screws which he did, knocking them into the woodwork as if he was hammering the devil himself.

After I heard the whole story, I could not but burst out laughing. Mother joined in, glancing apologetically at father, but then he too, realising the ridiculousness of the situation, started to shake his head in almost disbelief and laughed and laughed. 'What a stupid trap to fall into,' he kept repeating, 'to be caught like that by that loveable stupid fool Stiebert of all people.' But then he put on his serious face again, looked straight at me and said, 'I know that you will not pass on to anyone what I am saying here between our own four walls, at least not until these blasted Nazis have been wiped out of Germany for good. Please remember to the end of your life that it was not I who stuck this vile swastika flag out of our window. I would never have believed that one day I would have been forced so low. It was old stupid Stiebert who made me do it and I could do nothing about it, not a thing. And how am I going to explain it to my workmates tomorrow?'

After the Nazis came to power in 1933 many things in Germany were reorganised. One of the new developments was the division of the country into Gaue. A Gau was an old German word for something like a district, an area. The Nazis liked to rummage in German history to drag out what suited them. At the head of the Gau stood the Gauleiter (leader). Hitler himself had appointed each one of them, mostly for loyal services rendered. Almost all of them had been his party cronies in the early days, when they started their political campaign in the beer cellars of Munich. There was no doubt in anyone's mind that no group of people anywhere were more loyal to Hitler than his Gauleiters. Their decisive influence cut right across all other administrative power in their Gaue. The wider region of Hamburg was called the 'Free Imperial and Hansa City', which since the Middle Ages had been an independent city state with its own government. As a result, Hamburg became a Gau in its own right and Karl Kaufmann its first Gauleiter.

His appearance was typical of many top Nazis, short and stocky with a thick neck. Father's view was that their necks were so thick because their brains had slipped into them. It was easy to imagine Kaufmann in his younger days wading into anyone who gave the slightest impression of disagreement with the official speaker. They didn't ask questions before they beat people up and threw them out. Father made no secret of his intense dislike for the Gauleiters, but I do remember him saying that the people of Hamburg had been more fortunate than other Gaue for having

Karl Kaufmann imposed on them, as he seemed more civilised than the others. If I remember correctly, father's opinion was later shared by the British Commander who occupied Hamburg in 1945 and found that, against Hitler's orders, Kaufmann had not allowed wanton destruction of important places like bridges etc. in his Gau, which would have inflicted more unnecessary suffering on the people.

Kaufmann arrived one day at our school totally out of the blue. Before anyone realised what was going on, a couple of black Mercedes pulled up outside the school building, heavy jackboots were coming up the stairs and our corridor, followed by a quick knock knock and in stepped three or four men in smart brown uniforms. That was Kaufmann's way of surprising people, something he clearly enjoyed. We had all seen photos of our Gauleiter in the newspaper and recognised him at once. So did Herr Hinck, our teacher, who started to behave like a headless chicken, not knowing what to do, nor what to say. He just gaped at Kaufmann, but to collect himself, he went half-way towards him, raised his hand and said: 'Heil Hitler, Herr Gauleiter, this is my so-and-so class, my name is Johannes Hinck, and your visit is indeed an honour to us.' Kaufmann made it easy for him. He stretched out his hand and said something like: 'Heil Hitler, Herr Hinck, how nice to meet you and what a good-looking class you have here.'

He then turned to us 'Heil Hitler, class, what a joy to meet you and see so many happy and eager faces. Now don't let me disturb you, carry on as normal with your lesson. We just came up the corridor and as this was the first door, we knocked, as you must have heard and here we are. Try to ignore us, all I want is to stand here and listen and watch you at work.' Of course, he was asking the impossible. 'Just carry on as normal and ignore me.' How could we? Here suddenly in our class room stood the most powerful man in Hamburg, far more important than even the Lord Mayor. Herr Hinck, still all over the place, made a feeble attempt to continue. But as all of us were staring at the Gauleiter and none was taking any notice of what Hinck was saying, it all ebbed away into an embarrassingly empty silence. But then Kaufmann, realising the situation he had created, came to the rescue and broke the ice. Semi-apologising to Hinck, he strode right across the classroom close to where I was and asked my friend sitting next to me what his name was. My friend stuttered and spluttered as if he had forgotten it, when Kaufmann touched the crown of his head, sat down on the desk in front of us with his jackboots on the seat and asked him whether he liked it at school. My friend said something like, 'well, yes and no, but what I really would like is to step out into real grown-up life, and the earlier the better.'

'Oh, I can understand that only too well,' Kaufmann quipped. 'You might not think so judging by my crinkled face and greying temples, but I can well remember the time when I was as old as you are now. Like you,

I could not get out of school quickly enough. But that was before the Great War when dark, threatening clouds were already drifting towards the Fatherland and times were extremely tough for all of us Germans. I was lucky to get an apprenticeship and was full of myself, convinced that the good life was just round the corner. But that warm feeling did not last long. Once I had started to go to work, my enthusiasm for it disappeared like the air out of a pricked balloon. I had to get up very early to be at work at seven and it did not take me long to wish that I were back at school, that I had all my free time again and could play football with my friends. Having spouted out all the big words before about going out into life and to work, I could not simply retract all that and tell my parents and friends that I did not like going to work any more. So take a valuable tip from me and do not wish your life away, most certainly not your school life. For if you do, I am sure that you will regret it.'

He then asked several others including me what we intended to do with our lives. I told him that I did not yet know, but that I thought of perhaps becoming an engine driver, as my father was a railwayman, or a pilot with Lufthansa. He said that it was good that youngsters should have their dreams and high expectations but that there would not be enough room in the sky to accommodate so many wishful pilots. Pondering a bit, he then asked me whether there was something I disliked about the school, twinkling with one eye towards Hinck as if to ensure that he was only asking it as a joke. But being so suddenly confronted with a question from a Gauleiter of all people, I was unable to think straight and blurted out that I was annoyed that there never was enough toilet paper in the lavatory. Of course the class exploded, everyone laughed including Kaufmann and even Hinck managed a thin embarrassed smirk. Needless to say, I felt awful. No one told me off afterwards for that spontaneous answer, but it worked, at least for a while. From that day on there was enough toilet paper hanging from the wooden rolls in our lavatories.

Kaufmann then turned to the class in general and mentioned the greatness of our Fatherland, which Adolf Hitler had given back to us. The outside world, as it should, was now treating Germany with respect again, after many years of insults. We all were assured a great future if we stood loyally together and by our Führer which he did not have the slightest doubt we would. After this the door opened and in came our rector Herr Duggen who must have heard about Kaufmann's visit to our class. One could see that he was very nervous, had a red face and spoke with a strained voice, apologising that he had not been present simply because he had not known about the visit. But Kaufmann, being in a friendly and jovial mood, rejected the unnecessary apology and put him at ease by saying that it was really he himself who was to blame and promised that he would not overrun the school like that again, that next time he would give proper notice beforehand, hoping that Herr Duggen would forgive him. After an all-round 'Heil Hitler' with arms shooting into the air, they all left with Hinck visibly relieved. I was so proud that the Gauleiter had spoken to me and rushed home to tell mother. When father came home he managed to dampen my enthusiasm by asking whether I had noticed Kaufmann's pot belly.

The study of *Mein Kampf* was part of the history curriculum at school. Our teacher usually read sections out of it to us, before going on to discuss the book. He emphasised its greatness, probably one of the greatest books ever written, so full of understanding of history and human nature. I cannot remember one instance when anything in it was as much as questioned, everything had to be swallowed uncritically. We were encouraged to read it at home and were asked several times by our Nazi teacher Sieg whether our families possessed the book. Once he went round the class asking us individually. About a third said they had but I doubt whether that was true. But as father had taught me that there were lies and lies, I told teacher Sieg that my parents would probably present me with one for Christmas. Needless to say that was the last thing they would have done.

However I myself borrowed it from the local library and read it from cover to cover when I was about fourteen years old. I am fairly sure that very few in our class did likewise. It was hard work and I understood very little of what I read. But I was determined to be able to honestly say to others that I had read it. When I said to my friends that I thought that it was one the greatest books ever written, I was sincere in what I was saying, although the usual response was 'Ah well, I really must settle down one day in the winter and read it myself.'

A little more than about a dozen years ago when I visited the then GDR, I found the opportunity of reading it a second time. My friends there had saved it when most people had acted more prudently and had got rid of it, together with the swastika flags and other Nazi emblems, before the Red Army reached their towns. My friend's mother had hidden it high up on her bookshelf and for protection had put it into the dustjacket of Dostoievski's *The Idiot*, which it fitted into in more ways than one, and she was still laughing about her 1945 trick when I visited her. Reading it this time, I simply could not stomach reading every word of it. So much of the book now seemed idiotic and I had difficulty in understanding, even taking into account my youth, why I did not recognise what a load of dangerous rubbish it was.

CHAPTER VII
Conflicting Loyalties

As I grew up, I was well aware of the interest that my father and his friends took in what was going on in Russia. It seemed to me that they looked at the unfolding events there as if they were of great importance not only for the people in that vast country but for us and humanity as a whole. This puzzled me, for I was taught at school that outright evil had been unleashed on the poor people of Russia by their communist oppressors.

When on the long winter evenings the friends sat around our kitchen table with the lamp above it pulled down shading their faces from the light, the word Russia kept creeping up again and again. I knew that Russia was that huge country to the east of us, by far the largest in the world and that it straddled the Ural Mountains from Europe into Asia, and though its people were poor it was potentially enormously rich. To me there seemed something mysterious about it, a country I was unable to understand but which fascinated me greatly. It held a kind of wonderment – and at the same time of threat – a strange feeling which I did not feel for any other country, and which I have not really lost to this day.

The name of Joseph Stalin was often thrown into the discussion and I remember one of father's friends saying 'that man is holding down one of the most important and probably hardest jobs in the history of the world.' I also noticed that some doubt was voiced as to whether he was the right man to have taken over from Vladimir Lenin, who was, as far as I could tell, held in high esteem by all in our kitchen. I gathered that there had been a revolution in Russia a few years before I had been born, by which the ordinary folk had got rid of their Tsar and had taken over the running of their vast country themselves. One of father's friends expressed grave doubts about whether the new Russian government, unless a revolution took place in Germany, would be able to hold out for long.

The discussion then focussed on the possibility of a German revolution. Though it seemed to me that though they were all strongly in favour of it, the opinions on how to achieve it, were much divided and the discussion sometimes became rather heated. But then father remembered me sitting in the corner on the floor by the stove, winked at mother who was doing her needlework on the chair next to me and I had to go to bed.

The next morning I asked him what the word 'revolution' meant, and he gave me one of his knowing smiles, saying that I was not old enough to understand such a complex issue, but that he would tell me about some of his own experiences to give an idea of what it was about. Towards the end of the war father's regiment had been transferred to Poland where from their dug-in positions they could look across towards the Russian lines. There was already political turmoil behind those lines in that unhappy country. It was known that many of the soldiers had deserted their regiments, had simply left their positions and had walked back to their homes in the villages where they knew their loved ones were starving. They also had a very good idea about the corruption amongst their leaders.

This was in 1917 and no real fighting was going on any more at the front line. No shots were fired from either side, when one sunny winter's day masses of Russian soldiers had come walking across no-man's-land. They had no weapons on them but waved greetings towards their German 'enemies'. Most of the German soldiers, father amongst them, felt very disgruntled about the war, so they also climbed out of their dug-outs and met the Russians halfway.

At first it all seemed a very eerie experience. No one could be sure what to expect from such a strange situation. But when they actually met, there was joy and laughter, even tears were shed and they took each other into their arms. The calls went out for interpreters as few could speak each other's language. Their hearts were so full and they wanted to say so much to each other. They looked for presents in their pockets but none had anything worthwhile to give. Both sides were as poor as the other. But somehow they managed to breach that language barrier and expressed their desire for friendship, peace and love, and bringing the killing to an end. The Russians said that they had simply had enough of war, refused to take orders from their 'betters' any more, and in some cases, had resorted to killing them.

All they wanted now was to end the war against the Germans. 'But when they asked us,' father said 'whether we too did not want to end the senseless slaughter and what we were going to do about it, we were not really prepared for that question and felt rather uneasy about it, and there was a sense of shame in the air. But we had the impression that they understood our position because they did not press us, which would have only spoiled the atmosphere.' But when the German soldiers had come back from their meeting in no-man's-land they were told off by their officers. One of them, as an example, was punished because he had given a piece of his uniform, the property of His Majesty the Kaiser, as a present to a Russian soldier. They received strict orders not to go and meet the enemy soldiers ever again.

On the next day when the sun was at its highest, the Russians came again. They were many more now and it looked as if a long brown wave was coming towards the German line. There was much waving and one could hear their joyous shouting. Some of them carried what looked like presents. Then the German officers gave orders to fire over their heads. Many of the Russians fell on their knees into the snow, unable to shoot back as they had no weapons on them. They were obviously unable to understand what had happened after the friendly meeting of the previous day. It was a very sad picture to watch them walking back slowly, some carrying their presents, others putting them on the snow and waving to their enemies to come and collect them later. And as they went away, they kept looking back and waving.

I noticed that when telling me that, he still felt bitter and sad and was holding back tears of emotion. 'They wanted peace and our friendship, most of us were prepared to give it to them. But our officers, the bastards, did not allow us to go. Next thing we heard that real revolt, indeed revolution had broken out all over Russia. Though we received very little real information, they wanted to keep us in the dark, but some news always had the habit of trickling through. And because the suffering of the people and the soldiers had been so great, the revolution took root. Out of that at first aimless and confused revolt, grew leaders who were able to channel it into positive aims. For if frustrated people act in unison, they have more chance of success than if they struggle in isolation. Their common action got rid of Tsarist rule – a year later we too got rid of our Kaiser – and started to set up a new sort of society which was a very difficult task indeed.

'That, Henry, is what is called revolution, the Russian Revolution of 1917, Lenin's Revolution. Whatever might happen to it, history will, like the French Revolution of 1789, acknowledge it as one of the most important events of our century. Whether it will succeed, who knows. If the forces of capital are able to turn the clock back one day it will be tragic, for then people will have to start the same process all over again.'

Perhaps as father had said, I was still too young to understand such complex issues, but what he told me gripped my imagination. All this occurred in the days before the advent of the Nazis. Afterwards the Nazis got hold of me and 'educated' me with their way of thinking which so very tragically caused much bitterness between my father and myself.

CHAPTER VIII
Racing towards War

It was around this time that the name of the American Air Force Captain Charles Lindbergh, who was of Swedish origin, appeared frequently in our press. Many of the reports were about the kidnapping of his baby son and there was much sympathy for Lindbergh in our country. Father told me that he had been the first to cross the Atlantic in a mono-plane, a feat which he much admired. Captain Lindbergh, though still relatively young, had also invented an oxygen pump which kept animal organs alive outside their bodies. He was also good looking, at least I thought so from the newspaper photos and that's where father's criticism of him, as well as his admiration, came in. Lindbergh represented the prototype of the Nazi race ideal, he had the reputation of hating Jews and coloured people and had given money to the Ku Klux Klan.

At that time only a very few foreigners could afford to openly support Nazism. For Göbbels, Lindburgh was a God-send, and as a result, the German media carried reports about him very frequently. Everyone in Germany knew his name and we children, even though he was not quite German, made him our hero. Father was saddened by this. He could not understand how a man with such undoubted courage and intelligence could sink so low as to lend his name to making the Nazis respectable. Lindbergh visited Germany many times, was invited by Hitler to Berchtesgaden and hobnobbed with Göring and other high-ranking Nazis. Whenever there was an opportunity, he was depicted in the cinemas and the newspapers.

The Führer presented him with a medal and it was announced that he had chosen to settle in Germany for good after he had denounced America as a Jewish-run rathole. For German youth the influence of Lindbergh was very powerful, especially as he attended Hitler Youth rallies and stayed in camps. If a young man of his standing so openly and fervently supported Nazism, the Nazi ideology was bound to be good. Such went our line of thinking.

What I am writing about now happened more than half a century ago which makes it awkward for me to present events in proper chronological order. At about this time an event occurred which is known to history as

Kristall Nacht (Crystal Night). I remember a cold wintry morning when the news broke. A low-ranking embassy official, Ernst vom Rath, had been shot dead in the foyer of the German Embassy in Paris, after having been requested to come down from his office by a visitor. The latter shot him through the heart without a word and did not resist arrest. When it became clear that this cowardly deed had been perpetrated by a young Jewish male, Herschel Grünspan, all hell broke loose in the German media and the incident was blown up into a Jewish conspiracy against our Reich, our nation.

When father said that what had happened was the result of a homosexual quarrel, I was furious with him. As I did not understand what homosexual lovers were, I challenged him to explain it to me. But he found it awkward to do so, so as a result I suspected that this was a propaganda lie, which we were told in the Hitler Youth were often circulated by underground political leftist groups. I felt that there was treason all around me and, worst, within my own family.

I think that it was on the next night or the one after, that open terror rained down on the Jewish community and their businesses. News came from the Göbbels Ministry that the German nation's anger had been too severely tested at this vile murder of a German official by a dirty Jew. People had taken, understandably enough, the law into their own hands and had smashed thousands of Jewish shops all over Germany, mainly in the large cities. Hundreds of synagogues had been burnt down and looted and burial grounds desecrated.

I went after school to have a look at some of the shops in Altona. Only a small number were affected, including the Department Store owned by the Finkels. I don't think that many more than half a dozen were affected. The displays in the windows had been wrecked and destroyed. All the large plate-glass windows at Finkels had been smashed and though a police guard stood outside to keep people away, everything within the shop was in total disarray and it appeared that looting had taken place on a large scale. That same evening I wanted to go to Hamburg with some of my friends to have a good look there, as we had heard that especially in the fashionable shopping streets around the Alster a large number of shops had been destroyed, some of them gutted. However my parents urged me not to go because they had heard that several totally innocent and defenceless Jewish people had been clubbed to death, while others had been thrown into the Alster river and left to drown. They felt that going and gaping at these places, where people had been murdered, would be ghoulish and degrading. I took heed of their advice, though I remember I had difficulty explaining to my friends why I didn't want to go.

When Göbbels afterwards announced that it had all been done spontaneously, few people believed him, as it had happened within the span of a few short hours at many places hundreds of miles apart. It quickly became an open secret that many of the windows had been smashed by SA men in civvies and that many of them had later drunkenly boasted about it. Father pointed out that SA rowdies who previously did not possess two pennies to rub together, suddenly flaunted high quality cameras, were expensively dressed, and their womenfolk wore furs for the first time in their lives.

Apart from the brutality itself, revealing to the whole world how thin the veneer of civilisation was in Germany, Kristall Nacht created a very damaging economic reaction. The Jewish shop owners and other business people whose property had been destroyed were safely insured with German insurance companies, and these were unable to avoid their legal obligations through invoking 'an act of God' – unless Josef Göbbels was quickly elevated to that exalted status. However, the Hitler Government then carried out its master stroke by turning the whole issue upside down: by punishing the Jewish victims with a financial penalty for the disturbances caused by their unwanted presence. The money raised covered the insurance costs. The reaction in the Hitler Youth to Kristall Nacht was a smirking one, with an undertone of 'it serves them right.' At school it was not mentioned at all, at least not in our class by Herr Hinck. My parents were devastated and called it Scham Nacht (Night of Shame).

It was in the spring of 1936 that news came in of the civil war in Spain. My parents, as soon they heard about it, were extremely worried, though most people, so it seemed, could not care less. Father often complained how poorly informed and educated working class people were. They had enough worries of their own and Spain was very far away. Being by that time fourteen years old, I was very interested in what was happening there, but of course was in no position to either properly understand, nor far less, analyse the unrolling events on the Iberian peninsula. From one side I was overwhelmed by information from the official media and from the other, I had to listen to the daily comments my parents made on the subject. I could do no other but try to steer a middle course between the two and probably without wanting to, benefited from that experience, which forced me to think for myself but which in turn made me suspicious of anything coming in on me, from whatever quarter.

What I did glean was that a government had been properly and democratically elected by the people, but that a revolt had broken out amongst top army officers led by a General Francisco Franco, who openly announced his intention of toppling the elected government in Madrid. It was an open secret that the rebellion was supported by the wealthy classes and the hierarchy of the Catholic Church. Father's prediction was that as the rebellion was a fascist attempt to strangle any development towards democracy, it would not take long before Franco's political blood brothers Mussolini and Hitler intervened. All too quickly his suspicions proved to

be accurate, as reports came of German Junker planes flying Franco's
Nationalist troops from North Africa to Seville in southern Spain. It was
clear that without these transport planes Franco would never have been
able to carry through his plans, and that he must have made sure of
German Government support beforehand.

Then a very important development occurred, whereby the new
Spanish Government gave long-sought-after autonomy to the Basque
region, creating a new regional government in the city of Guernica. At the
same time Germany and Italy recognised Franco's Government with its
seat in the city of Burgos. By that time German Heinckel and Junker
bombers had already been sent out on small missions in support of
Nationalist troops. That was known to most of us, but it came as a big
surprise when it was announced that planes from the German Legion
Condor had bombed what was an unprepared and totally defenceless
Guernica with high explosives. Much of the city was destroyed and the
cost in human lives was horrendous. In the Hitler Youth we learned a new
song about our heroic flyers of the Legion Condor. We sang it so often,
that I still know most of its words, about bringing freedom to Spain with
bombs.

I had come from a Hitler Youth meeting that evening where we had
been told about our fliers' successful mission. The thought that our pilots
and crews had been in real action, gave us all a tremendous feeling of
pride and I was full of it, when I told my parents. But they already knew.
Mother put me straight away in my place by pointing out that there was
nothing heroic about attacking an undefended city from the air and killing
masses of innocent people. What right did we have to bomb anything in
Spain anyway? What had those people done to us? In her view it was not
only a breach of fundamental international law but a ghastly crime against
humanity which ought to be dealt with in an international Court of Justice.
How would we react if French or any other pilots bombed the German city
Karlsruhe, because they disagreed with our choice of government?

All the time while mother spoke, father had been sitting back, listening
and saying nothing, but when I came out with something about 'the
damnèd communists of Guernica have got what they deserved', he shot
up, rushed around the table and grabbed me by my tie. He bent down so
that his face was at the same level as mine, looking at me straight in the
eye. This time I could see that he was really furious but I could not see how
I could retract and extricate myself. In most cases when something like
this happened, he acted in a controlled manner, but this time and before I
was fully aware of what was happening to me, I received a hard slap on
the cheek. Standing there in my brown shirt, more surprised than really
hurt, I realised that I had wildly overstepped my mark. He did not raise
his voice, on the contrary it came out more as a hissing sound. 'What did
you say? Did I hear right that the massacred people of Guernica deserved

what they have got? And is this the son of my own blood who is saying this?' It was then that mother came between us, trying to ease his grip on my tie which threatened to strangle me.

'Talk to the boy, Fritz,' she said, 'please don't hit him, he doesn't understand what he is saying and it is not his fault that they teach him these ghastly things in the Hitler Youth.' Father looked at her and then at me and let go. 'Sit down right here and now. And now you listen to me, young man, and I don't want one word from your silly brown lips until I have finished what I want to tell you and give you permission to talk.' All I could do was to nod without a word, as I could see this time he was really furious. With mother sitting very close to me 'just in case', he gave me a long and serious talking to. I listened to his every word.

He explained the Spanish situation, that the Spanish people had dared to elect a people's government who stood for bettering the lives of ordinary working people by way of socialist measures. But when the wealthy in the country realised that the leaders in the government meant what they said, namely that in order to tackle the problem of poverty it would be necessary to deal with privilege and wealth first, they saw their whole world under threat. When it became clear to them that the people were no longer listening to their priests any more but wanted change, real change and not the one graciously handed down from above, they reached for their last trump card. They brought in the army under Franco, in order to smash the elected will of the people. They had played success-fully with dangling carrots for generations, but the suffering masses were beginning to see through that game of mass deception and foolery. So the big stick had to come out.

In the same way, he pointed out to me, as the German establishment had brought Hitler and his Nazis in to save the social and economic status quo, the Spanish establishment was doing the same with Franco. And that, he stressed, was behind the brutal bombing of the people of Guernica, not allowing the people to elect a socialist-oriented govern-ment. And the Spanish Catholic Church, being one of the richest land-owners in the country, was of course one of the mainstays of the old establishment.

He then made it clear to me that he would not allow me to ever use such cruel words and sentiments in our home again, and outrightly forbade me to sing that arrogant 'Legion Condor' song in his or mother's presence. By the time he had finished with me, he had visibly calmed down and said: 'Well, Henry, I can see that all this must have been a bit much to grasp and I am sorry for not being one of the best explainers, but maybe the day will come when you come to accept what your father has tried to tell you.'

It was in the late spring or early summer of 1939 that the Legion Condor under the command of General von Richthofen, a relative of the 'Red Baron' of the Great War, arrived back from Spain at Hamburg.

When the ship *Wilhelm Gustloff* unloaded its soldiers off the gangway, Reichsmarschall Göring was there, wearing one of his self-designed fancy light-blue uniforms, greeting the 'victors of Guernica' as father so sarcastically called them. I stood close behind in the ranks of the Hitler Youth, watching the soldiers coming off and being greeted by the white-shirted girls of the BDM (female section of the Hitler Youth) with flowers and kisses. I was so elated, so proud of being a German. Surrounded by the military razzmatazz, the stirring martial music, the singing and the happy confident faces, I believed with all my heart that our people, surely the greatest on earth, was now on the march. But when I came home and excitedly told my parents what I had taken part in, my mood saddened when mother started to cry and father looked at me and shook his head as if to say, 'is there no end to this?' When I asked her what the matter was, she said that everything looked so bleak, so hopeless, that she and father feared that we were steering straight into another war, and that they were especially worried about me, as conscription was now in full swing.

We sang many songs in the Hitler Youth about German Austria and, when in the spring of 1938 the Austrian problem literally exploded on to the political scene, we sensed that the European ice was at last beginning to crack. Hitler, having been born in Austria, the issue of that country becoming part of our Reich was never far from German political thinking. Almost all the seven million Austrians were German-speaking and the coming together of the two (Anschluss) probably also made economic sense. For years this Austrian Anschluss had looked like an unstoppable event, it was not so much a question of if any more, but of when. Then came the murder of Austria's Chancellor Engelbert Dollfuss, an authoritarian Catholic. Most people in Germany assumed – and probably in Austria too – without daring to say so openly, that the crime had been committed by Austria's Nazis, guided by their brown blood brothers from north of the border.

Kurt Schuschnigg then became Chancellor and had to withstand grotesque demands for a Union from Hitler. The latter once all but ordered him to appear before him in Berchtesgaden where he shouted and bawled at him, saying that his patience was running out and that he had had enough. With political and economic pressure both from inside Austria and Germany, the situation thus developed in March 1938, that Schuschnigg had to resign to make room for a Sayss-Inquart to become Chancellor. It was he, a member of the Austrian Nazi Party, who handed Austria on a plate to Hitler by signing the documents of the Anschluss. Though this had been in the air for quite some time, when it came, it arrived somewhat out of the blue. One day Austria, Österreich as we called it, had been an independent European state and neighbour, and on the next day, it had become a part of what we now called Greater

Germany. The name Österreich then totally disappeared from the maps and it was renamed 'Ostmark'.

Our entire school was called together on that day in the large Aula and the Rector Herr Duggen reported on the situation. I remember him stressing in his speech that we were now finding ourselves with new neighbours, Hungary, Yugoslavia and Italy, which was bound to alter our European perspective. We then listened to the Führer's speech. All of it was so enormously electrifying. We were full of joy when we heard the Führer's voice, telling us that since early morning German troops together with their Austrian comrades were dismantling all border posts and were now marching together into the heart of the country towards Linz and Vienna, joyously received by the people. We could sense the sincere emotion in his voice saying that we were lucky to be living in such a great period of German history, thanking – at times he became suddenly religious – 'den Allmächtigen' (the Almighty).

The Nazis celebrated the Anschluss with many festivities, some of which were organised by the Hitler Youth. Many special marches were laid on to honour the event and our troop sent invitations to Austrian Hitler Youth groups to stay with us on an individual private holiday. When I told my parents that I had put my name down for an Austrian boy to stay with us, they were angry and told me never to do that again. But they did not order me to cancel the invitation, and luckily nothing ever came of it.

Altogether it was a wonderful time of uplifting elation for us youngsters, a cause for national pride and joy. We studied the new map of Europe at school with our Deutschland having become a powerful block right in the heart of the continent. Had Czechoslovakia not pushed its ugly shape like a threatening fist towards our Reich's centre, Deutschland's shape could have been called almost round. Just to look at Czechoslovakia on the map gave many of us rather suggestive thoughts. Father reminded me that Cardinal Innitzer of Vienna had used the Heil Hitler salute and had made disparaging racist remarks about the people of Czechoslovakia. He wondered what Nazi Germany and the Vatican were brewing up together.

It was in the following summer that we went camping in a Thüringian castle in Central Germany where we met up with a group of Austrian Hitler Youth. Being so excited about meeting them, I asked them so many questions on the Anschluss and was rather disappointed that the reaction of some of them was less than enthusiastic. I had the impression that they were not all that keen to talk about it. It was a strange and totally unexpected experience for me. I then asked one of them, a Viennese, whether he had seen Hitler on his first visit to the city after liberation. He responded with a sullen laugh, looked at me and said, 'liberation did you say, what do you think then we were liberated from?' I thought that he was joking or that I had not heard right and therefore did not respond to his question. But he followed it up, by saying: 'Come on, you have asked me a question, I have answered by throwing a question back at you and now you look at me like a dumb fish and say nothing. Answer me. I have asked you what you think you have liberated us from.'

Now I was severely taken aback because I realised that he was dead serious and also that I found it impossible to give him a meaningful answer. And then he helped me by telling me: 'You have indeed liberated us from our freedom and probably also from much of our gold. I can assure you that of the many thousands who shouted 'heil' when your Führer entered our city, a large number now regret that he came and wished that they could turn the clock back to the times when we were an independent Österreich.' I was so shocked that I did not know what to say. Because it had all come so unexpectedly, it had hit me right between my Nazi eyes. But searching for a quick way out, I asked him why, if he thought like that, he had donned the brown uniform of Hitler's youth. Did he think that was honest?

'Honest,' he said, 'where does honesty come into this game when you arrive with several armies at our border after having previously organised a fifth column around Seyss-Inquart in our midst? As to my brown shirt, have you ever heard the word 'blackmail'? I will not give too much away to you, only say that I was accepted to go to university until it was discovered that my father had opposed the Anschluss. Now I want a job as an engineer and I know that without being a member of your Hitler Youth I would not stand a chance. And you think that I am not honest.' This was all too much for me. I simply could not understand, turned round and left him standing, thoroughly upset. One thing, and I am now very glad about it, I did not go and report him. Had I done so, it could have been very unpleasant for him. Maybe I did not do it as a result of my father's influence, instilling into me that, whatever the circumstances, never transgress a clearly marked line of honour in personal relations which my conscience always helped me to find.

On the next day my Viennese protagonist, probably having noticed my miserable face and having thought about the risky situation he had put himself into, offered me his hand and urged me not to be so serious about it. He was probably a couple of years older than I was and urged me to use my brain a little bit more and perhaps not to follow so uncritically the propaganda furrow which others had ploughed for me. 'Let's wipe a sponge over it,' he said, 'let's be friends on a personal basis, not political comrades, and enjoy our stay here together in your beautiful Thüringia.' On the last day before parting he came into our room to say 'good bye'. We shook hands and earnestly looked at each other for quite some time. I wished him a safe journey home and said 'Heil Hitler'. 'No, not Heil Hitler, please, but adieu, peace, good health and a good trip back to your grey north.' He laughed and clapped me on the shoulder. In spite of our clash, I liked his eyes and the open way he looked at me. And when his group marched out through the gate I had made it my job to stand there. He seemed to be pleased that I had bothered, turned his head towards me, and waved several times before he disappeared behind a sharp bend in the road.

Being so young, I quickly forgot about this strange incident, perhaps I simply wanted to shut it out of my mind because I was unable to reconcile it with my presumptions. Memory of the incident came back to me several years later, when together with a number of Austrian soldiers, we were retreating from Stalingrad through the snow. Under these conditions there was no need to argue about the Anschluss or liberation. I myself did not bother any more and I suppose that my then Austrian comrades would have hated the very words and what they meant to them. For without Anschluss they would not now he tramping through the snow, completely demoralised. My thoughts went back to the meeting in the Thüringian castle and one of them said: 'Henry, what is on your mind? You are smiling to yourself.' I told him about the conversation I had had with that Viennese friend. It was he who then pointed to the blinding icy desert around us and said something about 'history throwing long shadows in the snow.'

Not far from where we lived was the flat of Ernst Thälmann, the then General Secretary of the German Communist Party. Thälmann, especially before 1933, was much in the news. He had the reputation of great personal courage, was often leading demonstrations against unemployment, hunger, rearmament and other symptoms of the underlying sickness of our economic system. He was much respected by working people especially in Hamburg, but was hated by most members of the middle classes. Working people knew that he lived their lives, came from their surroundings and knew what he was talking about. Father, I well remember, always had appreciative words to say about 'our Ernst'. He had been to his meetings, listened to his speeches but, though he never let on, I had the impression that he knew him personally.

After the Nazis came to power, it had not taken them long to arrest Thälmann and lock him up in a concentration camp. Father was very bitter about it. 'How low have we been pressed so that we are unable to prevent a working class leader like Thälmann being carted away like a common criminal?' Being of the young generation and only knowing Thälmann by name, I had no strong feeling about what was happening to him. We had learnt in the Hitler Youth that communists were criminals and anti-German. But the fact that I knew where he lived, that he had been a Hamburg docker and that he spoke the same Plattdeutsch language as I did, made me nevertheless feel a bit disturbed about his fate.

When father said that 'our Ernst' would never have stayed quiet if one of his comrades had been unjustly arrested, I made the mistake, which I straight away regretted, of suggesting that he, father, should go and protest about Thälmann's arrest. He looked at me as if not believing what he heard, his face reddened and he almost lost control again, shouted at me and was close to hitting me when mother came out from the kitchen and saved us both from ourselves. He then showed what I now realise was his supreme integrity. He acknowledged that he had gone too far again, sat down, put his chin on his chest and said: 'Sorry Junge, I should not have shouted at you like that. I do apologise. But you too should have been thoughtful enough and not suggest something like that to me.' With that I was quickly in his arms with mother joining us in the embrace, and all was forgiven and forgotten.

Having by that time reached the age of about sixteen, I increasingly realised the terrible knot of contradictions within me. There was my great love for my father – but also for my Führer and my country. How was I to sort it all out in my brain and heart? When I went to the Hitler Youth that night, I hardly listened to the lecture, almost got in trouble over it and was deeply unhappy.

As is now history, Ernst Thälmann was murdered by the Nazi guards in Buchenwald a day before the Red Army reached it. Not so many years ago I visited Buchenwald not far from Weimar where I paid respect to Goethe's house. I found the place where Ernst Thälmann had been killed. Outside the gate there was a van which sold sausages, but also flowers. I bought a bunch, took them back through the gates and placed it amongst others in front of his plaque as a tribute to Thälmann – and to my father.

As any political opposition to Nazism had been made impossible by the outright brutality of the Nazi state, there was no other way for those who still had the courage to do so, but to go underground. Being an all-out supporter of the regime, I of course knew little or nothing about that. A clever weapon used by the opposition were jokes. They were often very funny and everyone, even sometimes Nazis, could not but laugh at them. I certainly did, and what was more, I passed them on because I realised that telling jokes was welcome in any company. When one of us went so far as to tell one at a Hitler Youth Dienst, he was told off in no uncertain manner and we all were given a severe lecture on this morale-undermining practice. But the telling of political jokes went on unabashed. A joke was a joke, we thought, and surely our Führer, having been told all along what a great sense of humour he possessed, would easily laugh them off.

One of them went like this: Adolf Hitler was rowing on his own in a small boat on the Wannsee just outside Berlin, when his boat capsized and a boy rowing near-by managed to save him from drowning by pulling him, choking and spluttering, into his boat. Hitler then asked the boy whether he recognised him to which he replied, 'Yes of course, mein

Führer.' Hitler then told him that he would be eternally grateful to him and asked him to express a wish, any wish, which he, the Führer would fulfil. After some considered hesitation the boy answered that he would like a state funeral. Hitler, taken aback, remarked that it was a rather unusual wish for so young a boy. But the latter replied: 'Well mein Führer, it is like this, if I go home and tell my father that I have saved you from drowning, he will say, "What!" – and then surely will strangle me.'

A rumour was making the rounds that Hermann Göring was collecting anti-Nazi jokes and that he was paying a few marks for every new one by return of post. I never heard of anyone who had actually done that and secretly had to agree with father when he said: 'yes, by return of post, but the postman would be wearing a brown uniform and taking that naive joker with him.'

It was during the very early part of the war that radio newscasters were obliged to read news reports very quickly without pausing, either between words or sentences. The reason was that pirate interceptors kept cutting into the broadcasts in a very witty manner, challenging everything, pointing out the lies and ridiculing the rest. We all thought that it was very funny and I am sure many who hitherto had not bothered to listen to news, did so now to just hear the pirate. What he was saying, so it seemed, had become more important to many listeners than the official broadcast. No doubt the Gestapo set up listening posts to catch him. But as far as I know, they never succeeded. His interceptions though, became less and less frequent, probably because he had to play safe and move from place to place. Needless to say, many jokes circulated about the pirate and the Nazis. I am not sure any more whether the pirate always had the same voice, but he was witty, precise and very knowledgeable. The suspicion was that he was a high-up Nazi, perhaps a civil servant or another official, as his interruptions suggested a high level of education and knowledge.

England, we seldom called it Britain or Great Britain, always had a special place in German thinking. For us it was a kind of love-hate relationship. One reason of course was that the English, the Angle-Saxons, were our acknowledged cousins. The other was that they ruled over a world empire on which the sun never set. That achievement, we all agreed, demanded due respect and there was much in our political philosophy and especially in the Nazi one, which strove towards the same historic ends. The English had been on the side of the victors in the Great War and while the French, at least that was our naive view, were pushing for the full implementation of the Treaty of Versailles, England was less harsh on this issue, which made us like them better. But we were not so foolish not to recognise that they always had their own interests foremost in their minds. We were taught at school and in the Hitler Youth that a fundamental English policy was that of 'divide and rule', which was

167

always directed against the strongest continental power. It was perhaps a crude view, but a telling one.

The first time I heard and read about Mr. Neville Chamberlain was when he took over the Premiership from Mr. Baldwin in the middle thirties. That was the time when the Empire, though beginning to wobble, was still largely intact and I thought that the position of the English Prime Minister must be one of the most powerful in the world. The next time he sprang into prominence was when it was announced that he was in strong favour of a large armament programme for the British Navy. Naturally, German propaganda made much of that British armament programme in order to convince the German populace of the necessity of our own. Father warned me about them all whether they be German, British, French or American. He told me about deals between Krupp, Schneider-Creusot and Vickers during the war and how they all covered their tracks, all in the pursuit of profits.

Then came the late summer and early autumn of 1938 when events began to roll over each other. To those who read of these developments, it became clear that Germany was positioning itself for supremacy over Europe and perhaps more. And it was in connection with the resulting political tension that Chamberlain stepped into the limelight again. All the main industrialised countries were in deep economic and therefore social trouble. Mass unemployment was prevalant everywhere except Germany and we had the feeling that sooner or later something was going to give.

Hitler made a series of wild speeches, when it was suddenly announced that Prime Minister Chamberlain was coming to Germany to meet our Führer. To us this was terrific news. We had been aware that ever since Hitler had come to power, our state had been treated like a kind of pariah. And now this! We were not going anywhere, they were coming to us! Was this not the proof that our Führer's peace policies with the clenched fist in readiness was succeeding? To our thinking this was a turning point in power relations in Europe and ultimately the world at large.

I suppose it was not difficult to present Chamberlain as a public figure who really belonged to the bygone century. Everything about him seemed old-fashioned and somewhat odd. His way of dressing and bearing suggested to us a very strange type of English gentleman who had been left behind by modern developments. As we had also seen photos of ordinary English working people, it strengthened our view that Britain must be a very class-divided society, very much different from other nations.

The first time I saw Chamberlain on the newsreels was when our Führer welcomed him at Berchtesgaden. The difference, just by looking at those two, between these two most important European players, could not have been greater. The thought of Hitler stalking around with an umbrella was to the German mind unthinkable. Of course I was all too young then and full of myself, far too inexperienced to analyse and weigh up the issues at stake, but I did sense that Chamberlain's arrival in Germany indicated that the situation had become very serious and was approaching a climax.

Following the Berchtesgaden visit, Chamberlain flew to Cologne to meet Hitler again, this time at the Hotel Dreesen, overlooking Bad (Spa) Godesberg and the Rhine. All that became known was that the two had extensive discussions on the Sudeten crisis. Hitler simply wanted to annexe the Sudetenland into the German Reich, because most of it was inhabited by German-speaking people. Göbbels' propaganda machine informed us that the Czechs were committing unspeakable atrocities against the German people there which could no longer be tolerated. When the Czechs denied it, we were told that was just what was expected of them as they were like all other Slavic people, habitual liars.

The Hotel Dreesen meeting was quickly followed by the Munich one which ended in the infamous pact signed by Hitler, Chamberlain, Mussolini and the French Premier Daladier. What came out of the signing of the Munich Pact was that Czechoslovakia had to cede the Sudetenland to Germany. As the former's main military defence lines were now in German-occupied lands, its entire defence situation was totally undermined. What was left was in every sense a rump country. Naturally I was cock-a-hoop about it all while father called it one of the most shameful betrayals in European history, the throwing of a small country to the German wolves.

When Daladier went back to Paris after the signing, he was feted as the saviour of peace by people lining the road, which given that he expected to be lynched, greatly surprised him. The Czech diplomats had not been allowed to take part in any of the negotiations. They had to wait in an anteroom into which the main players came with beaming faces. Yes, they had saved the peace in Europe and the Czechs were told that they had to pay the price for it.

At the Hitler Youth meeting following the Munich signing we were told that our Führer had acted with the greatest foresight and wisdom and had achieved for Germany the opening up of Lebensraum, a success unequalled by any other German leader in its entire history. I was sincerely convinced that Adolf Hitler was a really great superman.

Father, having worked in the engine sheds of the Deutsche Reichsbahn (Railways) since the end of the war, was able to secure a locksmith apprenticeship for me at the railway workshops in Hamburg-Ohlsdorf. The first question I had to answer on my application form was 'when did I join the Hitler Youth?' I am sure, that had I answered in the negative, I would not have even got a low-status job like that. I was excited about the prospect of now joining real adult life and very much looked forward to my first day at work.

As Ohlsdorf was at the other end of the city and work started at seven o'clock, I had to get up at four-thirty. I never had given much thought to this problem beforehand. Father had to get up at five o clock, but when mother woke me, I could not believe what was happening to me. Work generally started early in German industry and when I joined the workers' train, mother's sandwich box under my arm, I learned that if I wanted a seat for the forty-minute journey, I had to be on the platform in good time. I also learned that no one felt like talking that early in the morning, most travellers looking very grumpy.

We were fourteen new apprentices and when we first assembled in the foyer of the management office, we sat on our lonely chairs around the wall, too shy to say anything to each other. Naturally, over the next three years we became great friends and stayed in correspondence with each other as soldiers, when one after the other, I think nine of the fourteen, died during the war.

An official welcomed us with an introductory speech containing the warning that the easy life of school was now over and that the serious side of life was about to begin. We were led along the rail track to the workshop where the older apprentices were already lined up outside, waiting for us to join them. Even here everything was done in a military style. The workshop master and his two assistants stood in line at the side. A senior apprentice stepped forward, greeted us with 'Heil Hitler, new ones', after which he quoted a passage out of Hitler's *Mein Kampf* which urged us to be loyal and work hard for our employer and therefore for Deutschland. Then the swastika flag was hoisted to which we raised our arms in the Nazi salute. At the end of each working day the flag was hauled down to which we had to line up again.

We had to change into our work clothes after which we were shown to our work benches, and given the first batch of basic tools such as hammer, files and pliers. We were shown how to work the basic machines like drills and instructed in safety regulations. The assistants then handed us a small iron block which we had to put into our vices on to which we were let loose with our files. The working day was eight hours, four on Saturdays. We had one week's holiday a year. I never admitted it to my parents nor to my friends or anyone else, but from my first day at Ohlsdorf I did not like anything about the entire set-up. Though I got used to it later, my first and enduring impression was that I had landed in some sort of a slave camp. I don't think that I had a lazy nature, I wanted to work all right, but the pressures there were such that one was no more than a worker-soldier. Maybe this was to make us feel like a part of the overall plan, to prepare German youth for what was to come: war.

The workshop was very old-fashioned with little light coming in the metal framed windows. Discipline was harsh. If you stayed too long in the lavatory, you were told to cut it shorter next time. One of the assistants was constantly on to us. Several of us, though not I, were physically beaten by the works master for some breach of discipline. We discussed whether to complain to either management or the Hitler Youth, but then decided against it as none of us was prepared to take the lead. It was also known that our works master was a party member.

One afternoon a week we had sport, going by train to a railway sports ground. I liked it there because we played football, competed in athletics and had other fun. However, it did not last long, and new regulations were introduced which gave more emphasis on military preparation and we were shown how to throw hand-grenades and march properly, which was really unnecessary as we had learnt all that already in the Hitler Youth. Although at the time I agreed with the 'necessity', believing that we did it all for Deutschland and our Führer, there was also something in me which did not like it, though I was unable to properly formulate this obvious contradiction.

I was glad when after three years workshop training I was called up to the forces. I had thought that would give me greater freedom to develop my personality as a soldier. But that too did not take me long, hardly more than a day, to realise that I had made another miscalculation. Deep down I knew that the only one who could help me to understand the contradictions within me was my father. But it had all gone too far by then and I was too proud to ask him.

After the Wehrmacht had annexed the Sudetenland in the autumn of 1938, the occupation of the rest of Czechoslovakia was a foregone conclusion, no more than a question of time. Whenever something of that kind happened, father and I loved to get the old atlas out. He pointed to the shape of that long Slav country which stuck out dangerously like a spear into the heart of Germany and prophesied that sooner or later Hitler would pick it like an over-ripe plum. If we two untrained minds were able to recognise this near-certainty, it was inconceivable that statesmen like Chamberlain and Daladier could not have foreseen it when they signed the Munich Pact.

Of course father's suspicions were well-founded. For suddenly another Czech crisis developed. We were informed that the Czech authorities were making life difficult for the minority of Germans who were still living in that country. The aged President Hacha, an ex-university professor from Prague, was in effect ordered to go to Berlin, where he was told that his country's behaviour was an unacceptable disgrace which had to be dealt with. The unfortunate old man had a heart attack as a result of Hitler shouting at him. After he recovered, he was informed that the areas of Bohemia and Moravia were to become Reichs Protectorates, and that Slovakia was to become an independent state under the presidency of the fascist Catholic priest, Father Tiso – in other words, a puppet state of Germany. Hacha had no other choice but to sign, having no friends left anywhere.

Within a day, the Wehrmacht moved in and occupied the entire country, including Prague. Hitler himself went to the city and drove to its ancient castle, the Hradschin, the home of the Bohemian kings. Watching the newsreels of the occupation, I saw the Führer standing behind an open castle window, looking down on the city, the river and the Karlsbridge. He did not come too close to the window, 'just in case' – while driving through the town he had been subject to hostile demonstrations. Film of the demonstration showed people crying and raising their fists against the soldiers. Hitler, so it was said, was disappointed because he had expected a warm welcome, like that he had received in Vienna eighteen months earlier.

The famous Skoda Works were now safely in German hands and fully incorporated into the war machine. Also, our Führer had opened a new door to the east and the Balkans. The age-old German dream was developing into reality. In the Hitler Youth we were in no doubt that we were about to step through these doors into our glorious future. Again father fetched the atlas and put it on the table. He asked me what I thought this newest alteration on the map would mean to future developments. Well, it was of course all too obvious. This time, with Czechoslovakia neatly incorporated into the Reich, it was Poland which stuck into our country like an ugly threatening thumb.

'Correct!' responded father, 'and you can put your entire savings on it, that it will be the next item on your Führer's list. The German establishment, the mighty Ruhr barons, the junkers and the bankers will prod our mad Chancellor not to let a chance like that slip through his fingers. After all, to fulfil their aims, that's what they have appointed him to do. And I will prophesy that one day all these grandiose plans will end in nothing but blood and ashes. The jumped-up house painter will not stop with Poland, mark my words, he will go on as any power-drunk dictator would do after these early successes. But in the end he will fall on his belly, as he so richly deserves. The only trouble is, we will all fall with him.'

I just laughed gleefully, youth is like that, I suppose, because I simply could not see father's predictions in that light. I was grateful that I had been born into such a momentous German epoch and I thought that father, as much as I loved him, had completely misread the flow of modern history. I was so full of myself, thinking that I was the one who had understood history – and all that was left for father was to stand back and shake his head in sorrow. It was only a few short years after this, when I trudged back with our beaten army through the snow of Russia, that father's words became meaningful to me.

As is well-known, war broke out on the 1st September 1939. For some time previously, our news reports were full of Polish border violations, military overflights and atrocities against innocent German civilians living in Poland. Then the infamous 'Gleiwitz incident' occurred in which Polish soldiers were said to have crossed the border into Germany by night, occupied the Gleiwitz radio station and urged the Polish people on the German side of the border to rise against the German authorities and liberate themselves. Even though it was later proved at Nuremberg that these 'Polish' soldiers – all of them had conveniently been killed – had been concentration camp prisoners stuck into Polish uniforms, the propaganda ruse worked very well at the time. Public opinion was infuriated. Göbbels made a rousing speech and then Adolf himself followed it up by announcing that since the early hours of that morning German guns had started to 'shoot back'. He said that his patience had finally been exhausted and many of the German public, including myself, howled in support. The wheels of war had finally clicked into gear. Our mighty Reich was on the march and death to those who dared to stand in our way!

Father, especially after what had happened to Czechoslovakia, wondered whether the British would stand by their Polish ally with whom they had concluded a pact. And when Chamberlain sent an ultimatum to Hitler which the latter declared unacceptable – how dare the man with the umbrella – no one was surprised. As father had said so many times, the main aim of his life had been to save his son from going through the same criminal madness as he had been forced to go through, as a soldier in the war. To him all that lay now in ruins. On top of all that, it must have been doubly painful for him to watch me rushing into it full of enthusiasm.

The Hitler Youth ensured that we followed the flag. The arrival of war was explained to us as a liberation from the pressures of unbearable uncertainty. It was as if honest reality had dawned and had come out into the open. The Führer, when he made his Poland speech, had put on a different uniform. It was grey now, the same colour as that of his soldiers.

What happened after that is now history. German troops with incredible speed swept into the heart of Poland and beyond. After about two weeks Soviet forces moved in from the east to reclaim what the Poles had taken from them eighteen years earlier. And a week later Poland as a state had simply ceased to exist. It was then that Hitler made one of his most arrogant speeches. He beamingly declared that 'Mit Mann und Ross und Wagen hat sie der Herr geschlagen' (With man and horse and cart they were punished by their master), and the entire German nation broke out in jubilation. There were only a few like father who did not join in the howl. All that was left for him to say was 'When will we ever learn . . . ?'

It was during the early part of the war, just before I was called up, that father fell ill. Though he tried to keep it from me, thinking perhaps that it was merely a sort of passing tummy trouble, I had noticed that he was not well. For once he did not seem to be in the mood to argue with me and when I tried to needle him with our Blitzkrieg victories, he became angry and sad and told me to leave him in peace with my grotesque Hitlerite nonsense. Then came the terrible morning when two of his workmates

173

brought him back home and a doctor was called, who sent him straight into hospital. Within a day or two he had his operation, stayed in the intensive care ward for a few days, and seemingly recovered in the general ward. It was a long walk to the hospital from where we lived. But I went every evening after work to bring him the newspaper, as I knew that he loved to keep up with what was going on the world. I did it because I loved him so much.

But then he turned yellow. Mother as well as uncles and aunts became very disturbed. But I simply could not accept that my father was seriously ill. I felt sure that he would be out of hospital in a week or two and that he would start arguing with me again and that all my family's worries were unfounded. But the doctors decided that he should have a second operation, only a minor one, they said, to clear up a small matter.

I visited him the next day. He was back in the intensive care ward and had drips and all sorts of funny things hanging down from behind the bed which frightened me. We were alone. Mother was going to come later and he said he wanted to talk to me. His voice was already weak and I realised that he had great difficulty in speaking.

On the bedside table next to him stood a small bowl with water and a cotton wool stick, which the nurse used to touch his lips from time to time to quench his thirst. He asked me to hold the bowl for him so that he could drink, because he was so terribly thirsty. But then the nurse came in and told me that I must not do it, as it would kill him. After she had gone out, he told me not to take any notice of her and to hold the bowl to his lips so that he could drink. And when I refused, he became very angry with me, and said that it was all over with him anyway and that all he wanted now was this last drink.

I did not know what to do. I ran to the door to look where the nurse was – and when I couldn't find her, decided to give him the bowl of water. He emptied it with greedy gulps. And I felt tears running down my cheeks. I was so sad, so confused.

The next morning, it was a Sunday, he died peacefully. Mother was with him, I was alone at home and wanted to go later. After she came back to tell me, we cried in each other's arms. I did not tell her what I had done, never told her nor anyone else. I kept it all to myself. But for a long time I believed that I had helped kill my father. All that I had wanted was to ease his pain – for I loved him so very much.

Epilogue

Sixty years and more have passed since the events in this book occurred. After father's death my own life went through a wild and turbulent period, and the worst of what father had predicted came true, when eighteen years old, I was called up to the Panzers. After a short interlude in France, I was transferred to the Eastern Front, where the previous summer the German Army had already conquered large areas. Before I was nineteen years old, I took part in my first battle at the Crimea in Manstein's Eleventh Army. The silent fear and the emotional turmoil in me was considerable. Next I went with Paulus's Sixth Army on its push to the Volga, taking part in many battles until we reached Stalingrad. It was there that our noses were ground into the snow and then into final defeat.

I was very lucky to get away. With the German Army destroyed, I set out with its remnants on the Napoleonic retreat through the winter. I was a member of different Kampfgruppen (battle groups) for almost all units, such as divisions, regiments and battalions, had been torn to pieces. We ordinary soldiers felt abandoned by our leaders. This was perhaps the worst time in my whole life, one morning we measured a temperature of minus fifty-four degrees centigrade. We suffered badly but I can also bear witness to the incomparable suffering of the civilian population who got caught up in it all. There were many times when I thought, 'Oh mother, why did you give me life?'

To my shame now, up to Stalingrad I had still been full of Hitler Youth 'ideals'. Only after that battle and the retreat did they begin to crumble. The very nature of the battle in the east was that we often stayed at one place for a period, and during one these periods, I fell in love with a Russian girl, Anna. I learned to appreciate her great human quality which at the same time was a recognition that my conviction of German racial superiority, was nothing more than nonsense.

Especially during the winter's retreat, we often stayed with the peasants in their primitive but mostly warm cottages. I had many conversations, arguments and quarrels mainly with the women – their menfolk were at war – whom I learned to respect and even trust as fine human beings. When some of them asked me why I had come to their country to conquer, burn, kill and destroy, I half-heartedly gave a stock Nazi answer in terms of a quest for glory and national honour. Their rejection of this banality revealed the emptiness of my words, and I stood naked and totally devoid of any meaningful explanation to give them, and when they suggested that I had come in the service of my masters, the mighty arms manufacturers, bankers and landowning Junkers to secure for them the enormous mineral wealth and land of Russia, I painfully realised that at root they saw things through the same eyes as my father.

Once I became ill and was lying in the corner of a very primitive hut on straw, when a Russian woman, Madga, nursed me back to health. Why had she done it, I wondered? After all, I was an enemy soldier who had invaded her country. Also, she had two sons of about my age in the army, whom she had not heard from for a considerable time. Father's answer to that question would have been, that 'she acted as a human being first and foremost, a quality so many of us western Christians only pay lip service to.'

I once had the bad luck to get captured and be taken prisoner by a Russian unit, until a German counter-attack liberated me the next day. I was well aware of course how badly Russian prisoners on the whole were treated by us Germans and I can only state that my treatment by them, though necessarily harsh, was fair and humane.

The manner in which our retreat developed and continued convinced me that any smouldering hope for a German victory was lost. As we were approaching the Polish border, I heard that Hamburg had been pulverised in an air attack as Coventry had been before it. I knew that we were the guilty party, that we had started it, but I did wonder how history would judge the two Christian states who, an eye for an eye, wiped out each others' cities. Tens of thousands died in Hamburg on one night alone. Later I was told that mother had been wounded, while our home and all we had possessed had been blown to smithereens. Mother never fully recovered, as in addition to her ordeal, I had been declared 'missing, presumed dead'.

After having been wounded, I was taken back to Germany where I passed through our destroyed cities such as Leipzig, Magdeburg, and Halle. I asked myself, 'What was all this for, why have I been fighting in the east helping to destroy their cities?' – and I remembered what my father had tried to tell me would happen – in vain of course. Hardly able to walk properly, I was released from hospital to join a unit without a name, only a number. Our declared aim was to stem General Patton's advance, along with the other armies marching towards our western border. But it was as good as all over by the time I was captured in the town of Schifferstadt, defending the line of the Rhine.

I was taken as a prisoner-of-war to America to pick cotton in Arizona and California, and work on farms in Montana. Especially in Arizona close to the Mexican border I witnessed the ruthless exploitation of poverty-stricken migrant workers who had come across from the Rio Grande, by the plantation owners in pursuit of profit. We had been told that America was the land of the free, but it was all too obvious, even to us, that people who had no money were anything but free.

After less than two years in that large and beautiful country, a thousand of us boarded ship at New York to cross the Atlantic, to go back home, we thought, to rejoin our loved ones. But instead of landing at a German port, we were unloaded at Liverpool where the US Army handed us over to the British. We protested, saying that they had no right to do that, that it was peacetime now (it was the end of 1946), and moreover none of us had fought the British Army, nor had any of us been accused of war crimes.

But might proved right. Britain needed farm workers and I worked as such for a shilling a day until I was finally released in 1948, three years after the war had ended. I am not complaining, how could I after what German power had done to others. I am only stating facts. But I nevertheless do sometimes wonder how guilty I was for being a participant in the Nazi war-machine – or, on the other hand, to what extent was I a victim of that vile system which governs us all?

I know what father's answer to that question would have been, for he had told me in so many different words at so many different times: 'Junge, don't you ever forget it as long as you live, that while we have a system in which the poverty of the many is the very condition for the wealth and the economic power of the few, justice and peace on earth can be no more than a distant human dream.'

DATE DUE

APR 3 0 2013			
GAYLORD			PRINTED IN U.S.A.